EUROPEAN YEARBOOK OF BUSINESS HISTORY

EUROPEAN YEARBOOK OF BUSINESS HISTORY

Editors

Terry Gourvish	Business History Unit, London School of Economics
	Houghton Street, London WC2A 2AE
Wilfried Feldenkirchen	Lehrstuhl für Wirtschafts-, Sozial- und
	Unternehmungsgeschichte, Universität
	Erlangen/Nürnberg
	Findelgasse 7–9, D–90402 Nürnberg

Editorial staff:

Jane Waller	Deputy Archivist, ING Barings
Andrea H. Schneider	Association for European German History e.V.

Edited in association with:

Harold James	Princeton University
Geoffrey Jones	University of Reading
Akira Kudo	University of Tokyo
Alain Plessis	University of Paris
Manfred Pohl	Historical Institute, Deutsche Bank AG, Frankfurt
Gabriel Tortella	University of Madrid
Herman Van der Wee	Leuven University
Mira Wilkins	Florida International University
Vera Zamagni	University of Bologna

NOTES FOR CONTRIBUTORS: *The European Yearbook of Business History* is an annual publication of the Society for European History - SEBH e.V. The journal is concerned with the history of individual European enterprises and entrepreneurs, as well as multinational corporations, and will also publish new research and surveys in the wider field of business history. The journal aims to cover all Europe, not just those countries of the European Union, during, but not exclusively, the nineteenth and twentieth centuries.

Prospective contributors should contact the SEBH office (see address below) for guidelines on producing contributions for the *Yearbook*. All contributions will be refered. Research articles should normally be of 10,000 words including footnotes, whereas surveys should be shorter at 5,000 words. Contributions should be sent as hard copy and on disk, or as e-mail attachment to:

Society for European Business History –
SEBH e.V.
Zimmerweg 6, D-60325 Frankfurt am Main
Tel.: + 49 69 7103 5993/4; fax: +49 69 9720 3308
E-mail: ejohnston@compuserve.com

SUBSCRIPTIONS: *The European Yearbook of Business History* is published annually in June. A subscription to the *Yearbook* costs £50, including postage. Orders should be sent to your usual bookseller or subscription agent, or direct to Customer Services, Ashgate Publishing Ltd, Gower House, Croft Road, Aldershot, Hampshire GU11 3HR; tel. +44 (0)1252 317707; fax +44 (0)1252 343151.

PERMISSIONS: Requests for permission to re-use material published in the journal should be sent to Ashgate Publishing Ltd, Gower House, Croft Road, Aldershot, Hampshire GU11 3HR.

European Yearbook of Business History

Vol. 2, 1999

edited by
Wilfried Feldenkirchen and
Terry Gourvish

Published by ASHGATE on behalf of the
Society for European Business History

Published by
Ashgate Publishing Limited
Gower House, Croft Road
Aldershot, Hampshire GU11 3HR
Great Britain

Ashgate Publishing Company
Old Post Road
Brookfield, Vermont 05036–9704
USA

Ashgate website: http://www.ashgate.com

ISBN 0 7546 0090 4   ISSN 1462–186X

Typeset by Manton Typesetters, 5–7 Eastfield Road, Louth, Lincolnshire, LN11 7AJ, UK.
Printed and bound in Great Britain by MPG Books Ltd, Bodmin, Cornwall

Contents

The European Yearbook of Business History

The aim of the *Yearbook* is to reflect the changing structure, experience and aspirations of European business as it approaches the Millenium. The challenge of globalization, co-operation within a single European market, and an increasing interest in corporate governance and environmental issues are illustrative of the changes which not only affect contemporary business enterprises, but also stimulate new types of scholarship among European business historians, and encourage new preservation strategies by business archivists. Increasingly, an interest in single industries in one country is being replaced by comparative analysis embracing several countries, whilst the definition of 'business history' has widened to embrace social and political issues.

The *Yearbook* intends to exploit these changes by serving as a forum for debate in Europe. It publishes new academic research on any aspect of European business history, but with special emphasis on works of synthesis, comparative studies of business activity, and reviews of current research work in individual countries, including assessments of major source materials and archives. At the same time, theoretical contributions are also welcome, as are extra-European perspectives on Europe, particularly from the United States and Japan. Published in English, the *Yearbook* aims to bring work on individual countries to a wider, European audience.

The Society for European Business History

The Society is based at the Centre for European Business History in Frankfurt. It is generously supported by European companies. The Society aims to promote all aspects of European business history.

Office
Emma Johnston
Secretary General

Marion Hausmann
Assistant

Society for European Business History e.V. – SEBH
Zimmerweg 6
D-60325 Frankfurt am Main
Germany

Tel.: +49 69 7103 5993/4
Fax: +49 69 9720 3308
E-mail: ejohnston@compuserve.com
         hausmann@businesshistory.de
Homepage: www.businesshistory.de

Details of membership can be obtained from the Society at the above
address.

Company History and Business History in the 1990s

Geoffrey Jones

University of Reading

The 1990s represent something of a paradox in business history's evolution as an academic subject. In institutional terms, the subject has in relative terms flourished. The Japan Business History Society continues to dominate the field with over 800 members, in addition, the US Business History Conference now has 475 members and the European Business History Association, only founded in 1994, has 300. While faculty positions in economic history have declined in many countries, new posts have been created for business historians, even though many business schools continue to neglect or marginalise the subject. Yet, it is not evident that the intellectual advances made by the subject have been so great. The Chandlerian synthesis has been criticised, but no new synthesis has replaced it. Many well-researched company histories have been published, but it is hard to say that they have made a decisive improvement on the methods employed by their distinguished predecessors.

This article examines some general trends in business history research and the writing of company histories over the 1990s. The focus is on Europe, but developments in the United States and Japan are also considered. Needless to say, given the size and diversity of business history research, the discussion is selective and subjective, not to say opinionated.

RECENT TRENDS IN BUSINESS HISTORY

It has been a long-term aim for many (if not all) business historians that their subject should evolve from producing well-written empirical historical case-studies to delivering valid generalisations about business structures and behaviour. It would be an exaggeration to say that the 1990s have seen great advances in this respect, but a bold generalisation might be that there has been movement in this direction. While in the past many writers would launch into their stories with little more than an introduction saying they had discovered new and interesting facts, it has become quite common for articles and some books in business history to begin with a more general problem or theory, and then launch into their empirical research. The extent to which this new approach has taken hold seems to vary between countries. Oddly, it is in highly empirical Britain that business historians have been especially concerned to relate their research to wider issues, debates and theories, and the same trend is observable in Scandinavia. In contrast, in the United States – where Chandler has done so much to conceptualise and generalise – much research remains profoundly rooted in the empirical case-study approach.

The influence of Chandler remains strong in the 1990s. Chandler's primary achievement has surely not been his provision of historical accounts of the growth of big business in the United States, and later Britain and Germany, but the providing of a set of testable propositions about the growth of organisations and their sources of competitive advantage. In his three major books to date, we have learned that new organisational structures resulted from changes in the strategic direction of firms; that large firms grew when it was rational to replace markets to co-ordinate flows of goods and services; that the 'organisational capabilities' of firms rest on a commitment to investment in production, distribution and management; and that firms that become 'first movers' are able to retain their positions as industry leaders if they continue to invest in their organisational capabilities.[1]

These highly plausible propositions are of central concern to mainstream management researchers and it is not surprising that Chandler remains the most commonly cited business historian in management literature. In the 1990s, the Chandlerian agenda has continued to pre-occupy business history research, outstandingly so in the United States,[2] though recently attention there has begun to shift towards new directions for research. Business historians from Spain to Australia continue to compile lists of the largest firms.[3] The degree to which business strategies and structures in different countries paralleled or differed from the patterns outlined by Chandler for the United States continue to preoccupy business historians, even if it might be questioned whether the use of the unique case of the United States as a benchmark is helpful.[4] A landmark publication of the 1990s was the volume edited by Chandler, Amatori and Hikino which extended the Chandlerian analysis not only to southern Europe, but also to Argentina, South Korea and even the USSR and Czechoslovakia during the Communist era. Although individual authors in this book differ in the degree of their Chandlerian orthodoxy, they all show the heavy influence of Chandler in their approach to interpreting organisation and strategy.[5]

Yet, during the 1990s some Chandlerian certainties have been challenged. Ironically – given the severe structural problems of Japan and other Asian businesses at the end of the 1990s – the competitiveness problems of American firms in the 1970s and 1980s have led to the widespread criticism of Chandler's explicit assumption of the superiority of the American business system. Without rehearsing all of these well-known criticisms, it is widely recognised that some important actors, such as governments, were largely omitted from the Chandlerian story – the focus on the creation of managerial hierarchies has led to a neglect of the role of business systems as a source of organisational capability; and the very concept of 'organisational capability' is recognised as being in need of more precise formulation. Chandler's assumption that technological changes produced a given set of organisational changes has also been challenged in the light of a growing recognition that technological change can take a number of alternative organisational forms. There has been a recognition too that a focus on high-tech manufacturing industry leaves much unsaid about other sectors of the economy, notably services.[6] An especially powerful assault on Chandlerian certainties came from Langlois and Robertson with their assertion that, since the late nineteenth century, the large and centralised corporate enterprise has been at most only one route to innovation and economic growth.[7] Scranton's *Endless Novelty* provides another powerful exploration of the world beyond big business by examining American batch and speciality production from the late nineteenth century to 1925.[8]

But perhaps the most important challenge to Chandler and the intellectual advances of the 1990s came with a renewed interest in small and family firms. Whatever their performance in the United States, family firms have been shown to be viable forms of business organisation in other countries and within certain industries.[9] British business historians have taken particular exception to Chandler's view that 'personal capitalism' was to blame for Britain's alleged misfortunes from the late nineteenth century, and this has encouraged stimulating research on how family firms functioned.[10] The role of the 'networks' linking many small and family firms – and their viability as compared to Chandler's 'hierarchies' – has become an especially important topic of research. This reflects the evident importance of enterprise groups in Japan's business history,[11] the growth of interest in networks by institutional economists and organisational theorists,[12] and the trends towards the disintegration of contemporary big business through outsourcing and strategic alliances.

Business history research exploring the significance of 'networks' has proved to be among the most exciting over the last decade. In the United States, Scranton's research on networks of small firms in Philadelphia's textiles and clothing industries has been especially influential, and has now been reinforced by his new research on 'network specialists' in the furniture trade in Grand Rapids and machine tools in Cincinnati.[13] Some of the most innovative research in British business history in the 1990s has also employed network concepts, such as Tweedale's study of Sheffield's steel firms,[14] and Boyce's revisionist view of the pre-1919 British shipping industry, which makes explicit and successful use of network theory.[15] Important work has been done drawing parallels between Japanese enterprise groups and corporate groups in Europe.[16] There is, however, room for a great deal more research on the relations between firms, as well as on developments inside them.

Research on networks can be related to a growing interest in another area almost wholly neglected by Chandler: culture. While 'culture' used to be the last refuge of the scoundrel in economic history – the residual explanation for an event when all rational explanations failed – major advances in sociology, organisational studies and institutional economics now offer business historians a highly respectable set of analytical tools to address problems of key concern to them. Hofstede's work on cross-cultural management and Schein's on organisational cultures have been especially fundamental.[17] From a transactions cost perspective, Casson has examined cross-national differences in levels of 'trust', and the implications of such disparities for entrepreneurship and the choice between the use of hierarchies or networks, studies which suggest that high trust cultures provide a more supportive environment for network-like arrangements to function than do low trust cultures.[18] A number of publications in the mid-1990s in both the United States and Britain suggest a renewed attempt to put 'culture' onto the mainstream business history research agenda, despite the complex methodological problems faced by historians relying on archival materials to research 'culture'.[19] Significantly, Chandler et al.'s *Big Business and the Wealth of Nations* (1997) ends with an essay on culture. 'If the notion of organisational capabilities will grow in theoretical stature', its author concludes, 'then it must also integrate managerial values and interpersonal communications, that is, the structure and creation of the means of co-ordination, co-operation, control, and trust inside business firms'.[20]

The application of concepts of networks and culture to business history raises the question of whether business historians should seek to develop their own concepts – the approach of Chandler, though he was certainly influenced by sociological and other theories – or view their subject as a testing ground for other people's models. The present author argued a few years ago that both approaches were appropriate.[21] In practice, the 1990s has seen the transfer of ideas from other subjects, notably new institutional economics, into business history,[22] but it is hard to think of major conceptual advances emerging from the discipline. Chandler has been critiqued, corrected and amplified, but new conceptual tools have remained elusive. This is disappointing, as subjects such as entrepreneurship appear to be crying out for major conceptual innovations. Empirical data continues to be assembled on entrepreneurs – the recent Belgian 'dictionary' of entrepreneurs was another breakthrough in this respect[23] – but business historians remain reluctant to perceive general patterns.

Moving beyond Chandler, a number of issues have attracted considerable attention from business historians in the 1990s. The internationalisation of business which, following the pioneering research of Mira Wilkins in the 1960s and 1970s, took off on a large scale in the 1980s, has continued to generate extensive research in the 1990s. Wilkins herself, having published the first volume of her massive study of foreign investment in the United States in 1989, is now well advanced in the second volume, which will take the subject from 1914 to the present day.[24] Wilkins's research is indicative of a new interest in inward rather than outward multinational investment. Mark Mason made an impressive contribution to the Japanese business history literature with his study on why US multinational investment in Japan is so low.[25] The role of foreign multinationals in Franco's Spain is another area which has seen important research contributions.[26] The international growth of German, Swiss, Dutch, Scandinavian and other European firms have also been researched;[27] and Harm Schröter has made especially important contributions to understanding the growth of multinationals from smaller European countries.[28] The present author has sought in his own research in this area, and through edited volumes, to extend research from the manufacturing sector to services, notably multinational banks and, more recently, multinational trading companies; while he and others have in addition sought to re-examine international cartels and other non-equity arrangements.[29] He also attempted a synthesis of the now enormous literature on the history of multinationals.[30]

The methodologies employed in this research on the history of multinationals are worthy of mention. Since the 1980s there has been quite extensive application of the theories and concepts associated with international business to the realm of historical research, and this area more than any other in business history continues to see the interaction of theory and empirical research methodologies. Company case studies continue to be widely employed to illustrate the process of internationalisation.[31] However this area has also seen in the 1990s the construction of databases consisting of large numbers of firms, again in the area of inward rather than outward investment. Examples of the latter include the Bostock and Jones database on inward investment in Britain between 1850 and 1962,[32] and Antje Hagen's database on German FDI in Britain before 1914.[33] The use of databases to examine large populations of firms or people has been used in other areas of business history research in the 1990s – such as entrepreneurship[34] – and its potential to inform many debates remains underexploited.

It is perhaps appropriate here to mention that the whole issue of multinationals raises special issues for company archivists concerning the location of corporate archives. Considerations related to corporate efficiency will often dictate the concentration of records in one place – usually but not invariably in the home country of the multinational. However, in some countries the business history of entire sectors lie among the records of the foreign firms, so archival research can only be conducted at great expense, sometimes only from thousands of kilometres away. A country like Singapore, whose modern economic growth is almost entirely due to foreign firms, is an extreme case. However, the same general issue applies to a European country such as the United Kingdom where foreign-owned companies have grown steadily in importance generation after generation, and which, by the 1990s, control large parts of its industry and over 30 per cent of total exports. If corporate records are held by parent multinationals, the twenty-first century business historian of the British automobile, consumer electronics, investment banking and many other industries will need to travel to the United States, Japan and elsewhere in Europe to do her/his research, and learn a few foreign languages as well. The issue of the location of archives becomes especially sensitive when old established domestic firms are acquired by foreign multinationals – should their records be retained in the host country or transferred to the parent?[35]

A second area of considerable research interest in the 1990s has been human capital formation. The pioneering research on management education by Robert Locke in the 1980s[36] and, more generally, widespread recognition of the importance of skill formation and training in explaining national patterns of innovation and economic growth, has led to stimulating new research in this area by business historians. British business historians have been concerned to explain why British investment in training and management skills was so low, and to explore if this really mattered.[37] More widely, national differences in management education systems and their consequences have attracted important research,[38] and have led into debates concerned with how management systems were transferred between firms and countries.[39] Business historians have much to contribute to the wider debates on the acquisition and diffusion of information and knowledge.

Arguably, some major themes have been somewhat under-represented in the literature. The formidable theoretical literature on the economics of innovation and technological accumulation, which has argued that technological change is a cumulative, incremental and path-dependent process,[40] has not had as great an impact upon business history research as might have been expected. Much of the historical research in this area has been undertaken by scholars with little or no historical training or historical knowledge. Among the business historians who have addressed issues of innovation within firms, David Hounshell and Lou Galambos from the United States have been especially prominent over the last decade,[41] though important research has also begun to appear in Europe. An example is Amdam's study of the role of professional networks in innovation in the British and Norwegian pharmaceutical industries during the interwar years.[42] From a different perspective, there has also been important business history research on the early history of the computer industry, but a great deal remains to be done, especially outside the United States.[43] The whole issue of the collection and use of information within firms has attracted fascinating research, more noteworthy for its quality than its quantity.[44]

There has continued, in the 1990s, to be considerable variation in the research agendas of business historians within different countries. This reflects differing national debates within the historical profession, as well as different contemporary concerns. In Germany, reunification stimulated an interest in aspects of the transformation of former East German companies into capitalist enterprises. Germany in the 1990s has also seen another surge of interest in the history of business enterprises during the Nazi period. The role of their business leaders and firms in this period continues to be a highly sensitive topic not only in the more obvious countries such as Switzerland, but also in Norway, The Netherlands and elsewhere, and much research remains to be done in finally laying to rest the ghosts of this era. On the subject of ghosts, British business and economic historians have spent decades trying to explain why their country 'declined' or 'failed' from the late nineteenth century. Their usual benchmark was the United States rather than – more appropriately – other European countries. A new theme of the British literature in the 1990s has been the discovery that their country and business sector had not failed at all![45] Meanwhile business historians in the United States began to focus more on issues of gender and ethnicity, subjects which preoccupy their society and historical profession, but which their business historians had long seemed to be avoiding.[46]

In Italy, as elsewhere, contemporary preoccupations have influenced historical research agendas. The slow process of change in the Italian banking system following the Amato bill in 1992 has result in a new interest in the universal banking model in operation before 1936. The perceived Italian failure in contemporary science-based industries has led Italian researchers to look for the historical origins of these problems in industries such as nuclear power and pharmaceuticals. Privatisation policies have stimulated research on the role of the state as entrepreneur in the course of Italy's industrial development, and a renewed interest in the histories of enterprises owned, or formerly owned, by the government, for example, public utilities and banks such as Banca Commerciale Italiana and Credito Italiano. Generally, not only in Italy but in other southern European countries such as France or Spain, the role of the State is attracting – and needs to attract – much research.[47] The state-owned firms in these countries played a strategic role in their economies and political systems, and functioned as alternative business organisation models.[48]

While national research agendas remain to some extent distinctive, a general trend of the 1990s has been the publication of studies of both wide themes and textbook overviews. US authors, most notably Chandler but also others, had a good track record in publishing syntheses about their own and other countries,[49] but European and Japanese researchers in business history – as opposed in this instance to economic history – had more problems in generalising from the massive accumulation of company case-study evidence. In the 1990s both the Japanese and Europeans have been more willing to write 'big books'. In the business history literature on Japan, Suzuki on management structures and Morikawa on the *zaibatsu* are noteworthy in this respect. Moutet's study of the spread of scientific management in interwar France and Caron's recent majestic survey provide two examples in the French literature.[50] British business historians have shown a new interest in using multi-company archives to produce studies of the evolution of industries over long time periods. Examples include the present author's study of British multinational banking and Gourvish and Wilson on the British brewing industry.[51]

The 1990s saw a welcome willingness among business historians to write textbooks, despite persistent gaps in research on many aspects of business history. For some time, Britain only had Leslie Hannah's attempt to transfer the Chandlerian framework to that country, first published in 1976,[52] but the mid-1990s saw the publication of two business history textbooks by Kirby and Rose and Wilson. Among other national surveys, there is the chapter on Dutch business in the van Zanden text,[53] as well as the many national chapters in Chandler et al's *Big Business*. Cassis's *Big Business*, a study of Britain, France and Germany is another major contribution, welcome not only for its comparative dimension, but for providing a pioneering overview of the business history of France.[54] A Spanish textbook will shortly appear edited by López and Valdaliso. A new trend is the writing of business history texts designed for business studies students. A Norwegian and a US text were published in 1997, and a British one in 1998.[55]

The importance of texts and surveys in business history can hardly be exaggerated. As long as the literature consisted of multiple firm histories, articles in specialist journals, and conference volumes, it was hard for non-specialist scholars to penetrate, even should they have wanted to do so. Books that discern patterns and make generalisations open the subject up for others and can even inform business historians of how their subject has advanced. However many countries continue to lack national business histories – as opposed to economic histories – while the first business history of Europe remains to be written. On a more positive note, business history research has continued in the 1990s to spread out from its 'core' areas of North America, Northwest Europe and Japan. There is now a rich and vibrant literature on both Italy and Spain, and growing interest in Portugal.[56] Carlos Dávila's recent edited volume showed how much research has now been accumulated on some Latin American countries, as well as highlighting continuing gaps.[57] Rajeswary Brown's research has represented an important application of business history concepts to the Chinese, Indian and Western firms active in Southeast Asia.[58] There is less evidence that business history is 'taking off' in the transition economies of eastern Europe, perhaps because most of their university systems are in sufficiently dire straits to exclude new initiatives.

COMPANY HISTORIES IN THE 1990s

If attempting to discern themes in the area of business history as a whole is a highly subjective exercise, it is even more subjective to do so with regards the history of companies more narrowly defined. But, in the work considered above, there are strong continuities with past generations. The 1990s has continued to see numerous company histories produced, ranging from commemorative pamphlets to heavily footnoted scholarly studies by leading academics. There has been a welcome appearance of substantive firm histories from countries such as Switzerland whose business history has long remained under-researched. Peyer's study of Roche, in particular, is worthy of attention.[59] Substantive 'academic' histories of course remain a tiny minority, but in this context it is most relevant to concentrate on trends in these 'academic' business histories. Despite anecdotal evidence that the commissioning of such a history is a danger signal, casting doubt upon the vitality of a firm's management, major firms have continued to ask academics or academically qualified researchers to write histories of their companies. The interest now extends far beyond manufacturing firms, which perhaps used to provide the main customers for such work. Banks (which actually have a long tradition in some countries of commissioning histories) continue to be the subject of major historical accounts.[60] Firms from accountants to oil companies to utilities have had their company histories written in the 1990s.[61]

In some European countries a trend towards commissioning more 'academic' histories seems discernible in the 1990s. In Germany, for example, there was a strong tradition for firms to ask their own archivists to write their histories.[62] Although this practice certainly continues, there appears to have been a trend towards companies engaging professional historians to write their histories, perhaps in order to enhance the firm's external reputation for objectivity. Examples include the recent study by Wilfried Feldenkirchen of Siemens before 1945 and, especially, the multi-authored history of Deutsche Bank. The latter history, written by five academics including a Briton and an American Jew, dealt in detail with Deutsche Bank's role in the Nazi era, its policies towards Jews, and other issues of great sensitivity in recent German history. The outcome might be criticised as more of a political than a business history of the bank, but the depth of research and the willingness to confront controversy is beyond question.[63]

Academic company histories continue to be written under a variety of circumstances. In countries such as Britain, where business historians hold 'permanent' academic positions, company histories continue to be commissioned, in return for a fee and – in most cases – a guarantee of no substantive censorship. However some major company histories in Britain were not commissioned but were the results of historians approaching firms and securing access to their confidential records. Weir's study of Distillers, the whisky company, and Fieldhouse's history of the United Africa Company, the West African trading company owned by Unilever, fall into this category.[64] A rarer variant is when a company employs the business historian on its staff. This was the case with the BP History Project, whose second volume appeared in 1994 and whose third volume should be published in 1999.[65] In other European countries, 'contract research' has been the chief means by which business historians are funded, even if they hold university posts. The company histories produced by researchers in leading business history centres in the Netherlands, such as Rotterdam and Utrecht, are essentially the outcomes of such contract research.[66] In Japan, all company histories are commissioned and are published anonymously.

The company histories discussed above – and many others not mentioned here – are for the most part not only full of rich empirical data, but their authors often make shrewd, critical judgements on past managerial strategies. The great majority of the scholarly histories of the last ten years can be regarded as 'objective', though there appear to be instances when things have been omitted due to company pressure, and there are perhaps even more cases of 'self-censorship'. But, the degree of 'objectivity' does not appear to be related to the means by which the history was financed. A far greater problem, discussed over a decade ago by the distinguished British business historian Donald Coleman in a classic article of relevance for the subject generally, is that these volumes do not appear to be read either by business practitioners or by most other academics. 'The end products, in the form of numerous handsomely produced volumes from prestigious publishing houses sit impressively on sundry bookshelves', Coleman wrote in 1987. 'They are very largely unread by anyone except other business historians.'[67]

In fact, although the present author is unaware of any study in this area, the extent to which 'academic' company histories are unread seems to vary between countries. In the 'instant' culture of the United States or profoundly anti-intellectual Britain, few managers – let alone the elusive 'general public' – are to be found devouring lengthy scholarly histories of even the most famous firms. In France, and in the smaller European countries where a few firms can play a much bigger role in their economies, it would appear that readership levels might be higher. Perhaps a more general problem is that so few academics read company histories. There is good reason to believe that they are unread not only by management researchers and industrial economists, but also by economic and other historians. Indeed, most company histories appear unread even by other business historians. It is only when the same material is reused in other contexts – such as journal articles – that it appears to gain attention.[68] This situation is evidently related to the poor reputation of company histories in general among other academics, as high quality scholarly works get tarnished with the same brand image as public relations leaflets. However, there are also problems with the 'products' themselves, especially their excessive length and a lack of direct relevance to wider academic debates.

In his article, Coleman suggested one way forward would be to persuade companies to sponsor research on specific issues. While some companies expect commissioned histories to cover everything and everybody, this is surely one of the approaches which can all too easily lead to unreadable or at least unusable books. A discernible trend in the 1990s has been for company histories to focus on particular themes. In his history of the British chocolate company Rowntree, Fitzgerald focuses on the theme of marketing, reflecting that firm's great importance in the evolution of consumer marketing in Britain, especially in the interwar years.[69] In her study of the Dutch food and biochemicals company CSM, Sluyterman focuses on management strategy.[70] Amdam and Sogner's study of the Norwegian pharmaceutical company Nyegaard looks at the circumstances behind innovation within the firm, such as the business culture and the firm's external linkages.[71] In countries where writing a company history can be done within the context of a Ph.D. degree, such histories tend of necessity to be focused on specific themes. Examples include Cailluet's study of organisational capabilities at Pechiney between 1880 and 1971, and the on-going projects on the Dutch post office and central statistical office at Erasmus University, Rotterdam.[72]

The writing of more thematic studies surely offers one of the more promising avenues for company histories to move forward in academic terms, as well as to be of more value to the firms that commission them. Rather than focus on a holistic approach to the company's past, an approach which all too easily becomes a view of corporate strategy as seen from the boardroom – it would surely be preferable for 'key' topics to be explored systematically and in depth. This approach might involve commissioning independent studies of different aspects of a firm's history, which the Swedish Match history published almost two decades ago showed could deliver excellent results.[73] Or, if a single book is commissioned, it might be organised around key themes dealt with systematically and over time. These 'key' themes will naturally vary according to industry, firm and time period, but would surely include the (inter-related) areas of organisational structures, organisational capabilities, innovation, human resources management and corporate culture.

These topics require somewhat different archival resources than have been used in the past. In many cases the archives which survive in a firm are those that concern its statutory obligations – reports and accounts, etc. – and records of high level decision-making, such as Board papers. The latter are most prized by business historians as they provide a short cut to getting an overview of the firm's history. On the other hand, issues of capabilities, innovation and culture will necessitate looking at what happens 'lower down' within a firm's structure. It is necessary to look at routines rather than big decisions. The study of intangibles such as the knowledge possessed within a firm, flows of information, and the corporate culture – and how all these things changed over time – can involve a very wide range of historical records far removed from documents on strategies. Valuable records will range from technical data on how computer systems were arranged and functioned within firms, to photographs of how offices and plants were laid out, to videos of how people performed work tasks. Oral history – of staff employed at all levels – is of especial use in examining issues of culture, information flows and systems.

A second trend of the 1990s has been to place the histories of firms within their wider contexts. This provides another central means of making company histories more accessible, for studies that focus sharply on specific firms (and rely exclusively upon that firm's archives) often lack perspective and relevance. It remains surprising how many excellent firm histories fail to address the distinctiveness of their firm vis-à-vis their competitors. However the context needs to be properly defined, for there are numerous examples of earlier generations of company histories in which the context was so broad that there was insufficient detail about the firm itself.[74] Recent banking histories seem especially good at putting their subjects into a wider context. King's four-volume history of the Hongkong Bank has a great deal to say about the diplomatic and political history of China as well as the business of the bank.[75] The history of Belgium's Generale Bank likewise is informative about the banking system as a whole.[76] However the placing of a firm's history within its wider context has not been confined to banks. The recent two volume history of the Norwegian Post Office places a strong emphasis on the wider social and economic context, while the first volume in particular also puts some stress on the consumers' perspective on the institution.[77]

Again, there are implications here for corporate archives. Records generated within the firm may be uninformative or misleading about the external environment of the firm. It would be reasonable to argue that a company archive cannot be expected to collect material relating to the broader industrial, economic and political milieu, and that that is the responsibility of other archives and archivists, including those of the state. However, there are subjects 'external' to the firm but forming an essential part of its history – its customers, its suppliers and its interaction with the natural environment. Given the research trends discussed above concerning the growing interests in networks and the relations of firms with other firms, it seems likely that company historians of the future will increasingly have need of records which are not generated within the boundaries of the firm, but which may be of great importance for understanding both the performance of the firm and its wider role within society. An example of this approach is Gálvez's study of the Spanish Tobacco Company between 1887 and 1945, which explores patterns in the relationship between gender, technology, labour organisation patterns and managerial constraints in the case of this state-controlled company. Galvéz used not only company records, but also those of municipal and central government, the press, literary surveys and oral history, and this enabled her to examine both 'routine' and 'strategic' decisions and to explore the difference between the strategies of the company and its routine practices.[78]

CONCLUDING REMARKS

This article has tried, in an arbitrary and subjective fashion, to find some trends in the enormous literature published in business history during the 1990s. The subject is spreading geographically and in the range of subjects addressed. There is a welcome growth of internationally comparative research. The Chandlerian preoccupations with the strategy and structure of large managerial companies, especially in the manufacturing sector, have been supplemented by new research interests in small and family businesses, inter-firm networks, human capital and culture. These research areas are delivering exciting results. At the same time, the appearance of more surveys and texts is making business history accessible to non-specialists and students.

Methodological advances do not seem to have kept pace with this evergrowing stream of empirical research about our business past. On the plus side, there is a new willingness to relate research to general issues, and the appearance of more surveys and texts is welcome. The transfer of concepts and ideas from new institutional economics has produced especially interesting results. However, business historians themselves have proved better at criticising Chandler than developing new concepts. There have been no major conceptual breakthroughs from business historians in understanding entrepreneurship, innovation or firm competencies, even though evolutionary approaches to such subjects are in vogue in the social sciences. In some respects, business history has become highly fashionable, so long as it is not written by business historians.

Many good company histories have been written in the 1990s. This article has only highlighted a few of them. Yet it is hard to say that this genre has moved much beyond the achievements of earlier generations, such as Wilson's *Unilever*,[79] and this is probably a cause for concern given that the readership for such books remains problematic or – to rephrase – that the potential of such studies to inform contemporary managerial decision-making, influence public opinion, and enhance scientific knowledge of firms – seems to have remained unrealised. The reasons for this situation are complex, but two trends discernible in the 1990s might lead to an improvement in the situation in the twenty-first century. The first is for company histories not to attempt to cover everything but to look in more detail at key themes. Secondly, there has been a renewed trend to place the history of companies within wider contexts. Both approaches involve the adoption by business historians of rather different methodologies, and they also have implications for the acquisition and retention policies of corporate archives.

NOTES

* The first version of this article was presented at a conference organised by the Statens Arkiver Erhvervsarkivet in Arhus, Denmark in February 1998 and will be published by that organisation. I would like to thank Andrea Colli, Lina Gálvez-Muñoz, Antje Hagen, and Keetie Sluyterman for helpful comments on earlier drafts of this article. They are not responsible for my views.

1. Alfred D. Chandler, Jnr, *Strategy and Structure* (Cambridge, Mass., 1962); idem, *The Visible Hand* (Cambridge, Mass., 1977); idem, *Scale and Scope* (Cambridge, Mass., 1990).

2. A perusal of *Business and Economic History*, the annual journal of the Business History Conference, and of *Business History Review*, demonstrates the continuing influence of Chandler. However, see *Business and Economic History* 26, 1 (1997) for a special issue on 'The Future of Business History' which had many new ideas.

3. A. Carreras and X. Tafunell, 'La gran empresa en España, 1917–1974. Una primera aproximación', *Revista de Historia Industrial* 3 (1993); C. Schmitz, 'The World's Largest Industrial Companies of 1912', *Business History* 37

(1995); D.T. Merret and S. Ville, 'The development of large-scale enterprise in Australia, 1910–64' (Mimeo, 1998).

4. For example, Jean-Pierre Daviet, 'Stratégie et structure chez Saint Gobain: un modèle français dans les années 1930?', *Enterprises et Histoire* (1992); R. Giannetti, G. Federico and P.A. Toninelli, 'Size and Strategies of Italian Industrial Enterprises (1907–1940): Empirical Evidence and Some Conjectures', *Industrial and Corporate Change* 2 (1994).

5. Alfred D. Chandler Jnr, Franco Amatori and Takashi Hikino (eds), *Big Business and the Wealth of Nations* (Cambridge, Mass., 1997).

6. B. Supple, 'Introduction', in Barry E. Supple (ed.), *The Rise of Big Business* (Aldershot, 1992), p. xxv.

7. R.N. Langlois and P.L. Robertson, *Firms, Markets and Economic Change: A Dynamic Theory of Business Institutions* (London, 1995).

8. P. Scranton, *Endless Novelty: Speciality Production and American Industrialization, 1865–1925* (Princeton, 1997).

9. Roy Church, 'The Family Firm in Industrial Capitalism: International Perspectives on Hypotheses and History', *Business History*, 35 (1993); Keetie E. Sluyterman and Hélène J. M. Winkelman, 'The Dutch Family Firm Confronted with Chandler's Dynamics of Industrial Capitalism, 1890–1940', *Business History* 35 (1993); Keetie E. Sluyterman, 'Het Familiebedrijf als speciaal aandachtsveld binnen de bedrijfsgeschiedenis', *It Beaken* 54 (1992).

10. Mary B. Rose, 'Beyond Buddenbrooks: the family firm and the management of succession in nineteenth century Britain', in J. Brown and Mary B. Rose (eds), *Entrepreneurship, Networks and Modern Business* (Manchester, 1993); idem, 'The family firm in British business, 1780–1914', in M.W. Kirby and Mary B. Rose (eds), *Business Enterprise in Modern Britain* (London, 1994); Stana Nenadic, 'The Small Family Firm in Victorian Britain', *Business History* 35 (1993).

11. W. Mark Fruin, *The Japanese Enterprise System* (Oxford, 1992).

12. M.J. Piore and C.F. Sabel, *The Second Industrial Divide* (New York, 1994); W.W. Powell, 'Neither Market Nor Hierarchy: Network Firms of Organisation', *Research in Organisational Behaviour* 12 (1990); M. Ebers (ed.), *The Formation of Interorganisational Networks* (Oxford, 1997).

13. P. Scranton, *Figured Tapestry: Production, Markets and Power in Philadelphia Textiles, 1885–1941* (Cambridge, 1989); idem, 'Build a Firm, Start Another: The Bramleys and Family Firm Entrepreneurship in the Philadelphia Region', *Business History* 35 (1993); idem, *Endless Novelty*.

14. G. Tweedale, *Steel City: Entrepreneurship, Strategy and Technology in Sheffield, 1743–1993* (Oxford, 1995).

15. Gordon H. Boyce, *Information, Mediation and Institutional Development: The Rise of the Large-Scale Enterprise in British Shipping, 1870–1919* (Manchester, 1995).

16. T. Shiba and M. Shimotani (eds), *Beyond the Firm. Business Groups in International and Historical Perspective* (Oxford, 1997).

17. G. Hofstede, *Culture's Consequences* (Beverley Hills, 1980); E.H. Schein, *Organisational Culture and Leadership* (San Francisco, 1985).

18. Mark Casson, *Economics of Business Culture: Game Theory, Transactions*

Costs and Economic Performance (Oxford, 1991); idem, 'Entrepreneurship and business culture', in Brown and Rose (eds), Entrepreneurship. Another important contribution is Mark Granovetter, 'Coase Revisited: Business Groups in the Modern Economy', Industrial and Corporate Change (1996).

19. K. Lipartito, 'Culture and the Practice of Business History', Business and Economic History 24, 2 (1995); A. Godley and O.M. Westall (eds), Business History and Business Culture (Manchester, 1996). Two recent British-authored textbooks also emphasised the role of culture. John F. Wilson, British Business History, 1720–1994 (Manchester, 1995) and Geoffrey Jones, The Evolution of International Business (London, 1996).

20. Jeffery R. Fear, 'Constructing big business: The cultural concept of the firm', in Chandler et al., Big Business, p. 569.

21. Geoffrey Jones, 'Business history: theory and concepts', in Mila Davids, Ferry de Goey and Dirk de Wit (eds), Proceedings of the Conference on Business History 1994 (Rotterdam, 1995).

22. See the special issue of Business History 39, (October 1997) on 'Institutions and the Evolution of Modern Business', edited by Mark Casson and Mary B. Rose.

23. G. Kurgan-van Hentenrijk, S. Jaunin and V. Montens (eds), Dictionnaire des patrons en Belgique. Les hommes, les entreprises, les resaux (Brussels, 1996). Mention here should be made of the valuable Encyclopedia of American Business History, published at regular intervals since 1988.

24. Mira Wilkins, The History of Foreign Investment in the United States before 1914 (Cambridge, Mass., 1989).

25. Mark Mason, American Multinationals and Japan (Cambridge, Mass., 1992).

26. Antonio Gómez Mendoza, El 'Gibraltar Económico': Franco y Rio Tinto, 1936–1954 (Madrid, 1994); Salvador Estapé-Triay, 'Controlling Subsidiaries under Economic Nationalism: Ford and the Franco Regime (1936–54),' in Ulf Olsson (ed.), Business and European Integration since 1800 (Göteborg, 1997).

27. Geoffrey Jones and Harm G. Schröter (eds), The Rise of Multinationals in Continental Europe (Aldershot, 1993); Rolf Petter Amdam and Even Lange (eds), Crossing the Borders (Oslo, 1994).

28. Harm G. Schröter, Aufstieg der Kleinen (Berlin, 1993); idem, 'Unternehmensleitung und Auslandsproduktion: Entscheidungsprozesse, Probleme und Konsequenzen in der schweizerischen Chemieindustrie vor 1914', Schweizerische Zeitschrift für Geschichte 44 (1994); Jones, Evolution.

29. G. Jones (ed.), Banks as Multinationals (London, 1990); idem, British Multinational Banking 1830–1990 (Oxford, 1993); idem, (ed.), The Multinational Traders (London, 1998); idem, Merchants to Multinationals (forthcoming Oxford); idem, (ed.), Coalitions and Collaboration in International Business (Aldershot, 1993); A. Kudo and T. Hara (eds), International Cartels in Business History (Tokyo, 1992); D. Barjot (ed.), International Cartels Revisited (Caen, 1994).

30. Jones, Evolution.

31. E.g. Robert Greenhill, 'Investment Group, Free-Standing Company or Multinational? Brazilian Warrant, 1909-52', Business History 37 (1995); Antje

Hagen, 'Export versus Direct Investment in the German Optical Industry', *Business History* 38 (1996).

32. F. Bostock and G. Jones, 'Foreign multinationals in British manufacturing, 1850–1962', *Business History* 3 (1994); G. Jones and F. Bostock, 'U.S. Multinationals in British Manufacturing before 1962', *Business History Review* 70 (1996).

33. Antje Hagen, *Deutsche Direktinvestitionen in Grossbritannien, 1871–1918* (Stutgart, 1997).

34. E.g. H. Berghoff and R. Miller, 'Tired Pioneers and Dynamic Newcomers? A Comparative Essay on English and German Entrepreneurial History, 1870–1914', *Economic History Review* 47 (1994).

35. However, the acquisition of companies by firms of their own nationality can pose the same or a greater threat. In the 1980s the British conglomerate BTR acquired the old-established tyre company Dunlop and proceeded to destroy its historical records.

36. R. Locke, *The End of the Practical Man* (Greenwich, CT, 1994); idem, *Management and Higher Education since 1940* (Cambridge, 1989).

37. S.P. Keeble, *The Ability to Manage: A Study of British Management, 1890–1990* (Manchester, 1992); R. Fitzgerald, 'Industrial training and management education in Britain; a missing dimension', in N. Kawabe and E. Daito (eds), *Educational Training in the Development of Modern Corporations* (Tokyo 1993); H.F. Gospel, *Markets, Firms and the Management of Labour in Modern Britain* (Cambridge, 1992); Mary Rose, 'Investment in human capital and British manufacturing industry to 1990', in Kirby and Rose (eds), *Business Enterprise*; idem, 'Education and Industrial Performance: Influences on British Experience since 1945', in E. Abe and T. Gourvish (eds), *Japanese Success? British Failure?* (Oxford, 1997).

38. Rolv Petter Amdam (ed.), *Management, Education and Competitiveness. Europe, Japan and the United States* (London, 1996); N. Tiratsoo and J. Tomlinson, 'Exploring the 'Gospel of Productivity': United States Technical Assistance and British Industry 1945–1960', *Business History Review* 71 (1997); T.R. Gourvish and N. Tiratsoo (eds), *Missionaries and Managers. American Influences on European Management Education 1945–60* (Manchester, 1998); Lars Engwall and Vera Zamagni (eds), *Management in Historical Perspective* (Manchester, 1998).

39. Rolv Petter Amdam and Ove Bjarnar, 'Regional Business Networks and the Diffusion of American Management and Organisational Models to Norway, 1945–65', *Business History* 39 (1997); M. Kipping and O. Bjarnar (eds), *The Americanisation of European Business* (London, 1998).

40. R.R. Nelson and S.G. Winter, *An Evolutionary Theory of Modern Change* (Cambridge, Mass, 1982); N. Rosenberg, *Inside the Black Box* (Cambridge, 1982); G. Dosi et al., *Technical Change and Economic Theory* (London, 1988); R.R. Nelson, 'Why Do Firms Differ, and How Does it Matter?', *Strategic Management Journal* 12 (1991).

41. David Hounshell and John Kenly Smith, *Science and Corporate Strategy* (Cambridge, 1988); David Hounshell, 'Planning and Executing 'Automation' at Ford Motor Company, 1945–65' in H. Shiomi and K. Wada (eds),

Fordism Transformed (Oxford, 1995); idem, 'The Evolution of Industrial Research in the United States', in Richard S. Rosenbloom and William Spencer (eds), *Engines of Innovation: US Industrial Research at the End of an Era* (Boston, 1996); L. Galambos, 'The Innovative Organisation: Viewed from the Shoulders of Schumpeter, Chandler, Lazonick et al.', *Business and Economic History* 22 (1993); Lou Galambos with Jane Eliot Sewell, *Networks of Innovation. Vaccine Development of Merck, Sharp & Dohme, and Mulford, 1895–1995* (Cambridge, 1995).

42.   Rolf Petter Amdam, 'Professional Networks and the Introduction of Research in the British and Norwegian Pharmaceutical Industry in the Interwar Years', *History and Technology* 13 (1996).

43.   S.W. Usselman, 'IBM and its Imitators: Organisational Capabilities and the Emergence of the International Computer Industry', *Business and Economic History* 22 (1993); M. Campbell-Kelly, 'Development and Structure of the International Software Industry, 1950–1990', *Business and Economic History* 24 (1995); Ross Hamilton, 'Despite Best Intentions: The Evolution of the British Minicomputer Industry', *Business History* 38 (1996).

44.   J. Yates, *Control Through Communication* (Baltimore, 1989); Lisa Bud-Frierman (ed.), *Information Acumen* (London, 1993).

45.   Barry Supple, 'Fear of failing : Economic history and the decline of Britain', *Economic History Review* (1994); David Edgerton, 'The Decline of Declinism', *Business History Review* (1997).

46.   See the introduction by Scranton and Horowitz and several of the papers in *Business and Economic History* 26, 1 (1997); Alice Kessler-Harris, 'Ideologies and Innovation: Gender Dimensions of Business History,' *Business and Economic History* 20 (1991); Angel Kwolek-Folland, 'The African American Financial Industries: Issues of Class, Race and Gender in the early 20th Century', *Business and Economic History* 23, 2 (1994). For European perspectives on gender, see Anita Göransson, 'Gender and Property Rights: Capital, Kin and Owner Influence in Nineteenth and Twentieth Century Sweden,' *Business History* 35 (1993); and R. Oldednziel and V. Willemars, 'Vrouwen enhetideaal van Scientific Management: De geschiedenis van het International Institute for Industrial Relations, 1922–1946', *Neha-jaarboek* 58 (1995).

47.   On the role of the State as entrepreneur and public companies in Spain, see F. Comín and P. Martín-Aceña (eds), *Historia de la Empresa Pública en España* (Madrid, 1991).

48.   I owe this point to Lina Gálvez-Muñoz.

49.   In addition to Chandler's works, see also Louis Galambos and Joseph Pratt, *The Rise of the Corporate Commonwealth* (New York, 1988); Mansel G. Blackford, *The Rise of Modern Business in Great Britain, the United States, and Japan* (Chapel Hill, 1988); William Lazonick, *Business Organisation and the Myth of the Market Economy* (Cambridge, 1991).

50.   Aimée Moutet, *Les Logiques de L'Enterprise* (Paris, 1997); François Caron, *Les deux révolutions industrielles du XX siècle* (Paris, 1997).

51.   Jones, *British Multinational Banking*; T.R. Gourvish and Richard Wilson, *The British Brewing Industry 1830–1980* (Cambridge, 1994). The writing of

industry studies is by no means an exclusively British trend. For example, Jacques van Gerwen and Marco van Leeuwen at the Nederlandsch Economisch-Historisch Archief are researching a history of the Dutch insurance industry.

52. Leslie Hannah, *The Rise of the Corporate Economy* (London, 1976, 2nd edn 1983).

53. Jan Luiten van Zanden, *Ein klein land in de 20e eeuw. Economische geschiedenis van Nederland, 1914–1995* (Utrecht, 1997), ch. 3.

54. Y. Cassis, *Big Business. The European Experience in the Twentieth Century* (Cambridge, 1997).

55. Rolv Petter Amdam, Sverre Knutsen and Lars Thue, *Bedrift og Samfunn* (Bergen, 1997); Thomas K. McCraw, *Creating Modern Capitalism* (Cambridge, Mass., 1997). David J. Jeremy, *A Business History of Britain 1900-1990s* (Oxford, 1998).

56. For Spain, see G. Nuñez and L. Segreto (eds), *Introduction a la Historia de la Empresa en España* (Madrid, 1994). A more recent and substantial Spanish compilation is F. Comín and P. Martín-Aceña, *La empresa en la Historía de España* (Madrid, 1996). The best review of Spanish business history literature is F. Comín and P. Martín-Aceña, 'Rasgos históricos de las empresas en España. Un panorama', *Revista de Economía Aplicada* 4, 12 (1996). For Portugal, see the special issue of *Análise Social* 32 (1996) on 'História Empresarial en Portugal'.

57. Carlos Dávila L. de Guevara (ed.), *Empresa e Historia en América Latina. Un Balance historiográfico* (Bogota, 1996); Rory Miller, *Britain and Latin America in the Nineteenth and Twentieth Centuries* (London, 1993) makes an impressive attempt to incorporate business history research into a wider historical framework.

58. R.A. Brown, *Capital and Entrepreneurship in South-East Asia* (London, 1994); idem (ed.), *Chinese Business Enterprise in Asia* (London, 1995).

59. Hans Conrad Peyer, *Roche. A Company History 1896–1996* (Basel, 1996).

60. Richard Roberts, *Schroders* (London, 1992); Richard Saville, *Bank of Scotland. A History 1695–1995* (Edinburgh, 1996); Ulf Olsson, *At the Centre of Development. Skandinaviska Enskilda Banken and its Predecessors 1856–1996* (Borås, 1997). French banking history is especially active. Prominent examples include Hubert Bonin's research on Société Générale, e.g. H. Bonin, *Société Générale in the United Kingdom* (Paris, 1996).

61. Keetie E. Sluyterman, *Moret 100 Jaar* (Rotterdam, 1993); Edgar Jones, *True and Fair. A History of Price Waterhouse* (London, 1995); Michel Dumoulin, *Petrofina* (Louvain-la-Neuve, 1997); René Brion and Jean-Louis Moreau, *Tractebel 1895–1995* (Antwerp, 1995).

62. E.g. Horst A. Wessel, *Kontinuität im Wandel. 100 Jahre Mannesmann 1890–1990* (Düsseldorf, 1990).

63. L. Gall, G.D. Feldman, H. James, C.-L. Holtfrerich, H.E. Büschgen, *The Deutsche Bank 1870–1995* (London, 1995).

64. D.K. Fieldhouse, *Merchant Capital and Economic Decolonization. The United Africa Company 1929-1987* (Oxford, 1994); R.B. Weir, *The History of the Distillers Company 1877–1939* (Oxford, 1995).

65. J.H. Bamberg, *The History of the British Petroleum Company. Volume 2. The Anglo-Iranian Years, 1928–1954* (Cambridge, 1994).
66. E.g. J.J. Dankers and J. Verheul, *Hoogovens 1945–1993* (The Hague, 1993); Aart Camijn and Anne-Marie Kuijlaars, *Een Energiebedrijf in Beweging* (Rotterdam, 1994); Keetie E. Sluyterman and Huib H. Vleesenbeek, *Three Centuries of De Kuyper* (Schiedam, 1995); Dirk de Wit, *60 + 40 is waar schijnlijk hondred. Ahrend* (Rotterdam, 1996).
67. Donald Coleman, 'The Uses and Abuses of Business History', *Business History* 39 (1987).
68. This point was made to me strongly by Keetie Sluyterman in the case of her experience in the Netherlands.
69. Robert Fitzgerald, *Rowntree and the Marketing Revolution 1862–1969* (Cambridge, 1995).
70. Keetie E. Sluyterman, *Driekwart eeuw CSM: cash flow, strategie en menden* (Amsterdam, 1995).
71. Rolv Petter Amdam and Knut Sogner, *Wealth of Contrasts* (Oslo, 1994).
72. L. Cailluet (1995), 'Stratégies, structures d'organisation et pratiques de gestion de Pechiney des années 1880 à 1971' Ph.D. thesis, University of Lyon II; at Rotterdam, Mila Davids focuses on aspects of the privatisation of the PTT and Anne-Marie Kuijlaars focuses on the theme of centralisation versus decentralisation in the institutional history of the CBS.
73. Lars Hassbring, *The International Development of the Swedish Match Company 1912–1924* (Stockholm, 1979); Karl-Gustaf Hildebrand, *Expansion. Crisis. Reconstruction* (Stockholm, 1985); Hakan Lindgreen, *Corporate Growth, The Swedish Match Industry in its Global Setting* (Stockholm, 1979); Hans Modig, *Swedish Match Interests in British India during the Interwar Years* (Stockholm, 1979); Ulla Wikander, *Krueger's Match Monopolies 1925–1930* (Stockholm, 1979).
74. An example is F.C. Gerretson, *History of the Royal Dutch*, 4 vols (Leiden, 1958).
75. F.H.H. King, *The History of the Hongkong and Shanghai Banking Corporation*, vols 1–4 (Cambridge, 1987–91).
76. E. Buyet, I. Cassiers, H. Houtman-Desmedt, G. Kurgan-van Hertenryk, M. van Meerten, G. Vantemsche, *La Générale de Banque 1822–1997* (Brussells, 1997; English edn, Tielt, 1997).
77. Finn Erhard Johannessen, *Alltid underveis. Postverkets historie gjennom 350 år, vol. 1, 1647–1920*; Lars Thue, *Alltid underveis. Postverkets gjennom 350 år, vol. 2, 1920–1997* (Oslo, 1997). In contrast, the five-volume history of the Danish Post Office co-ordinated by Hans Christian Johansen takes a more institutional view of its subject.
78. L. Gálvez-Muñoz (1998) 'Familia y Mercado. El Género en el Proceso de industrialización de la Fábrica de Tabacos de Sevilla bajo la gestión de la Compañía Arrendataria de Tabacos (CAT) 1887–1945', Ph.D. thesis, European University Institute.
79. Charles Wilson, *The History of Unilever*, vols 1 and 2 (London, 1954).

'The first shall be the last': recent developments in Belgian Business History
A first introduction

Greta Devos

UFSIA, University of Antwerp

In comparison with neighbouring countries such as the Netherlands and Germany, Belgian interest in business archives and business history was rather late in developing. The General State Archivist Etienne Sabbe was the first in 1934 to draw attention to the importance of business archives for economic history. During the nineteenth century much interesting and valuable material was destroyed by archivists – for instance in Ghent – on the pretext that one cannot write history 'à l'aide de bouquins de boulangers et de cordonniers', with the help of books kept by bakers and shoemakers.[1]

The rather late initiatives after the Second World War concerning the saving of archives and the writing of business histories is difficult to reconcile with the fact that in the economic history literature Belgium is considered as the leading country on the Continent on the Industrial Revolution.

Indeed Belgium, or rather the Austrian Netherlands were at first hand to introduce new techniques which allowed modern industry to develop in the late eighteenth and early nineteenth centuries. The rich coal seams running from northern France to the Ruhr crossed Belgium from west to east. With the exception of the Limburg seams which were not exploited until the early twentieth century, the Belgian coal-producing area was completely confined to the Walloon part and this has largely moulded its economic development. Until the 1860s Belgium was self-sufficient as far as iron, zinc and lead ore for her industries were concerned. Coal and mineral ores were two crucial factors in the development of heavy industry during the Industrial Revolution, though not the only ones. Motive power was another. The Walloon area is crossed, especially in the east from Charleroi to Luxemburg, by streams which provided the power of a host of water mills and at the same time served as important means of communication and transport. The country has also enjoyed a well-developed infrastructure since the eighteenth century. The result was that the Industrial Revolution took root there more quickly and more firmly than elsewhere on the Continent. Textiles in the region around Verviers and Ghent, coal and iron in the Liège and Mons area and the Borinage were the leading economic sectors. Initiative and entrepreneurship stimulated further development, as the capital Brussels became a centre of *haute finance*, where large banks and holdings got a grip on national and international enterprises. Antwerp, at the lower end of the Scheldt estuary, had to close its port to international navigation in the seventeenth century. Towards the end of the eighteenth century, under French rule, the Scheldt was reopened and the city expended its vast energy on the redevelopment of the port and its trade. That is the reason the Industrial Revolution largely by-passed Antwerp. Economic factors combined with political developments and changing political situations favoured the whole movement.

THE KEEPING OF BUSINESS ARCHIVES

So although Belgium was one of the pioneers in the early nineteenth century, this did not stimulate the preservation and care of business archives, nor the publication of business histories. On the other hand, Germany and the Netherlands, which industrialised rather late in the nineteenth century, demonstrated their interest quite early; at the beginning of the twentieth century important German entrepreneurs such as Krupp, Siemens, Duisburg and Reuter kept and stored their archives carefully.[2] The first German regional economic archives, the *Wirtschaftsarchive*, date from 1906. In the Netherlands the NEHA (Dutch Economic Historical Archives) was founded in 1914. Another pioneer was Switzerland a few years earlier with the establishment of an Economic Record Office in Basel and an Archive for Trade and Industry in Zurich.

In Belgium there are no dedicated economic archives. Here public institutions, and especially the municipal archives of larger towns have led the way in ensuring the preservation of business archives. The first submissions in Flanders went to the municipal archives in Antwerp with the archives of the Chamber of Insolvent Estates (sixteenth, seventeenth and eighteenth centuries) and the archives of the General Indian Company, better known as the Ostend Company, in the eighteenth century, although one can be sure that these archives were kept for largely political reasons and interest rather than for economic ones. In Bruges are to be found the oldest accounting ledgers relating to currency and exchange trading. Cities such as Ghent (pioneers of the cotton industry) and Verviers (with early archives of the woollen mills) keep records for the textile sector.

After the Second World War more things changed as the National and Provincial State Archives initiated a more active acquisition programme. But still in 1960 Professor G. Jacquemyns of the Université Libre de

Bruxelles attributed arrears in economic and financial contemporary history to the absence or the inaccessibility of many business archives for the period. Indeed the situation in the early 1960s was deplorable. The few initiatives of the National State Archives after the Second World War were in 1971 joined by the Centre for Business History at the Antwerp University (UFSIA). Meanwhile other universities, museums and many private organisations and associations have followed their example. Some businessmen, particularly those running large enterprises, have come to realise the value of their documents and keep them 'on site'. In 1975 the Association of Archivists and Librarians in Belgium issued a directory, edited by Dr Hilda Coppejans-Desmedt. This has subsequently been updated and the supplement – which is more voluminous than the first part – has been published recently.[3] It contains references to the business archives deposited in public repositories as well as those retained by private institutions and sometimes by companies. In this way an attempt is made to bring some unity in the chaotic situation that developed especially after the 1970s. This has resulted in certain large and important archives being deposited in several different locations. The most poignant example is what happened recently to the archives of the Boelwerf, the last major shipbuilding company in Belgium which was active until 1994. These very extensive archives were deposited in no less than seven locations; at the local State Archives in Beveren (the routine documents); at the Centre for Business History in Antwerp (the general and most recent documentation on shipbuilding); at the National Maritime Museum (mostly construction drawings); at the Armed Forces Center for Documentation near Brussels (those documents relating to the construction of mine-sweepers and submarines); at the library for Maritime Technology at the Ghent University (database for laser technology); while most of the remainder went to the municipal archives of Temse, the small town where the yard was located.

In 1975 the business archives directory composed by Hilda Coppejans-Desmedt already listed about 800 different archival fonds. For the supplement 250 institutions and societies were contacted as potential keepers of business archives. Some seventy-two of them responded positively. In the meantime it has been established that since 1975 the volume of acquisitions has more than quadrupled. About 40 per cent relates to the mining and metallurgy industries, especially in the Walloon region. For Flanders the acquisitions of coalmining papers are more recent. They concern the documents transferred to the State Archives at the closure of the Campine coalmines in the early 1990s. Also automobile production and trading, and the chemical and energy sectors submitted details of important records. The different branches of the textile industry are now represented in more realistic proportions. The oldest company records date back to the fourteenth century, the most recent from just a few years ago.

Despite recent acquisitions many gaps remain, in particular for agriculture and horticulture, fisheries, canneries and tinning factories. Information remains scarce not only for traditional industries such as diamonds, leather, ropeworks and shoes, but also more recent branches such as the pharmaceutical industry, production of medical equipment, alarm and security systems, heating and cooling technologies, telecommunication, electric data treatment, aviation, tourism, etc. Seldom have the corporate archives that were transferred to public safekeeping been retained in their entirety, because a part was destroyed by the owner, because at the time of transfer some items were left behind or because a deliberate selection was made. Shortage of storage space makes archive selection necessary. Therefore the dispersion of archives can result in the preservation of a greater number of the records.

In recent years a more preventative method has been introduced. Following the example of the Netherlands Economic History Archives (NEHA) in Amsterdam, the Antwerp Centre for Business History initiated three years ago the registration of archives in the possession of companies in operation. Contrary to the Dutch NEHA project which took a national approach, the Antwerp University opted for a provincial or regional approach, in part because the five-year project, in collaboration with the Belgian State Archives, is being financed by the Province of Antwerp. Obviously local interests take precedence over national ones. With details taken from address books a total of 1792 companies in the province were selected and approached. The size of the companies – based on the current employment levels – and their geographic location in the province were taken into account, to ensure that the sample was representative. Special attention was paid to companies, more than fifty years old, which were important in the pre-war period. By Belgian norms the response was high at 17 per cent or in total 306 companies. All completed the questionnaire with company data such as location, date of establishment, any predecessor companies; and information on the archives themselves such as location; extent of current and non-current record holdings; accessibility; existing finding-aids; types of documents; iconography; personnel and company publications, jubilee editions etc. Each responding company is introduced with a short historical summary. One of the findings of the survey was that many companies systematically destroy their old documents when the legal retention period has expired. This applies particularly to accounting records and correspondence. Documents such as minutes, personnel files, annual reports and documents relating to their 'heritage' are generally preserved longer.

Nevertheless the enquiry offers a representative overview of the archives still in the possession of extant companies. Meanwhile similar projects have been started for the provinces of Flemish Brabant and Liège and for the city of Brussels. In addition to the information on business archives deposited in the public and some private archives, we will eventually possess a treasure trove of information on the basis of which proper valid choices regarding preservation can be made. Indeed, the purposes of this project are multiple. With regards to the registration of business archives, we firstly wish to obtain a review of the items still held by companies, also by publishing this data we can provide the interested researcher with a listing of available documents; at the same time we want to make the companies aware of the 'treasures' they hold and that they form part of the economic heritage within the province. The study of the different economic sectors since the end of the nineteenth century will assist the librarian or the archivist in the selection of the various archives. These data should allow selection on the basis of scientific evidence and the importance of the respective sectors based on added value and employment, although one must admit that archives of SME's still slip through the net.

In the field of 'macro-selection' valuable work has been carried out in the Netherlands where a macro-selective model was set up for the textile industry by Erich Fischer and Jacques van Gerwen.[4] But the theme provokes heated discussions between archivists and researchers, as was clearly visible at the Colloque organised by the Centre for Business History in Antwerp in 1997 on the subject. Macro- and micro-selection happen to be highly topical as a result of recent media protests regarding the taking over by the National State Archives of the extensive mining records for the Campine region. The creativity of the business historian is thus jeopardised. Too often in the past series of documents considered unimportant were partly or wholly destroyed.

THE WRITING OF BUSINESS HISTORIES

First of all with the exception of a few publications on different economic sectors in the nineteenth and early twentieth centuries, the literature on business history was almost non-existent before the Second World War. What is more stringent, the early stages of industrialisation did not particularly inspire economic historians, with the exception of the publication by Professor Lebrun of Liège on the woollen industry at the end of the eighteenth and the beginning of the nineteenth century, shortly after the Second World War (1948).[5] It was one of the first valuable examples largely based on business papers, but in reality it was once more the history of an economic sector. The recent foundation of a centre for pre-industrial production processes and labour relations at the Vrije Universiteit Brussels in collaboration with the IISG in Amsterdam promises a rich harvest on business history oriented publications for the *ancien régime*. Earlier, two of the initiators of this Centre Hugo Soly en Catharina Lis

completed an outstanding study on a textile plant in a small town in the
Antwerp province during the twilight zone between the eighteenth and
nineteenth centuries.[6]

However, the recording of business history itself has progressed, particularly during the last decade. When Professor A.K.L. Thijs of Antwerp
University gave a review on the backwardness of Belgian business history,
in 1989, as a report of a research day at the Catholic University of Tilburg
in the Netherlands on the subject 'Business history in the tension zone
between commission and scientific research', his conclusions were rather
pessimistic, perhaps too pessimistic.[7] He did postulate that some very early
and valuable work had been published relating to business history in
general – that being the history of industries and sectors. To this effect he
quoted the early example of the history of twenty-five years of Belgian
railroads written by the publicist Auguste de Laveleye in 1862. About the
history of separate individual companies he was less optimistic. He indeed
referred to the importance of the 'Chamber of Insolvent Estates' records in
the Antwerp municipal archives, which had already been researched before the Second World War. This collection contains papers of bankrupt
commercial companies from the sixteenth to the eighteenth century, and
has generated several publications. The scientifically justified contemporary
business histories were rather scarce according to him, and he enumerated
a number of causes in explanation. Firstly he stated that the volume of
many business archives discourages both the student and the researcher.
The inadequate economic and technical formation of most historians and
the preference of economists for 'the actual' are additional faults. Furthermore, the university generated too few impulses to entice the interest of
thesis students towards business history. On the part of the corporations,
Thijs questioned the need for companies to publish histories on the occasion of important anniversaries. The authors too often are persons closely
related to the company: public relations people, retired managers or directors. The publications narrate the company's developments, seldom place
these in a wider socio-economic context, and too frequently these publications are not distributed to the general public.

Even if an entrepreneur engages a professional historian to write the
history of his company, tensions can arise between commission and science
because the Belgian entrepreneur is quite suspicious. After all, he never
knows for sure if the historian, to whom he allows access to his accounts,
his correspondence and the minutes of his board meetings, will actually
serve the interests of the company. Furthermore Belgian entrepreneurs feel
beset from all sides by the 'bureaucratic' state, left-wing politicians, labour
unions, etc. Evidently this is an historic development, and can be explained
by the very liberal-minded Belgian state of the nineteenth century, and the
progressive government interferences since the First World War. The state

tax collector, to some extent also controller of the freedom of enterprise, remains the enemy of the businessman. Very early on Belgian business was confronted with labour movements that manifested themselves as strongly anti-capitalist and anti-employer. These traumas are further reinforced by periodically surfacing publications, for example the publications relating to economic collaboration during the Second World War, to the internal strife within the 'upper classes' and to the resistance of the Belgian holding classes against the multinationals. Thijs concluded in 1989 that a number of conditions have to be met before decent business histories can be written: universities must make the necessary provisions to allow students to better prepare themselves for the role of scientifically operating business historians and the entrepreneurs must realise that only the truth about their companies will in the long term make clear the exact impact of business on society in the past.

Today, almost ten years later, a number of the conditions enumerated by Thijs remain unfulfilled. In spite of this it can be argued that not only the quantity, but also the quality of the publications have respectively increased and improved. This applies just as well to works commissioned by companies, employers' organisations, industrial federations, and so on, as to fundamental scientific research within the framework of long- or even short-term projects. The increased interest in this branch of history bears witness not only to the willingness of young researchers to study business history aspects or at least utilise business archives for their research. Seminars and workshops increasingly pay attention to business archives and histories. Particularly eminent is the Groupe d'Histoire du Patronat at the Université Libre de Bruxelles, along with the older Centre for Business History in Antwerp. Meanwhile the Flemish Society for Business History has announced the publication of a manual, involving some thirteen authors from the historical and other sciences. This interdisciplinary approach with attention to accounting, law, sociology, business economy, and so on, should make it easier for the student and the researcher to cross existing thresholds.

There is undoubtedly an increased demand in the business world for histories of enterprises, sectors and local economies. This tendency is also evident within the framework of industrial archeology, more specifically in relation to remarkable restorations and conversions of old company premises into offices and apartments, for example in the port of Antwerp. It should also be mentioned that in Antwerp certain business history publications are so popular that they have even given rise to a new business history genre: the comic strips, mostly compiled by company workers.[8]

A bibliographic review of Belgian business history is only now in preparation. A dedicated library does not exist,[9] nor does a Belgian-specific periodical, and nor does a business history university chair. With the exception of the Centre for Business History in Antwerp, founded in 1971, no centres occupy themselves solely with business history. Ten years ago, in co-operation with the National State Archives, the initially very Brussels-oriented 'Association pour la valorisation des histoires d'entreprises' was founded, better known as the Coppée-group after the then president, who was a member of the important Coppée family of entrepreneurs. This Association acquires business archives for deposit in the National State Archives in Brussels, catalogues them and commissions business histories. They usually employ the services of two 'freelance' historians, René Brion and Jean Louis Moreau, who have compiled histories of enterprises in different sectors in 'record time'.[10] The association assumes that all these services can be offered to companies against payment. Almost five years ago in Antwerp, the Flemish Association for Business History was established by archivists and academics. Here the dialogue between archivists and researchers of almost five Flemish Universities tries to promote scientific oriented business histories on an academic level. As per its articles of association, the association wishes to stimulate the scientific application of business history, safeguard business archives and transfer them to the National State Archives, improve access to available sources, campaign for better realisation among businessmen, students and researchers of the importance of scientific business history through the organisation of colloques, and the writing of manuals for researchers and archivists. Business organisations such as the Flemish Economic Union and the local Chambers of Commerce are approached to reach businesses. In this context an exhibition was organised by Chantal Vancoppenolle in Brussels four years ago on the Chambers of Commerce in Belgium[11] and three years ago the Centre for Business History, celebrating its twenty-fifth anniversary, arranged an exhibition on the Antwerp Chamber of Commerce. This was a good opportunity to draw up an inventory of the archive documents that the Antwerp Chamber was still holding and to plead for the opening of the archives to the public as well as the writing of a history on the occasion of its bicentenary in 2002.

As previously mentioned, it is not easy to give a complete review of business history research in Belgium. Still each university has its own centre dealing with business history to varying degrees. Foremost is the Antwerp Centre for Business History, where from the beginning attention was paid to the accumulation of archives and company or personnel publications, besides the publication of monographs on business history with specific emphasis on the entrepreneurial mentality and on maritime, commercial and financial business.[12] As an international port the city attracted foreign entrepreneurs for centuries, giving rise to many publications on the activities and integration of the newcomers.[13] At the Vrije

Universiteit Brussels the Centre for Contemporary Social History emphasises in their studies the social aspects, such as labour conditions, labour
relations, syndicalism, wages and consumption, making extensive use of
business archives.[14] The Centre for Economic Studies in Louvain tends to
conern itself with macro-economic problems such as the reconstruction of
national accounts for the nineteenth and twentieth centuries, and sectoral
studies.[15] Specific is the interest for the banking sector under the director-
ship of Herman Van der Wee,[16] a theme they have in common with the
Université Libre de Bruxelles and Ginette Kurgan. The Brussels Groupe
d'Histoire du Patronat pays specific attention to the entrepreneur and the
SME's.[17] The Université Catholique de Louvain is, among others, represented by Michel Dumoulin and collaborators in the Unité d'Histoire
Contemporaine who concentrate on the role of business and labour interest groups in Europe in the twentieth century.[18] The Université de Liège
studies industrial and technological aspects in the nineteenth and twentieth
centuries; their activities are outstanding in the economic history sphere,
as publications by Nicole Caulier-Mathy and Suzy Pasleau on testify. The
Nieuwste Geschiedenis department of Ghent University is active in the
social and political aspects of business. Of course individual researchers,
whether or not attached to scientific institutes, are active in the field.

In a recent article written by the Dutch historian Ferry de Goey on
business history in America, the Netherlands and Belgium (1940–95), their
issues, methods and themes, the author advances the discussion on the
definitions of business history in the wide sense, and entrepreneurial history.[19] While his separation of both definitions is not generally accepted, it
can be said that in the Netherlands the foundations of entrepreneurial
histories were laid at the end of the 1960s. In Belgium little consideration
has been given to the eventual differences, in fact entrepreneurial history
forms part of business history and is a weaker subdivision. In short,
entrepreneurial history for the nineteenth and twentieth centuries in both
countries is on the slow burner. However, the *ancient régime* has been the
subject of a number of remarkable studies since the end of the 1950s,
including the publication by Wilfrid Brulez on international trade by the
Flemish company Della Faille during the sixteenth century.[20]

Biographically oriented monographs for the industrial era are scarce,
however. The danger and even the fear of writing hagiographies have had
their effect. In many cases journalists and company members were attracted
to this kind of historiography, not always encouraged the historian to write
biographies. A very recent initiative in the right direction follows the English
example – the 1996 publication of the collective biography, the *Dictionnaire
des patrons en Belgique 1830–1980* by the Université Libre de Bruxelles in
collaboration with historians from other Belgian universities.[21] This publication not only gave rise to the compilation of an employers database. Through

the attention paid to the economic career, social role, political functions, cultural engagement, philosophical set-up, relationships, sociability, pluralities, intersection of interests, it will without doubt contribute to a more careful and realistic picture of the entrepreneur. The initiator of this project, Ginette Kurgan, is no stranger to the history of entrepreneurship; in the early 1980s she wrote about the financier Simon Philippart and railroad investments in the 1860s to 1890s. Recently a book was published on the leading figures of the Société Générale.[22]

Belgian historians and industrial archeologists cannot boast of a series of published works on technological history, as the Dutch and the British can. In fact, the history of technology has largely been neglected. A very recent remarkable study, written by doctor of Science W. Van Craenenbroeck on the Antwerp Waterworks 1860–1930 not only describes the economic developments of the firm but also explains the different projects and their pros and cons, richly illustrated with plans and sketches.[23]

Until now little attention has been drawn to the theoretical foundations of business history. The publications commissioned by companies lack by their very nature any theoretical introduction, while the use of business archives for studies with sectoral or thematic approaches do not demand specific business oriented theory. Contributions by Belgian authors based on theoretical ideas and published in foreign scientific reviews are non-existent. Even so, some work has been completed in Louvain and in Brussels. In fact, both concentrated on the size of entreprises. The Centre for Economic Studies was in the 1970s strongly influenced by A. Chandler's visions. The way was opened by the Louvain historically interested economist Herman Daems, who became a scholar of Chandler. It gave rise to the assembling of lists with the top one hundred enterprises in different periods and put the focus on large enterprises and holdings.[24] The Louvain group even laid the foundation for the discussion on the connections between organisation models and investment strategies at the International Economic Congress at Copenhagen in 1974. But in this 'big is beautiful' vision there was no room for the numerous small and medium-sized enterprises. This gap has been filled since the early 1990s at the Université Libre de Bruxelles, where small and medium-sized enterprises are in the limelight. Some introductory remarks, presented at the Tenth International Economic History Congress at Louvain in 1990, were further developed in the following years.[25]

SOME FINAL REMARKS

The publication of new inventories of business archives, and the introductory courses on business history and its sources, stimulate young scholars to study the history of enterprises or at least utilise business archives in their research. Seminars and workshops at the universities increasingly address to the problem. Within the scope of 'bridge building processes' in history, interdisciplinary interest is also growing among psychologists, anthropologists, marketing people, and industrial archeologists. Furthermore there is an increased interest shown by the business world itself for business histories, for the economic sectors and the local economy in the past, written by historians. It goes together with coincidental factors such as two important anniversaries: the fiftieth anniversary of the end of the Second World War and the centenary of economic revival and financial expansion abroad experienced in the late 1890s. Although one must admit that nearly every historical date provides an opportunity for commemoration. For the contemporary period, still, a great part of the monographs concentrate on history written on the occasion of an important anniversary, in other words on case studies of individual enterprises. Almost all these publications lack any theoretical introduction. Belgian business history still remains an empirical matter. With the exception of accidental references to Max Weber, Joseph Schumpeter or Alfred Chandler, it remains on the whole rather deficient in conceptualisation.

With regard to the future, many more initiatives will be required to make up for the relative arrears compared with neighbouring countries. On the subject of company archives, special attention will have to be paid to the matters of selection. For macro-selection the Dutch 'four-stage-model' (registration; study of industrial sectors; selection of archives; actions towards entrepreneurs) or micro-selection demands a better training of archivists to enable them to make a justified selection of sections of company archives for destruction. In this they need to be provided with assistance from business historians and technically competent members of the business community. As for business history itself, the universities in particular will have to make extra efforts to organise and improve the training of business history scholars. The publication of manuals, inventories, theoretical introductions, the writing of scientific monographs and the organising of workshops all constitute suitable tools to propagate business history.

NOTES

1. Cited by H. Coppejans Desmedt, 'Bedrijfsarchieven in België ter beschikking van onderzoek en studie: stand van zaken' in *Bedrijfsgeschiedenis, een uitdaging*, G. Devos (ed.), *Miscellanea Archivistica Studia 99* (Brussels, 1998), p. 83.
2. H.A. Wessel, 'Das Archivwesen der Wirtschaft und unternehmensteschichtliche Forschung in Deutschland' E. Fischer and J.L.J.M. van Gerwen 'Bedrijfsgeschiedenis en bedrijfsarchieven. De Nederlandse stand van zaken', in G. Devos (ed.), *De bedrijven en hun geheugen. Verslag van de studiedag*

32 DEVOS

rond bedrijfsgeschiedenis Antwerpen, 10 December 1993, Miscellanea Archivistica Studia 60 (Brussels, 1994), pp. 22–3 and p. 42.

3. Titles of the French version: H. Coppejans-Desmedt, Guide des Archives d'Entreprises conservées dans les dépôts publics de la Belgique (Brussels, 1975); H. Coppejans-Desmedt, Ch. Luyckx, D. Van Overstraeten and R. Wellens, Guide des archives d'entreprises accessibles au public en Belgique. Supplément, Archives Générales du Royaume-Guides 41 (Brussels, 1998).

4. E.J. Fischer, J.L.J.M. van Gerwen and G. Reudink, Stap voor stap. Een proeve van macro-selectie inzake Nederlandse Bedrijfsarchieven (Amsterdam Zeist, 1994), pp. 11–36.

5. P. Lebrun, L'Industrie de la laine à Verviers pendant le XVIIIe et le début du XIXe siècle. Contribution à l'étude des origines de la Révolution Industrielle (Liège, 1948).

6. C. Lis and H. Soly, Een groot bedrijf in een kleine stad. De firma De Heyder en C° te Lier, 1757–1834 (Lier, 1987).

7. A.K.L. Thijs, 'Bedrijfsgeschiedenis in België: peiling naar de ontwikkeling van mentale achtergronden', Economisch- en Sociaal-Historisch Jaarboek 25 (1989), pp. 31–41.

8. It applies to the shipping company Compagnie Maritime Belge (1995) and the Katoen Natie and its general manager (an enterprise specialising in the handling of goods in the Antwerp port).

9. An interesting overview is given by F.M.M. de Goey, 'Ondernemersgeschiedenis in Amerika, Nederland en België (1940–1995). Trends in vraagstellingen, onderzoeksmethoden en thema's: een overzicht', in NEHA-Jaarboek voor economische, bedrijfs- en techniekgeschiedenis, t. 95 (Amsterdam, 1996), pp. 21–65. But a lot of publications on business history are omitted by J. Blomme and P. Scholliers in their contribution on economic history in the 1980s, published in: NEHA-Bulletin. Tijdschrift voor de economische geschiedenis in Nederland, VII (1993), pp. 5–38.

10. E.g. R. Brion and J.-L. Moreau, Tractébel 1895–1995. Les métamorphoses d'un groupe industriel (Antwerp, 1995); R. Brion et al., Fédération des entreprises de Belgique: 10 ans pour l'entreprise (1895–1995) (Tielt, 1995); R. Brion and J.-L. Moreau, Histoire de la Société Générale (Brussels, 1998).

11. C. Vancoppenolle, Tussen Beleid en Belang. Geschiedenis van de Kamers van Koophandel in België (17de-20ste eeuw) (Brussels, 1995).

12. E.g. R. Baetens (ed.), Spiegels van Mercurius. Plouvier & Kreglinger. Tweehonderd jaar handel en maritiem transport (Tielt, 1998); G. Asaert, G. Devos and F. Suykens, The 'naties' in the port of Antwerp. Six centuries of activity in city and port (Tielt, 1993); G. Devos and G. Elewaut, CMB 100. A century of commitment to shipping (Tielt, 1995); on business strategies: H. Greefs, 'Foreign Entrepreneurs in Early Nineteenth-Century Antwerp', in C. Lesger and L. Noordegraaf (eds), Entrepreneurs and Entrepreneurship in Early Modern Times. Merchants and Industrialists within the Orbit of the Dutch Staple Market, Hollandse Historische Reeks, XXIV (The Hague, 1995), pp. 101–17.

13. E.g. G. Devos, 'Inwijking en integratie van Duitse kooplieden te Antwerpen in de 19de eeuw', in H. Soly and A.K.L. Thijs (eds), Minorities in Western

European Cities Sixteenth-Twentieth Centuries, Belgisch Historisch Instituut te Rome XXXIV (Brussels, Rome, 1995), pp. 135–56; idem, 'Die Firma Königs-Günther & Co. Ein Beitrag zum Häute- und Wollhandel deutscher Kaufleute in Antwerpen im 19./20. Jahrhundert', in W. Feldenkirchen et al. (eds), *Wirtschaft, Gesellschaft, Unternehmen. Festschrift für Hans Pohl zum 60. Geburtstag* II, (Stuttgart, 1995), pp. 862–75; H. Greefs, 'Enkele zwaartepunten in het onderzoek naar ondernemerschap en ondernemersstrategieën te Antwerpen 1794–1870', *Revue Belge de Philologie et d'Histoire* 76 (1998), pp. 419–42.

14. E.g. P. Scholliers, *Wages, Manufactures and Workers in the Nineteenth-Century Factory. The Voortman Cotton Mill in Ghent* (Oxford, Washington DC, 1996); idem, *Lonen in het chocoladebedrijf Côte d'Or, 1907–1931* (Brussels, 1980). Note also the work of D. Luyten on economic collaboration during the Second World War and on corporatism.

15. E. Buyst, 'De ondernemersfiguur in industrie en handel in België', in *NEHA-Jaarboek voor economische, bedrijfs- en techniekgeschiedenis 95* (Amsterdam, 1996), pp. 66–76.

16. E. Buyst, I. Cassiers, H. Houtman-Desmedt, G. Kurgan-Van Hentenryk, M. Van Meerten and G. Vanthemsche, *The Generale Bank 1822–1997. A Continuing Challenge* (Tielt, 1997); H. Van der Wee and M. Verbreyt in, *The Generale Bank* (Tielt, 1997); H. Van der Wee and M. Verbreyt, *Mensen maken Geschiedenis. De Kredietbank en de Economische Opgang van Vlaanderen 1935–1985* (Brussels, 1985).

17. G. Kurgan-Van Hentenryk, 'La petite entreprise de la fin de l'Ancien Régime à nos jours (Belgique)', in *Petite entreprise et croissance industrielle dans le monde aux XIXe et XXe siècles* (Paris, 1981), pp. 189–223; S. Jaumain, *Les petits commerçants belges face à la modernité (1880–1914)* (Brussels, 1995).

18. M. Dumoulin and A.-M. Dutrieue, *La Ligue européenne de coopération économique. Un groupe d'étude et de pression dans la construction européenne (1946–1980)* (Bern, 1993). Recent publications on business history include: M. Dumoulin, *Petrofina, un groupe pétrolier international et la gestion de l'incertitude. 1920–1979*, Recueil de travaux d'histoire et de philologie. 7e série, Fac. de Philosophie et Lettres, 4 (Louvain-la-Neuve, 1997); A.-M. Dutrieue, 'La Banque de Bruxelles au miroir de son conseil d'administration de 1871 à 1914', in *Etudes et Documents* IV (1992); M. Dumoulin (ed.), *Franki. Building a World* (Tielt, 1992).

19. F.M.M. de Goey, 'Ondernemersgeschiedenis in Amerika', pp. 21–65.

20. W. Brulez, *De firma Della Faille en de internationale handel van Vlaamse firma's in de zestiende eeuw* (Brussels, 1959); See also: H. Soly, *Urbanisme en Kapitalisme te Antwerpen in de 16de eeuw. De stedebouwkundige en industriële ondernemingen van Gilbert van Schoonbeke* (Brussels, 1977); H. Houtman-De Smedt, *Charles Proli, Antwerps zakenman en bankier 1732–1786: Een biografische en bedrijfshistorische studie* (Brussels, 1983); and R. Baetens, *De nazomer van Antwerpens welvaart. De diaspora en het handelshuis De Groote tijdens de eerste helft van de zeventiende eeuw* (Brussels, 1976).

21. G. Kurgan, S. Jaumain and V. Montens (eds), *Dictionnaire des patrons en Belgique. Les hommes, les entreprises, les réseaux* (Brussels, 1996).
22. G. Kurgan-Van Hentenryk, *Rail, finance et politique. Les entreprises Philippart (1865–1890)* (Brussels, 1982); idem, *Gouverner la Générale de Belgique. Essai de biographie collective* (Brussels, 1996).
23. W. Van Craenenbroeck, *Antwerpen op zoek naar drinkwater 1860–1930. Ontstaan en ontwikkeling van de openbare drinkvoorziening te Antwerpen* (Tielt, 1998).
24. H. Daems, *The Holding Company*, KUL, Fac. Economische en Toegepaste Economische Wetenschappen, Dept. Economie (Louvain, 1975); idem, *The Holding Company and corporate control* (Leiden, 1978); A.D. Chandler, *Managerial hierarchies: compared perspectieves on the rise of modern industrial enterprise* (Cambridge, Mass., 1980); H. Daems and H. Van der Wee, *The Rise of Managerial Capitalism* (Louvain, 1974); H. Van der Wee, 'Large firms in Belgium, 1892–1974: an analysis of their structure and growth', in D.C. Coleman and P. Mathias (eds), *Enterprise and history. Essays in honour of Charles Wilson* (Cambridge, 1984), pp. 199–211.
25. G. Kurgan-Van Hentenryk and E. Chadeau, 'Structure et stratégie de la petite et moyenne entreprise depuis la révolution industrielle: rapport général', in H. Van der Wee and E. Aerts (eds), *Debates and Controverses in Economic History. A-sessions. Proceedings of the Tenth International Economic Congress, Louvain, August 1990* (Louvain, 1990), pp. 167–91; E. Chadeau, G. Kurgan and M. Müller, 'Introduction', in *Structure and Strategy of Small and Medium-Size Enterprises since the Industrial Revolution*, Zeitschrift für Unternehmensgeschichte, Beiheft 83 (Stuttgart, 1994), pp. 7–19; See also: G. Crossick and S. Jaumain (eds), *Cathedrals of Comsumption. The European department store 1850–1939* (Aldershot, 1999).

The Changing Nature of the Business – Government Relationship in Western Europe after 1945

Matthias Kipping

Centre for International Business History, University of Reading[1]

INTRODUCTION

The role of governments in business matters is subject to considerable debate among scholars. The most restrictive view in this respect is without doubt taken by neo-classical economists. They argue that public involvement and intervention is only justifiable when the working of market forces alone would not lead to the optimal allocation of resources.[2] An important reason for such a 'market failure' are economies of scale which only allow *one* efficient producer to be present in a given market. What is usually referred to as 'natural monopoly' concerns especially utilities such as water, electricity or telecommunications, industries which, historically, have been regulated or owned by governments in most countries.[3] By contrast, neo-classical economists almost unanimously condemn any form of subsidy or protection which distort the working of the market mechanism.

More recently, however, there have been arguments in favour of a more active role for government. These have been advanced from two directions. On the one hand, there is the literature on the competitive advantage of nations.[4] The work of Michael Porter has been especially prominent in this respect. He stresses that the competitive success of companies in world markets is due to a combination of factors, including, for example, the available inputs and a network of related and supporting industries. At the same time, he underlines the need for the government to provide the necessary framework for these companies, namely by safeguarding domestic competition and ensuring overall economic stability, especially a low inflation environment. So far, this would have raised little contention among neo-classical economists. However Porter also advocates a more direct role for government, through the funding of basic and some applied research, the provision of the necessary infrastructure and an investment in human resources and training. Not surprisingly, these ideas were criticised by economists close to the neo-classical school.[5]

Most of these views lack a dynamic and temporal dimension. By contrast, a more evolutionary perspective has been adopted by those examining the contributions made by government in the rapid industrial development of Japan and the South East Asian economies.[6] In general, they highlight that, under certain circumstances, the 'active intervention by a strong developmental state in industrial development' can minimise the risk of co-ordination failures and ensure productivity growth at the same time.[7] Certain authors, especially in the United States, saw government intervention in these countries as an unfair advantage in international competition, consequently suggesting the use of political pressure or, if necessary, retaliatory measures to force Asian governments to open their markets and establish a more distant relationship with business.[8] Others have highlighted the role of entrepreneurial initiative in the rapid development and international competitive success of Japanese companies in certain industrial sectors, for example computers and steel production.[9]

Most of the above authors see government and, to a somewhat lesser extent, business as single, monolithic blocks and do not distinguish differences of opinion within each of them. By contrast, this article will examine the changes of the government–business relationship in Western Europe in the post-war period, based on an interest-group framework.[10] Such a view, derived from political science, looks at governments and businesses as a collection of interests groups which can also form coalitions across the divide.[11] As the article will show, government intervention is therefore not only the result of policy decisions to which companies or their representatives then react, but can also be a response to a demand from business or parts thereof. And neither should external influences, especially from the development of European integration and/or the world economy, only be seen as constraints placed on government and business. Both can actually influence them – to a larger or lesser degree – through their own actions.[12] At the same time, they can also use them as arguments and 'levers' to change the situation at a national level.

The article is structured chronologically. The first part gives an overview of the extension of public involvement in the economy during the post-war period until the early 1980s. The second part looks at the major shift which occurred with the adoption of the Single Market Programme by the European Union in 1987 and its consequences. The article concludes with a brief consideration of the future role of governments in a rapidly changing European and global economy. In each of these parts, the article will highlight the – sometimes considerable – differences between the major European countries in terms of government–business relations. France will be considered in some detail, because the country has long been identified as a special case. During the twentieth century, the French state has on average intervened more in industrial matters than any of its counterparts in Western Europe.[13]

THE INCREASING INVOLVEMENT OF GOVERNMENT IN BUSINESS MATTERS

From the end of the Second World War until the early 1980s, public involvement in the economy increased considerably in Western Europe in three major steps: (i) the immediate post-war period, which saw a redefinition of the role of government; (ii) the 1960s, when many countries pursued a national industrial policy; and (iii) the 1970s, characterised by attempts to alleviate the consequences of the two oil crises. While the evolution of government–business relations during each of these periods responded to a changing external environment, the European countries also influenced this environment and their own room for manoeuvre by increasing the level of economic integration. This factor came to play an important role subsequently.

THE EXTENSION OF GOVERNMENT INFLUENCE AFTER 1945

After the end of the Second World War, the wartime controls over the economy were initially maintained in many Western European countries in order to deal with shortages of food and basic raw materials. But even after gradually relaxing these controls, governments on the whole adopted a much more active role in economic and business matters than before the war.[14] The extension of government involvement was partly driven by political and ideological considerations, and partly by a recognition that the previous system had not produced the desired economic and social results during the Great Depression. Many countries therefore embraced some form of Keynesian demand management and a – more or less – limited redistribution of income. They usually also adopted a wide range of social and economic legislation which extended their influence into the sphere of private business. A number of countries nationalised certain key industries, a policy which had sometimes already been initiated during the inter-war period. In the case of Italy for example, almost all of the nationalisations had occurred under the fascist regime in the 1930s. None of them was reversed after the war.[15]

In France, the government increased its actual and potential influence over the economy as a whole and over individual industries and companies considerably after the Liberation of the country from German occupation. Companies in a number of sectors were nationalised between 1944 and 1948.[16] They included coal mines, electricity and gas supply, part of the transport sector, retail banking and insurance as well as a few specific companies, namely the automobile producer Renault whose founder and manager had been accused of collaboration with the German occupants. The government also adopted several social and employment measures, including consultative enterprise councils, a comprehensive system of health care and unemployment benefits, and retained the possibility to control prices.[17] A minimum wage (SMIG) was introduced in 1950. In addition, at the beginning of 1946, the government established a planning agency, the Commissariat Général du Plan (CGP), headed initially by Jean Monnet. Compared to its Soviet counterpart, the powers of the CGP were extremely limited. Representatives of business, government and labour were organised by sector in so-called modernisation commissions, which developed plans covering a four-year period. Only in the sectors where the government had direct control were the plans then implemented, most often with massive public financing. For companies in the private sector these plans were not binding, but served only as indications.[18]

It is interesting to note that the United States did little to prevent the massive increase in government involvement in France or other countries, despite its considerable political and economic influence over European governments.[19] It is especially surprising that the financial assistance given to Europe by the Marshall Plan from 1947/48 onwards was not used as a lever to protect private enterprise. The relative American inaction is due to a number of reasons. First of all, the Marshall Plan administration was – at least at the beginning – dominated by the 'new dealers' who also advocated a more active government role.[20] Secondly, the US government appeared most concerned about the possibility that communist parties could take power in countries like France and Italy and was therefore (a) prepared to accept almost any policy which could prevent this from happening and (b) reluctant to do anything which could be seen as interference in internal affairs.

Thirdly, Western European countries at the time made a clear commitment to market mechanisms, rather than centralised state planning or control. Following the American example, they moved to ban domestic and international cartels which had played such an important – and rather detrimental – role during the inter-war period.[21] The extent to which cartels actually disappeared has been questioned by some authors, who claim that many of them survived or were re-established.[22] But competition nevertheless increased as a result of the gradual opening of markets in Western Europe. This occurred first at a multilateral level with the General Agreement on Tariffs and Trade (GATT), signed in 1947, and then, more importantly, through the European integration process. The latter began with the European Coal and Steel Community (ECSC) which was established by France, Germany, Italy and the Benelux countries in 1951.[23] It was extend to the whole economy of these six countries with the Treaty of

Rome in 1957, which set up the European Economic Community (EEC) or Common Market.[24]

Many businessmen in Europe viewed the extension of government involvement and the introduction of more competition with suspicion. For example, in a speech during a visit to the United States in 1951, the head of the French and of the European employers federation, Georges Villiers, vituperated against the *dirigisme* in his own country and the extension of the welfare state in general as a 'socialist' effort towards equalisation.[25] He and his fellow business leaders also opposed the strict anti-trust provisions contained in the ECSC Treaty which was being ratified at the time. Their efforts to block the Treaty were counteracted not only by the governments involved, but also by a small, yet vocal and influential group of industrialists in many countries who actually favoured more open and competitive markets. Most of them came from the downstream or consumer goods industries, and some of them actually headed nationalised companies. A good example in this respect is Pierre Lefaucheux who had become CEO of the French car producer Renault when it was nationalised in 1945.[26]

Overall therefore, the government role in economic and business matters was considerably extended in most Western European countries in the immediate post-war period. In addition to adopting Keynesian demand management and laying the foundation for a – more or less comprehensive – welfare state, governments also started to open markets for more competition and established means to prevent and/or address market failures. Some countries, namely France, also created an apparatus, namely in the form of indicative planning, price and credit controls, which potentially enabled it to exercise a more direct influence over private companies. During the 1960s, the French and a few other European governments actually used this apparatus to pursue a more proactive industrial policy.

NATIONAL INDUSTRIAL POLICIES DURING THE 1960s

This further increase in government involvement was, once again, motivated by a change in the external economic environment, namely a considerable increase in international competition. Competitive pressures resulted, on the one hand, from a gradual removal of barriers to the free movement of goods, services, capital and people among the six member states of the EEC, which was accomplished in July 1968, six months ahead of the schedule established in the Treaty of Rome. At the same time, American multinationals reinforced their presence on the European Continent and became increasingly perceived as a major competitive threat by indigenous producers.[27] Britain came under similar pressures, especially because it applied and prepared to join the Common Market (Britain finally became a member in 1973).

The increased competition necessitated a considerable effort by European companies to improve their competitiveness, namely through further concentration. In certain countries, concentration was achieved with little or no government involvement. This was the case in Germany, where the business community traditionally aimed at preventing government interference, by resolving any potential conflict among themselves.[28] As a matter of fact, some of the few state-owned German companies, namely Volkswagen, were privatised during this period. In Britain and France, by contrast, government pressured private and state-owned companies to set up national champions in certain industries perceived to be of strategic importance.[29] A detailed examination of the French example demonstrates the – often nationalistic – objectives of this proactive industrial policy, but also highlights its difficulties in terms of potential and actual resistance from the companies concerned.

An important precondition for a more active government role in the economy was the return of General de Gaulle to power in 1958. With popular consent he changed the constitution to establish a regime with a strong president at its top, a post he held himself between 1959 and 1969. His successive governments began to interfere more directly in industrial matters and made extensive use of the wide variety of powers at their disposal. Initially they focused on the need for further concentration, by promoting the formation of so-called national champions, namely in high technology. In the computer industry, for example, the government managed to 'convince' three French electronics producers (CGE, CSF and Schneider) to combine their interests into a single entity, the Compagnie Internationale de l'Informatique (CII) in December 1966. The 'deal' offered to them in exchange was that 'the State provides the CII with financing, guarantees both R&D and sales for the company, as long as it develops a range of computers "which are original and have nothing to do with American technology"'.[30] This was not only directed against the predominant US producers, namely IBM, but also against the other French computer company Bull which was partly owned by General Electric.

It should be noted that business shared some of the objectives of the national industrial policy, namely the need for further concentration and a modernisation of infrastructures. However, the carrot and, if necessary, stick policy of the French government did not always produce the desired results. For example in the chemical industry, the different producers for a long time refused to combine their activities.[31] And even in the case of the nationalised industries, this process was often less smooth than it appears. Here, the government seemed – at least theoretically – well placed to influence the process throughout the whole value chain from the R&D stage to the customer. First of all, graduates of the country's elite higher education system, the so-called 'Grandes Écoles', were in charge of the institutions or organisations involved at each of the steps and also at the corresponding regulatory or political authorities. Secondly, the final products were usually purchased either by the government itself or a state-owned enterprise. However, many of the Grandes Écoles graduates at the company level resented and, sometimes, openly opposed any government interference.

In the late 1960s, government attention shifted towards investments in the so-called major projects (grands projets).[32] Most of them concerned an improvement and a modernisation of the country's infrastructure, for example the replacement of the outdated telephone network. But the government also financed other projects, like the development of a high-speed train together with the construction of a corresponding railway infrastructure. Unlike the industrial policy under de Gaulle, some of these projects were now carried out in collaboration with partners from other European countries, albeit under French leadership. This was the case with, for example, the rocket Ariane and the civil aircraft Airbus. In contrast with the earlier – disastrous – Franco-British supersonic Concorde project, the latter already showed a certain shift towards a more market rather than supply and technology driven approach.

But while some of them, such as Ariane and Airbus, can probably be characterised as successful, many others, as time progressed, appeared less so. The real costs and hidden failures of the national industrial policies became only obvious after the oil crises of the 1970s. At the same time, European companies came under increasing pressure from Japanese and, subsequently, other East Asian producers. What proved most consequential in the long run was the fact that the majority of these and the earlier projects had been largely financed through inflationary means, with a corresponding weakening of the French currency.[33]

GOVERNMENT ATTEMPTS TO DEAL WITH THE CRISES IN THE 1970s

Like most of its counterparts in Europe, the French government initially responded to the slowdown in the world economy and the major losses it caused at many companies, whether state-owned or not, with more rather than less public involvement. From the mid-1970s onwards, the government provided massive subsidies to the loss making companies and also protected them from foreign competition, by obtaining a – temporary – exemption from the free movement of goods under article 115 of the EEC Treaty. In both respects France, Italy and – to a somewhat lesser extent – Great Britain were the major 'offenders'.[34]

In France, the interventionist policies of bail outs, further concentration and protection were quite often pursued with major inconsistencies and frequent changes in direction. This was the case for example in the computer industry where the government initially favoured a European solution for the national champion CII through the formation of Unidata together with the German Siemens and the Dutch Philips in 1973, only to abandon it two years later. In 1976, the government finally merged CII with the other French producer Bull, now majority owned by the American Honeywell, providing four billion francs of orders and the same amount as a subsidy.[35] Government intervention reached its apex with the nationalisation of many large companies carried out in 1982, one year after the election of the socialist François Mitterrand to the presidency. The new government acquired the majority control of Bull and several other large industrial firms, namely in the electronics, engineering and chemical sector, the two major industrial holding banks (Paribas and Suez), many smaller banks as well as the remaining shares in the large, already publicly owned retail banks Crédit Lyonnais, BNP and Société Générale. The government combined the nationalisation with an ambitious investment programme and an expansionary macroeconomic policy.[36]

However, only two years later the government changed its course, embarking on a gradual – and extremely costly – disengagement from ownership and direct intervention in industry. Here, like in many other countries which experienced similar problems, developments at the European level played a major role in redefining the relationship between government and business and redrawing the boundaries between public and private.

THE INFLUENCE OF EUROPEAN INTEGRATION

The 1980s and 1990s saw major changes in the government–business relationship in Western Europe. Most of these changes were prompted by the relaunch of European integration, especially the so-called Single European Act of 1987 and plans for Economic and Monetary Union laid down in the Maastricht Treaty of 1993. These developments affected all the member countries of the European Union to varying degrees. But some of them had already made some decisions and moves towards reducing the role of the state in economic and business matters.

A REDUCTION OF GOVERNMENT INTERVENTION

This was especially the case in Britain and France, the two countries which had probably pursued the most proactive national industrial policy in the preceding decades. In the British case, the Conservative prime minister Margaret Thatcher who came to power in 1979, moved relatively quickly to privatise an increasing number of government-owned companies, including for example British Steel and British Airways, and to deregulate most of the public utilities, such as telecommunications, electricity, gas and the railways. Most of the latter were also privatised, sometimes beforehand, sometimes subsequently.[37] Her motivations were largely ideological and inspired by the example of the United States, where Ronald Reagan from 1981 onwards accelerated a deregulation effort started by his predecessors.

In France, the government also changed its economic and industrial policy quite drastically in 1983, to the surprise of many observers. The extent of this change and the surprise it caused is probably best summarised in the foreword of a book, published in 1985, which assessed the industrial policy under the Fifth Republic: 'Only less than two years ago, everybody expected the industrial policy, the real one, the one which was going to get the country out of the crisis. Today, even the expression is banned from the public discourse and spirit: the State has lost its godliness'.[38] Thus, state-owned companies could no longer assume that deficits would be covered automatically by the state and were requested to return to profitability in relatively short time periods. At the same time the government embarked on a major austerity programme, cutting public spending and increasing some taxes.[39]

These quite dramatic shifts in attitude and actual policy were driven on the one hand, by mounting losses in many of the state-owned companies (in the steel industry alone they accumulated to more than 50 billion francs between 1981 and 1985) and by the inflationary effects of the earlier increases in public expenditure, on the other. After three devaluations between 1981 and 1983, the French government decided not to devalue the French currency again, in order to stay within the European Monetary System (EMS). The EMS had been established in 1979 with the aim of stabilising exchange rates within the European Community.

From 1986 onwards, the government – now a centre-right coalition – also embarked on a privatisation programme, gradually returning many of the state-owned companies to the private sector, including for example Paribas, Suez, and Société Générale, the glass producer Saint-Gobain and the engineering and electronics firm CGE. Privatisation was halted, when the socialists returned to power between 1988 and 1993. But at the same time, they continued the policy of financial prudence initiated in 1983. In 1993, with the return of the centre-right to power, privatisation was resumed, now on an even larger scale. It now also concerned some of the 'holy cows', such as the car producer Renault, which was partially privatised in 1994 and the state holding reduced below 50 per cent in 1996. After finally returning to profitability, the steel producer Usinor-Sacilor was also sold off in 1995.[40]

THE CRUCIAL ROLE OF THE SINGLE MARKET PROGRAMME

These developments in France and elsewhere in Europe were also driven by a re-launch of the European integration process from the mid-1980s onwards. They concerned namely the idea to complete the internal market for the movement of goods, services, capital and people or 'four freedoms', which was initiated by the European Commission in Brussels with a White Paper in 1985. The main aim of the Commission and its President Jacques Delors was to overcome the 'Eurosclerosis'. But the initiative was also prompted by the intervention of a group of CEOs from a few larger European companies, assembled in the so-called European Round Table (ERT), who were concerned about their international competitiveness.[41] It led to the Single European Act (SEA) of 1987 which specified a whole catalogue of measures aimed at removing the remaining non-tariff barriers by a specific deadline, 31 December 1992. By that date, the European Union adopted around 300 directives which had to be adapted into national law by its member states. Some of them are still being implemented at the moment.[42]

The motivations of the individual member states of adopting what appears – at least in retrospect – as a rather radical agenda are less easy to assess, because they differed considerably.[43] The British government under Margaret Thatcher hoped to extend its own privatisation and deregulation efforts to the rest of Europe, possibly providing British companies with better market access. The French saw the single market as an opportunity to improve the competitiveness of European industry relative to its American and especially Japanese rivals. One of their objectives might also have been to extend their own national industrial policy, which had proved too costly, to the European level, i.e. to create European instead of national champions.[44] However, there were also groups who expressed concern about the consequences of more open markets in Europe. While broadly positive, the German and French unions for example feared a lowering of their high social standards. By contrast, the Southern member states saw their industries threatened by imports from the more advanced producers in Northern Europe. Both were eventually compensated through the establishment of a social policy and an increase in funding for underdeveloped regions/countries, respectively.

The Single European Market (SEM) had important consequences for European business and for government ownership and influence. Its actual impact differs considerably from one sector to the next and one region or country to another, but its main results were (a) a wide-ranging deregulation of economic activities, often followed, sometimes preceded by privatisation in cases of state-owned industries or companies; and (b) a major increase in the extent and intensity of competition for most industries.[45] This obviously concerned first and foremost public utilities. Some of them, like telecommunications, have been completely deregulated in recent years. In other cases, such as electricity, the opening of markets to domestic and, more importantly, foreign competition is still ongoing.

Another regulated industry with high levels of public ownership prior to the SEM was air transport.[46] Over the last decade, European airlines have undergone major changes, many of which also had a direct and visible impact on consumers. In a number of steps, Europe moved from bilateral agreements to a completely free internal market by April 1997. European operators can now fly between any two EU countries without any restrictions. Prices came down and passenger numbers increased, especially as a result of the establishment of a number of so-called low cost or budget airlines. The existing carriers were affected by these changes to different degrees, namely depending on whether the air travel in their own country had already been liberalised. This was especially the case with British Airways, which was already privatised in the mid-1980s. Lufthansa also managed a fairly quick turnaround when its profitability started to deteriorate in the early 1990s and has meanwhile become majority privately owned. Many of the other airlines are still state-owned today, but this is changing fairly rapidly, because the European Commission makes its agreement to further public subsidies conditional on a future privatisation.

However, the current situation of rather pronounced competition might only be temporary, if the American experience is anything to go by. In the United States deregulation was already carried out in the late 1970s. But since then there has been a gradual shake out of the budget airlines and increasing concentration with the formation of a few mega carriers. This also seems to be the trend in Europe, where the number of alliances is increasing – though it is not certain that they will lead eventually to fully-fledged mergers. It is difficult to believe that European countries are willing to see their national flag carriers disappear.[47] In addition, attention has shifted more to the global level recently, where a number of international alliances have been formed.

There are other regulated sectors which saw major, albeit less visible changes as a result of the SEM. Financial services was one of the areas specifically targeted by the 1992 programme. But so far, hardly any bank or insurance company has rushed to establish offices or branches abroad. This is mainly due to the fact that it would have been very difficult and costly to acquire customers and create loyalties to new and foreign service providers. Instead there have been a series of mergers both at national and at European levels. This has increased the level of concentration both in the banking and the insurance sectors considerably.[48] Once again, in order to level the playing field, the European Commission insists on future privatisation in cases where governments want to support ailing financial service providers. The best known case in this respect is the state-owned bank Crédit Lyonnais in France. Its rescue is expected to cost the French taxpayer approximately US$35 billion (*Frankfurter Allgemeine Zeitung*, 23 December 1997). After long and tedious debates between Paris and Brussels, it is now scheduled to be privatised in 1999.

Finally, there are sectors where the impact of the SEM has so far been fairly modest, because they were already subject to European and, more importantly, global competition and/or they remain at least partially sheltered by specific temporary exemptions. This is for example the case of the automobile industry. While none of the major producers is any longer fully state-owned, the production of cars and related products has continuously received a lot of government attention, because it is the single most important industrial sector in Europe, accounting for close to ten per cent of employment. The most important driver for change in this industry over the last decade was not the SEM, but the evolution at a global level, namely the international expansion of Japanese automobile producers during the 1980s.[49]

In this respect the SEM had, however, two indirect effects. First of all, it forced certain European countries, namely France and Italy, which had imposed restrictions on the import of cars from Japan, to gradually reduce these barriers. A gradual opening of these markets and the European Union as a whole between 1992 and 1999 was negotiated between the European Commission and the Japanese Ministry of Trade and Industry (MITI) under active participation of the European car producers and their trade association ACEA.[50] To deal with the increased competition proved difficult for some of the national producers like Fiat, whereas those in more open markets, e.g. Volkswagen of Germany, had already made the necessary adjustment. Secondly, the SEM made it possible for the Japanese manufacturers to assemble cars (with a high local content) within the European Union. Most of the investments were made initially in the United Kingdom, but other countries also benefited, by supplying parts, and some of them are set to receive major new investments in the future.

Despite the increased presence of Japanese producers, cross-border competition in automobiles remains limited for the time being. This is mainly due to the fact that car manufacturers were granted a so-called block exemption from the SEM rules concerning distribution. This means that the national distributors can only actively promote and sell cars within their countries. As a result, the differentials between prices for the same model in different countries are still quite considerable, even after accounting for the differences in taxation. And car prices in Europe overall are significantly higher than for example in the United States. The original exemption was granted for five years, renewed for a further five years last year, but seems unlikely to be renewed again. This in turn might result in more competition forcing prices down and, thus promoting further consolidation of the sector which is still quite dispersed in global comparison.

Overall, the SEM not only changed the competitive environment in Western Europe, it also had a profound impact on the government–business relationship. It was one of the major reasons which prompted governments to reduce their direct intervention and their ownership of industries and companies. At the same time, the SEM increased the influence of the European institutions in business matters. It should therefore come as no surprise that companies and trade associations have increased their lobbying efforts at the European level considerably over the last decade.[51] These developments are set to continue in the future.

CONCLUSION AND OUTLOOK

The article has shown that business–government relations in Western Europe were driven little, if at all, by economic theory. Instead, they evolved considerably over time, reflecting changes in the predominant outlook towards the government role in the economy and, probably more importantly, the evolution of the economic and competitive environment. Thus, from the immediate post-war period to the 1970s Western Europe saw an expansion of government involvement in business matters. Countries like France and Britain were especially active during the 1960s when they pursued an industrial policy promoting the concentration of domestic industry. They were also the countries to struggle most, when the repeated crises of the 1970s and the increase in competition from Asian companies exposed the weaknesses of these national champions. From 1980s onwards, these countries therefore pursued a reduction of government influence as well as the privatisation of many state-owned companies, albeit at different speeds. The gradual reduction of direct government influence in these countries has been very costly, in social and in monetary terms.

In the mid-1980s the European Union came to play an important part in the redefinition of the government role, especially through the so-called single market programme which resulted in a removal of the remaining barriers to the free movement of goods, services, people and capital. This entailed a commitment to end all subsidies to national companies and also led to the – still ongoing – deregulation of many previously protected sectors such as air transport, telecommunications and electricity. Concerning the actual extent of government involvement, there are nevertheless still differences between the European countries, for example between a more liberal British and a more interventionist French attitude. But Western Europe as a whole has now fully embraced what could be called the 'new orthodoxy', which combines market-oriented policies with a limited government influence.[52] This policy is summarised well by the French Finance Minister Dominique Strauss-Kahn: 'The government holds neither the view that the state should no longer play any role in the economy, especially on budgetary matters, nor the idea that public expenditure is always effective, regardless of its level and use.'[53]

The article has also shown that business and its representatives have not only been observers and passive recipients of government policy. Very often, influential industrialists have played an active role in shaping or rejecting these measures both at a national and at a European level. They seem to have played a particularly important part on two occasions: first, at the origins of European integration when the decision to establish an open and competitive market in Western Europe was made; then again in the 1980s when competition was extended with the single market programme. On both occasions, concerns to promote their own competitiveness appear to have been important drivers for the direct involvement of certain industries and their leaders. A key role was usually played by those sectors involved in downstream activities and active in international markets, like for example the automobile industry.

These trends will be reinforced in the future, namely as a result of European Monetary Union (EMU). Efforts towards monetary integration in Western Europe started shortly after the Second World War.[54] But the first successful step – in the long run – was made only in 1979 with the establishment of the European Monetary System (EMS) which aimed mainly at stabilising exchange rates. Following the creation of the single market, plans for Economic and Monetary Union were laid down in the Maastricht Treaty of 1993. EMU commenced in eleven out of the fifteen EU member states on 1 January 1999. Exchange rates between their currencies were irrevocably fixed, common notes and coins will be introduced in January 2002. Monetary policy has been taken out of the control of national government and handed over to the European Central Bank (ECB), with headquarters in Frankfurt. More importantly, EMU is likely to lead to further convergence among other government policies in Western Europe, because membership imposes quite strict financial criteria on the participating countries, namely in terms of budgetary discipline. In the future, this might also lead to closer co-operation and even harmonisation of fiscal policies.

For businesses, EMU removes the exchange rate risk for an important part of their market, but at the same time increases price transparency and therefore competition. In the long-run, this should increase their competitiveness and thus enhance their ability to compete successfully against their American and Japanese rivals.

NOTES

1. An earlier version of this article was presented at the December 1998 meeting of the Japan Association for Research in Business Administrative Behaviour (JARBAB). The author would like to thank Professor Sakurazawa for

organising his presentation, the Association's President Professor Kikuchi for inviting him, and all participants for many helpful comments. He is also grateful to his colleagues Mark Casson and Geoffrey Jones for a number of additional suggestions. The usual disclaimer applies.

2. W.J. Baumol, *Welfare Economics and the Theory of the State* (London, 1965).

3. R.H.K. Vietor, 'Contrived Competition. Economic Regulation and Deregulation, 1920s-1980s', *Business History* 36, no. 4 (1994), pp. 1–32.

4. M.E. Porter, *The Competitive Advantage of Nations* (London, 1990); R. Robert, *The Work of Nations. Preparing Ourselves for 21st-Century Capitalism* (London, 1991).

5. P. Krugman, 'Competitiveness: A Dangerous Obsession', *Foreign Affairs* 73 (1994), no. 2, March/April, pp. 28–44.

6. C. Johnson, 'Political institutions and economic performance: the government–business relationship in Japan, South Korea and Taiwan', in C. Deyo Frederic (ed.), *The Political Economy of the New Asian Industrialism* (Ithaca, 1987), pp. 136–64; J.E. Vestal, *Planning for Change. Industrial Policy and Japanese Economic Development, 1945–1990* (Oxford, 1993).

7. Ha-Joon Chang, *The Political Economy of Industrial Policy* (Basingstoke, 1994), pp. 134–35.

8. T.K. McCraw (ed.), *America versus Japan* (Boston, 1986); and K.P. Phillips, 'U.S. Industrial Policy: Inevitable and Ineffective', *Harvard Business Review* (July–August 1992), pp. 104–12.

9. M. Anchordoguy, 'Mastering the Market. Japanese Government Targeting of the Computer Industry', *International Organization* 42 (1988), pp. 509–43; and Seiichiro Yonekura, *The Japanese Iron and Steel Industry, 1850–1990. Continuity and Discontinuity* (Basingstoke, 1994).

10. The paper will not deal with the changes which occurred in Central and Eastern Europe over the last decade. These have been quite radical, because most of the countries of the former Soviet block have moved from central government planning to economies dominated by market forces.

11. S.D. Berger (ed.), *Organizing Interests in Western Europe. Pluralism, Corporatism and the Transformation of Politics* (Cambridge, 1981); F.L. Wilson, *Interest-group politics in France* Cambridge (Cambridge, 1987).

12. S. George, 'The European Union: approaches from international relations', in H. Kassim and A. Menon (eds), *The European Union and National Industrial Policy* (London, 1996), pp. 11–25.

13. R.F. Kuisel, *Capitalism and the state in modern France. Renovation and economic management in the twentieth century* (Cambridge, 1981); P. Fridenson, 'France: The relatively slow development of big business in the twentieth century', in Alfred D. Chandler Jnr et al. (eds), *Big Business and the Wealth of Nations* (New York, 1997), pp. 207–45.

14. B. Eichengreen (ed.) *Europe's post-war recovery* (Cambridge, 1995).

15. M. Maraffi, *Politica ed Economia in Italia. La vicenda dell'impresa pubblica dagli anni Trenta agli Anni Cinquanta* (Bologna, 1990).

16. C. Andrieu et al. (eds), *Les nationalisations de la Libération. De l'utopie au compromis* (Paris, 1987).

17. H. Dumez and A. Jeunemaître, *Diriger l'économie. L'Etat et les prix en France (1936–1986)* (Paris, 1989).

18. P. Mioche, *Le Plan Monnet. Genèse et élaboration 1941–1947* (Paris, 1987).

19. J. Killick, *The United States and European Reconstruction, 1945–1960* (Edinburgh, 1997).

20. J. McGlade, 'From business reform programme to production drive: the transformation of US technical assistance to Western Europe', in M. Kipping and O. Bjarnar (eds) *The Americanisation of European Business. The Marshall Plan and the Transfer of US Management Models* (London, 1998), pp. 18–34.

21. V.R. Berghahn, *The Americanisation of West German Industry 1945–1973* (Cambridge, 1986); M. Kipping, 'Concurrence et compétitivité. Les origines de la législation anti-trust française après 1945', *Etudes et Documents* VI (1994), pp. 429–55.

22. W.A. Brusse and R.T. Griffiths, 'L' 'European Recovery Program' e i cartelli: una indagine preliminare', *Studi Storici* 37, no. 1 (January–March 1996), pp. 41–68.

23. M. Kipping, *Intégration économique et compétitivité internationale. La France et les origines de la construction européenne 1944–1952* (Paris, forthcoming) (revised and extended translation of *Kartellen und Konkurrenz* (Berlin, 1996)).

24. W.A. Brusse, *Tariff, Trade and European Integration, 1947–57* (Basingstoke, 1997).

25. M. Kipping, 'Operation Impact: Converting European Business Leaders to the American Creed', in Kipping and Bjarnar, *The Americanisation of European Business* (1998), pp. 55–73.

26. Kipping, *Intégration économique et compétitivité internationale.*

27. J.-J. Servan-Schreiber, *Le défi américain* (Paris, 1967).

28. M. Kipping, 'Inter-Firm Relations and Industrial Policy: The French and German Steel Producers and Users in the Twentieth Century', *Business History* 38, no. 1 (January, 1996), pp. 1–25.

29. J. Zysman, *Political Strategies for Industrial Order. State, Market and Industry in France* (Berkeley, 1977); P.A. Hall, *Governing the Economy. The Politics of State Intervention in Britain and France* (Oxford, 1986); J. Hayward, *The State and the Market Economy. Industrial Patriotism and Economic Intervention in France* (London, 1986).

30. E. Cohen and M. Bauer, *Les grands manoeuvres industrielles* (Paris, 1985), p. 37.

31. Cohen and Bauer, *Les grands manoeuvres industrielles.*

32. E. Cohen, *Le Colbertisme 'high tech'. Economie des Telecom et du Grand Projet* (Paris, 1992).

33. E. Cohen, 'France: National Champions in Search of a Mission', in J. Hayward (ed.), *Industrial Enterprise and European Integration* (Oxford, 1995), pp. 23–47, esp. pp. 26–7.

34. D. Neven and J. Vickers, 'Public Policy Towards Industrial Restructuring: Some Issues Raised by the Internal Market Programme', in K. Cool et al. (eds), *European Industrial Restructuring in the 1990s* (Basingstoke, 1992), pp. 162–98.

35. Cohen and Bauer, 'Les grands manoeuvres industrielles', *Le Monde*, 9 September 1995.
36. V.A. Schmidt, *From state to market? The transformation of French business and government* (Cambridge, 1996).
37. V.V. Ramanadham (ed.), *Privatisation in the UK* (London, 1988).
38. Cohen and Bauer, 'Les grands manoeuvres industrielles', p. 7.
39. Schmidt, *From state to market?*
40. Schmidt, *From state to market?*
41. M.C. Green, 'Setting the Agenda for a New Europe: The ERT and EC 1992', *Journal of Common Market Studies* 33, no. 4 (1995), pp. 501–26.
42. D.G. Mayes (ed.), *The Evolution of the Single European Market* (Aldershot, 1997).
43. M. Kipping, 'European Industrial Policy in a Global Competitive Economy', in S. Stavridis et al. (eds), *New Challenges to the European Union* (Aldershot, 1997), pp. 489–517.
44. Cohen, *Le Colbertisme 'high tech'*.
45. J. Hayward (ed.), *Industrial Enterprise and European Integration* (Oxford, 1995).
46. K. J. Button et al., *Flying into the Future. Air Transport Policy in the European Union* (Aldershot, 1998).
47. Hans-Luidger Dienel and Peter Lyth (eds), *Flying the flag: European commercial air transport since 1945* (London, 1998).
48. D.G. Mayes and P. Hart, *The Single Market Programme as a Stimulus to Change* (Cambridge, 1994).
49. Ken'ichi Ando, 'The Single European Market and the Location Strategy of Foreign Car Multinationals', The University of Reading, Discussion Papers in International Investment & Management, series b, vol. XI, No. 249 (1998).
50. A. Mattoo and C. Mavroidis, 'The EC–Japan Consensus on Cars: Interaction Between Trade and Competition Policy', *The World Economy* 18, no. 3 (May 1995), pp. 345–65.
51. S. Mazey and J. Richardson (eds), *Lobbying in the European Community* (Oxford, 1993).
52. Commission of the European Communities, *An Industrial Competitiveness Policy for the European Union*, COM(94) 319 final, Brussels (14 September 1994).
53. *Financial Times*, 23 July 1997.
54. E. Apel, *European economic and monetary integration 1958–1999* (London, 1997).

Italian public economic sector: 60 years between managerial approach and political constraint (1933–1993)

Luciano Segreto

University of Florence

THE ORIGINS AND THE END OF THE 'MISSION' OF THE STATE-OWNED COMPANIES

In an official statement to the Parliament two years ago Mr Ciampi, the treasury minister at the time, declared officially closed the 'mission of IRI (Instituto per la Ricostruzione Industriale)' in Italy. There are two possible approaches to its history advances especially by the newspapers and partly by the political world. The first one proposes a linear interpretation, which says that its end is simply due to the different economic and political conditions of this decade in comparison with the previous period. Another one seems more closely linked to the internal history of state intervention in Italy, but ends with the assumption that IRI has been in a way a sort of anomaly of the Italian economic history, and that it has nothing to do or to share with other (private) economic factors. The story is quite different: role, morphology, performances and aims of the state presence in the economy changed deeply in the last six decades in relationships with the economic conjuncture, the evolution of the political situation and the transformation of the productive structure.

Three dates in particular have made a permanent mark on the relations between the private and public sectors in Italy: 1933, 1962 and 1993. The first corresponds to the creation of IRI, a public holding company which was assigned the task of rehabilitating and successively managing the industrial enterprises that until then had been controlled by mixed banks, which had also in turn passed under state-control. With the banking law of 1936, these banks were no longer able to carry out medium to long term credit brokerage or hold significant shares of industrial enterprises. The second date marks the nationalisation of the electrical energy industry and the end of a long period of a certain type of private capitalism in Italy that was in fact based on the enormous power (mainly financial) of the large electrical energy groups. Finally, the third date signalled a turning point in the structure of economic power in Italy. The privatisation of state-owned companies, and above all, the major banks (Banca Commerciale and Credito Italiano) controlled by IRI, in addition to the issuing of a new banking law in 1993 which signals the return of the universal bank among the protagonists of the Italian economy, all represent the fundamental ingredients of a delicate phase of transition towards a new structure of Italian capitalism.

The articulation of economic power, and within it, the dialectics between the public and private sectors was defined between 1933 and 1937–39. The large Italian industrial and financial groups survived the founding phase of IRI without much damage and were firmly in control of the situation. This was possible also because the new situation did not show any clear competition between public and private sectors. In fact, the industrial branches where the state-controlled companies were in a stronger or even dominant condition were also those in which the private groups were weaker, if not completely absent, and vice versa. This perfect, general equilibrium was altered just in the financial sector, given that almost the entire credit system was under the direct control of the state, through IRI or the treasury.[1]

NEW TERRITORIES AND NEW POLICIES FOR THE STATE-CONTROLLED COMPANIES IN THE POST WORLD PERIOD

The structure of Italian capitalism was not modified by the world conflict that followed. Yet, in the ten to fifteen years after the Second World War, some elements that were important in that context took on a different weight, as new protagonists came into the limelight. The 1950s were a decisive decade for public enterprise. In fact, its destiny and very nature were decided between 1947–48 and 1957. Actually the end of the war represented a decisive passage. The public enterprise played a prominent role during the reconstruction and the industrial development in the 1950s and 1960s. It has represented one of the major instruments by which the state widened its presence in the economy and its role in sustaining the economic development, along the same lines followed in many other industrialised countries in the same period. Through this instrument came one specific form of direct intervention, which gives to the state-holdings – and to each firm controlled by them – the capability to intervene autonomously in a specific field of activity. In this way these firms has been charged with a sort of suppliant role of state administration. This concrete change and the implicit link with the political level fell outside the original terms of reference of IRI.

IRI was established in 1933 with the specific aim of saving the largest banking institutions of the country, by restoring their liability and liquidity through the demobilization of the industrial shareholdings of the mixed banks. In the meantime, IRI had at its beginning specific tasks in financing industrial activities. The fresh capital was to come from the private sector through fixed bonds issued by IRI itself and guaranteed by the State. This organisation project was completed by banking legislation reforming the previous situation. The decision to transform IRI from a precarious to a permanent institution gave definitively to the state the main function of financial intermediate, previously played by the universal banks. The new situation also clearly showed the great relevance and the absolute necessity of industrial restructuring and the chaotic situation of the enterprises inherited from the mixed banks. The rapid passage to the Second World War actually prohibited any concrete programme of re-organisation and transformation of the enormous industrial apparatus (about forty per cent of the industrial stock holdings belonged to the state), with important sectors dominated by state-controlled firms reaching a quasi-monopolistic condition. The public presence was predominant mainly in the iron and steel industry, where the enterprises of IRI (controlled since 1937 by a sector holding company, Finsider) produced seventy seven per cent of the cast iron and forty five per cent of the steel in shipbuilding and shipping companies, where another sector holding company, FINMARE, had been established. The state was also present in the telecommunications sector through Stet (founded in 1934), which was at the head of three telephone companies (Stipel, Telve and Timo) and accounted for fifty two per cent of telephone subscribers in Italy.[2]

The main elements of economic relief of the controlled companies in the post war period are the following: the creation of FINMECCANICA, a holding company charged with bringing together the IRI firms of the engineering sector; the appointment of the new top managers of AGIP (the State oil company), thus giving the firm an opportunity to develop its activities; the new statute of IRI approved in 1948; the reconstructing and rationalisation plan for the Finsider plants (Sinigaglia Plan). In many of these new elements can be seen new motivations and functions driven to reach aims of general interest. From an organisational point of view, the creation in 1947 of Finmeccanica, a holding company for the many state-controlled firms of the mechanical sector, of Finelettrica in 1952 for the part of the electric sector already in the hands of IRI, and that of ENI in 1953, with the same role for the oil industry (assuming in the meantime the control of AGIP), confirmed the validity of the organisational choices of the 1930s.[3]

All these were holding companies that operated through firms working under private law, but their role in the Italian economy was very different. While the Finsider group took a decisive role in the Italian steel industry and in its relationships within the European Coal and Steel Community,[4] Finmeccanica did not show any new strategy of the state for the mechanical sector but the simple managing of a deep crisis which induced a large labour force reduction. In Finmeccanica there were too many different sub-sectors with very different problems, from the car industry to the heavy mechanical sector, from the defence industry to the shipbuilding industry. This last sector was finally separated from the rest of Finmeccanica in 1967 and passed into the control of a new state-holding, Italcantieri, which later on, in 1984, merged with some other shipyards under state-control and together they formed Fincantieri.[5]

Very different was also the attitude of the two holding companies in the power sector. While Finelettrica actually did not differentiate its strategy from the rest of the private companies of the electric sector,[6] ENI represented something very different. Its birth was not due, in contrast to IRI, to the necessity to rescue existing firms with industrial and/or financial troubles. The beginning of its activity in 1953 marked a decisive moment in the process of political re-orientation of the public enterprises, which had begun in the late 1940s and had its most important player in the major government party, the Christian Democratic Party.[7]

The real change was the reform of the statute of IRI in 1948. In a contradictory way in comparison with the choices made between 1945 and 1948, the new rules gave the government the right to nominate chairman, vice-chairman, general directors of the IRI companies, placing great limitations on the freedom of the managers. The managerial and/or industrial approach to the problems of the state-controlled companies was now largely subordinate to a political one, although the process was not yet concretely defined – thought this was not to take long.

However, the decisive turning-point occurred in 1956 when the Ministry of State Investment was established. The new law defined the legal and administrative framework in which it was easier to create new institutions and policies aimed at developing the state direct intervention in different sectors of the Italian economy. The government officially assumed the power of direction and control over state-enterprises. At the same time, strategic lines of action were specified which would have significant influence on the later events in public enterprises. From a managerial point of view the 1956 law on the public enterprises introduced two very important principles: 1) it says that the state-owned firms must be included in 'specific and autonomous managerial bodies', which must act following economically correct criteria; 2) the law adds that these firms had to leave any sector association, with the only exception being made for banks (who remained in the Associazione Bancaria Italiana, the Italian Banling Association), to clearly mark a distinction from the private enterprises and their lobbies. These very general instructions give an 'instrumental' function to the public enterprises in reaching the 'peculiar aims' which the state wants to obtain. The political institutions, and especially the government, are responsible for the identification of the objectives to which public enterprises must be subjected; to them is also given the task of covering the economic costs connected with reaching those objectives. In this way it seems clear that the respect for the economic criteria makes it easier to reduce the constraints in the management of the firms: the objective became no longer a 'greater profit, but a greater economic success'.[8]

THE APOGEE

Thanks to the new law the industrial policy of the public enterprises began to assume a strong expansionist connotation directly sustained by public money. A decisive factor in selecting the development strategies of these companies is represented by decisions and opinions defined by the government and the Parliament. The sectors where most of the interventions were made were highway construction (a law passed in 1955 and a ten year plan in 1961, permitting to build, among other tracks, the Autostrada del Sole, connecting without interruptions Milan with Reggio Calabria in 1969); the hydrocarbon and gas industries (a law was approved in 1957, giving the monopoly for twenty years to ENI for mining researches in the Po Valley),[9] the telephone sector (which passed completely under state-control in 1957 after the renewal of the concessions), the air transport sector (with the merger Alitalia-Lai in 1957)[10] and, of course, the steel sector (with the decision, taken in 1959 by the committee of ministers for the state-shareholdings to permit Finsider to build a new steel centre in Taranto, in the Apulia region).[11]

Furthermore, in 1957 Parliament decreed that public enterprises would have to direct sixty per cent of new investments and forty per cent of all investments to southern Italy. If the founding of IRI in 1933 could be considered a sort of large-scale rescue action for northern industries, this new legislation for public enterprise investments set the conditions not only to re-establish the equilibrium of previous choices, but for a major correction of the course taken in the field of industrial policy. This would be the cause of very serious consequences for southern Italy during the industrial crisis and restructuring of later decades (that is, the downsizing of the state's role in industry).[12]

During the end of the 1950s and the beginning of the 1960s the public presence was extended to the textile industry, which was going through a period of general crisis, particularly among some of the southern enterprises and the old industry leaders.[13] Meantime new holdings were set up in 1958 for the mining sector (EGAM, which actually began its activity only in 1971, declaring bankruptcy only five years later)[14] and for all the establishment controlled by the state in the spa sector (EAGAT) . The long phase of growth of the Italian economy (in spite of a slowing-down in mid-1960s) and the guarantee of state support were the basis of these decisions that lacked a fundamental requirement: a coherent strategy of intervention that was free from political conditioning and constraints.[15] However, there were other features that characterised the public sector's presence in the 1960's, through more co-ordinated programmes such as the reorganisation of the mechanical sector with the establishment of a new holding company, EFIM, in 1962, controlling 114 companies, from the financial sector to the aerospace industry, from the defence industry to the aluminium industry, from the transportation industry to the glass sector.[16]

All of these elements began to delineate a very particular situation in the Italian economy. If between 1948 and 1954 the growth of IRI sales, investments and occupation was about the same of that of the GDP, gross national investments and occupation, between 1955 and 1963 figures differ quite clearly. The growth of IRI sales was one hundred and fourteen point two percent, while that of GDP was between one hundred and nine point two percent and one hundred and sixteen point five percent (depending on the different sources): the total occupation in the IRI group increased by twenty seven per cent and in the entire country by twenty four point seven per cent, while the investments made by IRI grow by three hundred per cent and the gross national investments only between one hundred and thirty five point four per cent and one hundred and fifty two per cent (again depending the different sources used). Thus it seems obvious that the economic cycle was increasingly conditioned by public investments, whose rate of growth in the late 1960s and the beginning of the 1970s was more than fifty per cent, while the investments made by the private enterprises were rapidly sinking.[17] The very high level of the technical and professional capabilities of the managers of the state-owned companies was one of the main features of the public sector, and till the middle of the 1960s those managers were probably better, in general, than their counterparts in the private sector.

Apart from very precise examples, all these were clear illustrations of the concrete interest of the government to create a consensus on the activities of the state holdings. On the other side the Italian Socialist and Communist Parties (both in the opposition till 1962, when the Socialist Party entered the majority) shared since the end of the war the government approach to the role of the state-controlled companies. They saw them as a powerful obstacle to the power of the private groups, accused of maintaining a monopolistic position in the Italian economy, an evaluation which they did not extend – by definition – to those state companies which found themselves in the same situation in other sectors.

THE OTHER SIDE OF THE MOON AND THE ROLE OF THE 'REAL' MIXED BANK

The strong growth of the economy in the 1950s and the progressive integration in the international economy led to insufficient attention being paid to a problem that Italian private industry could no longer ignore: a lack of co-ordination and strategic initiatives. The only exception was probably the chemical sector. There the world of private industry saw its new technological frontier and a possible occasion to gain competitiveness both in Italy and at international level. Like Montecatini, also Edison, leader in the electrical energy industry, began to diversify its interests in this field during the 1950s. But they were not alone even there. Also the public enterprises, primarily through ENI, directed part of their investments towards this sector. In this way, the chemical industry became one of the favoured arenas (if not the most) in the clash between public and private.[18]

The end of the mixed bank in the 1930s had deprived Italian capitalism of the driving engine and co-ordination that had accompanied the country during its first phase of intense industrialisation. Bastogi, a financial holding deeply involved in the electric sector and controlled by the most important industrial and financial groups, both private and state-controlled,[19] did not seem to be able to carry out this function. After the war, its ownership structure had been progressively simplified, although for a few years it still maintained both public and private interests. In 1954, IRI left the controlling syndicate of Bastogi, but to compensate for the loss of the role of the public shareholder, Donato Menichella, Governor of the Bank of Italy, assumed the role of arbitrator for the interpretation and application of the pool agreement among shareholders. From that moment and for the rest of the 1950s and first half of the 1960s, Bastogi was controlled by a block syndicate in which pre-eminent and financially equal positions were held by Italmobiliare owned by Carlo Pesenti (the largest producer of cement in Italy, which joined the company at the beginning of the decade), IOR and the insurance company Assicurazioni Generali. Immediately after these came the 'historical' group of shareholders, consisting of Edison (the real giant of the electric sector, with a very strong financial structure) Sviluppo (part of the electric group SADE), Montecatini, Pirelli, Fiat and Ras (the second insurance group in Italy, controlled by Pesenti since the beginning of the 1950s). However, managerial problems and an incapacity to propose new wide-reaching strategic choices significantly reduced Bastogi's role in the financial equilibrium of Italian capitalism.[20]

In one sense, this situation was favoured by the choice made by the former mixed banks immediately after the end of the war to establish a medium-term credit institution. This would also function as a substitute for mixed banks (by now no longer foreseen by current legislation) in relations with large private groups, thus acting as an investment bank able to offer a wide range of financial services to private enterprise. The most important of these services would be the creation of underwriting syndicates for issues of shares and debentures. These were the aims and terms of reference that led to the foundation of Mediobanca in 1946, with the contribution of capital divided into equal parts among three national banks (Commerciale, Credito Italiano, and Banco di Roma).[21]

During those years the possibility for this new public organisation to operate effectively was proportional to its ability to offer adequate solutions to the needs of large private groups, and inversely proportional to a lack of strategic vision (mainly limited to a few directly interested parties – its principal shareholders), as in the case of Bastogi. The emerging strength of Mediobanca can be explained by its profile of a state-owned merchant bank, united to the three largest banks in the country by links to stock and financial markets (the three banks provided for the underwriting of shares or debentures issued by pools under Mediobanca), but which also acted as a financial brain for the large private groups, the 'real' mixed bank of the post mixed banks period. The contradictory nature of this new organisation – the new Centaur was in a certain sense certified by a secret agreement underwritten in 1958 between the three founding banks and some Italian and foreign private industrial and financial groups. This accord guaranteed the latter the possibility of jointly managing Mediobanca, regardless of its existing balance of shares between public and private capital.[22]

The role of Mediobanca grew in importance and was increasingly acknowledged during the 1960s after the nationalisation of the electrical energy industry in 1962. This choice was an essentially political one, tied to the delicate phase of transition from the centre party governments of the 1950s to the first centre-left wing governments which brought the Socialist Party first within the majority and then to the government.[23] In short, from that moment almost the whole energy sector (production and distribution of electricity, oil exploration abroad and exploitation of hydrocarbon deposits in Italy) were in the hands of the state.

From the point of view of the history of state intervention the birth of ENEL, the entirely state-controlled electric company, was a sort of anomaly. ENEL was an operation and not a holding company, as one should have expected following the historical model of the IRI group. In a way ENEL paid a high price for its entrance ticket. The company was established without any capital, unlike other public holdings, and with a very heavy debt represented by the fact the nationalisation of the electric sector was limited to the fixed assets of past electric groups and not their shares. On the other hand that decision partly favoured other public holdings, which were till 1962 involved in the electric sector. SME, SIP and Terni (a state conglomerate with interests in chemical, electric and steel industries) received, as many private former electric companies, fresh capitals, while ITALSIDER, the state holding for the steel industry, merged with some electric companies, thus obtaining a part in the rich distribution of fresh capital (in total the nationalisation meant a payment of 22,000 billion lire at today's value).

The dynamics of the movements of public enterprise (as noted, up against a rather heavy investment policy which no longer found an outlet in the world of private industry, nor in the general trends of the economy) at the time seemed quite aggressive for Italian private capitalism. The frontier has been moved and again new territories were 'captured' by state intervention. Therefore, the private sector tried to react with a defensive financial move: the merger between Montecatini (number one in the Italian chemical industry), the first five enterprises in the sector internationally (excluding the United States), and Edison, ex-number one of the electrical energy industry. Edison, which had already begun a process of diversification in the chemical industry in the 1950s, now had enormous cash holdings, thanks to the indemnities paid for the nationalised electrical plants.[24]

This complex financial operation was guided by Mediobanca, which in a certain sense inaugurated its new role as the financial engineer of Italian private capitalism. No longer the operational instrument for financial services to private enterprises of the three national banks, Mediobanca accentuated its role as an investment bank, thus becoming a real reference point for large private groups, the instrument to protect them from the increasing power of the politics, the government, the political parties and the state-controlled firms, which were acting as a *longa manus* of that world in the economic framework.

The nationalisation of the electric sector also engendered an important change in the criteria for selecting the management of the public holdings, the state-owned companies and the banks controlled by IRI and the treasury. Subsequently political loyalty became the decisive factor in the choice of the new managers. The political equilibrium among the government parties (with a prominent role of the Christian Democratic Party and the increasing importance from a political point of view of the Socialist Party) was more or less confirmed also in the nomination of the CEOs and all the members of the boards of these firms. This situation, along with the generation change which eliminated most of the old technocrats, who had ruled IRI from its birth and resisted the shift from the fascist regime to the new democratic Italy thanks to their technical capabilities, produced several consequences. Together with the frustration for most of the managers whose professional capabilities no longer counted, it contributed to the worsening of the performance of the state-owned firms in the following years.

In the same years as the triumph of the so-called 'state bourgeoisie',[25] many of the private industrialists that had symbolised the Italy of the 'economic boom' left the scene: the textile entrepreneur Piero Bassetti,

Zanussi, Borghi and Zoppas of the household appliances sector and some of the most important names in the food industry (Bertolli, Motta and Alemagna). Part of their enterprises ended up in public hands, especially those in the food sector which were controlled by a former electrical energy enterprise that was already half-owned by IRI before SME, which up until then had produced and distributed electricity in Southern Italy, Sardinia, and Sicily.[26]

The chain of collapses in some of these entrepreneurial families which had not even had time to establish themselves as real industrial dynasties can be explained by three factors. First, they were unable to successfully pass through the delicate transition from the first to the second generation or face the managerial limitations accentuated by the new problems in industrial relations after the contract renewals of 1969–70.[27] In addition, the costs structure in these enterprises was no longer able to stand up to competition in an increasingly open market. Moreover, the world of private industry showed all of its limitations in the investments of the immense liquidity introduced into financial circulation following the nationalisation of the electrical energy industry. Essentially unprepared for a moment that could no longer be postponed from a political point of view, private enterprises suddenly found themselves without an alternative strategy, thus showing evident signs of real entrepreneurial deficiency. Many of the former electrical energy entrepreneurs, as in the case of many industrialists of the 'economic boom' who disappeared from the scene in the 1970s, has not even achieved the dimensions (above all, economic) and the soundness necessary to ask for a stabilising intervention on the part of Mediobanca.[28]

For many years the role of the public enterprises had been changing. The drastic reduction of the economic development after the 1963–64 crisis gave them, together with previous activity in favour of the economic expansion, a new role in sustaining and rescuing the private firms in crisis. The main elements confirming this dual role are the doubling of the productive capabilities of the Taranto steel plant; the creation of Italcantieri, a new holding company for the shipbuilding sector; the new Alfa Romeo plant in Pomigliano d'Arco, near Naples; while the 'Red Cross' activities have been, since 1971, concentrated and co-ordinated by a new institution GEPI. GEPI was formed to help to maintain and increase the levels of employment in industrial firms in economic and financial difficulties at that time: it actually became a new hospital for private firms, whose control sooner or later passed to the state.[29]

The same function was played also in the chemical sector and specifically in favour of Montedison. The apparent financial soundness shown by Montedison in 1966–67 was almost immediately counterbalanced by the structural limits of the group and the incapacity of its management to tackle them. The only way to get the industrial project which was implied in the financial operation back in on its feet again was, in a certain sense, the negation of the operation itself. Created as a reference point for private enterprise hit by nationalisation and as a check on public enterprise, Montedison had to yield to the most aggressive of the public economic players: ENI, headed by Eugenio Cefis after the death of the state-owned oil company's founder, Enrico Mattei, in 1962. Encouraged and co-ordinated at the highest political and ministerial levels and by economic-financial establishment (Bank of Italy and Mediobanca), the joint intervention of IRI and ENI created the conditions for the essential public control of the giant of the Italian chemical industry, without however establishing the basis of a more discerning strategic vision of this sector.[30]

The development of the investments made by the public enterprises in the 1960s had a different timing in comparison with those of the private enterprises. After the workers conflicts of 1969–71 these investments had a significant anti-cycle role; they dramatically sustained the economic dynamic as a result of annual increases of fifty per cent and more, but at the same time the private investments sank very rapidly. The trajectories of the third cycle of investments made by the public enterprises had two main characteristics: their concentration in the big industries and a more evident localisation in the southern regions. The expansionist inclination of the public sector seemed clearly regardless of the cycle trend. It rather reflects two peculiar operative conditions of these enterprises: the increasing public importance of their action and the widening of the political aspect in the decision making process; the greater facility to gain access to the credit system and the support granted by the state resources through state endowment funds. This situation marked an abnormal allocation of the resources, inducing lasting consequences on the total efficiency of the productive system and on the economic and financial equilibrium of the public enterprises.[31]

THE CRISIS

The severe international economic crisis of the 1970s and early 1980s redesigned the relations between public and private enterprise. It was no longer possible to continue the expansion of investment in public enterprises by drawing on state-guaranteed debt. Having lost all possibility of an autonomous role, public enterprises were forced to strengthen their ties with the political world, thus finding themselves committed to making a difficult recovery from indebtedness.

The international economic crisis, exacerbated by the effects of OPEC, also caused the IRI group severe problems.[32] Pressures from very different political groups began to converge in the request to the state-controlled companies to sustain employment.[33] *Ad hoc* legislation, such as law no.

655 of 1977 confirmed this turn of events by closely integrating public enterprise action in the objectives of industrial restructuring and by subordinating the finance of public holding company programmes to the approval of a political body – the Comitato Interministeriale per la Programmazione Industriale (CIPI), the Interministerial Council for Industrial Planning. Thus, the entity of financing for public holding companies went from an average of 350 million lire in 1973 to 3.2 billion per year between 1978 and 1984, with a strong growth trend. Rather than constituting an instrument for a difficult and uncertain reorganisation which would have heavy consequences in terms of employment, these financial operations were an additional factor of distortion and inefficient allocation of resources, as well as a weakening of the potential of public groups.[34]

Some of these problems were also at the root of the decision of IRI and ENI to leave Montedison between 1980 and 1981.[35] If the chemical industry continued to be one of the sectors – if not the only one – that measured the balance of forces between public and private, clearly the return of the chemical colossus to the private sector was a point in its favour. In fact, over the next twelve years a ruthless battle was fought around Montedison (including two suicides, those of Raul Gardini, the head of the Ferruzzi group, and of Gabriele Cagliari, CEO of ENI) – first within the realm of private enterprise, then between public and private enterprise, and finally again in private enterprise.

However, the strategy of reducing state intervention in the economy and selling some of the public enterprises was not yet transparent enough to avoid experiences like that of the cancellation of the privatisation of the SME group (at that time a food industry holding) after that the government and some competitor intervened to block the agreement reached in 1986 by IRI with the De Benedettti group, at that time owner also of the Olivetti group.[36] But also the joint venture between ENI and Montedison in the chemical sector through the creation in 1988 of Enimont, an holding controlled in a precarious equilibrium by the private and public shareholders, showed that especially the government parties attributed still a great importance to the strategic presence of the state in some sector, which was supposed to guarantee the new Italian chemical colossus a leading position in Europe for seven product lines and a co-leader position for another three. Some years later became clear with the persecution of the managers of Enimont and of some of the most prominent politicians (former prime minister, secretaries of the Socialist and Christian Democratic Parties) what exactly 'strategic' meant for them: a regular and increasing flow of capital from the public enterprises to the ever thirsty cash reserves of those parties and sometimes of their rulers.[37]

This operation, which would have finally provided Italy with a chemical sector that was competitive on the international level and bring an end to the almost thirty-year 'war of the chemical industry', was undermined from the beginning by an irremediable contrast. Montedison did not bring any of its top-level production to Enimont, thus essentially recreating the situation of competition that the co-operation with ENI was supposed to avoid. Contrasts between the two shareholders and the management rapidly led to a paralysis of the company. With the fading of the dream of the Ferruzzi group and Montedison to carry out a process of integration in the Italian chemical industry under private management, but with public financing, the joint venture was dissolved. The private partner was paid off with a generous grant of public money, which was then partly deviated to government parties under the form of a maxi-kickback (this represented the focal point of the most famous trial in the 'Clean Hands' inquiry during the 1990s).[38] Instead, ENI had to settle its accounts with only what it had inherited from the company Enimont – many obsolete facilities and a high level of indebtedness. The result was two entities which operated in two distinctly different segments of the chemical market: Enichem for ethylene (the leading producer in Europe) and polyethylene (among the top producers on the continent) and Montecatini for polypropylene and fluoroderivatives (the leading producer in the world).[39]

THE END OF THE STORY?

For Italy the development of European integration meant the adoption of an increasing amount of normative and regulatory activities that were defined in Brussels, and their progressive preponderance over national disciplines in many fields. On the other hand, the concrete activity of the new 'internal European market' brought new challenges to national economies and single economic interests, both public and private.[40] Within this context, regulations were enacted between 1991 and 1994 with reference to brokerage firms, insider trading, take-over bids and investment trusts.[41] However, as a result of this external constraint some important steps were taken. Firstly, between 1992 and 1993 decisions were made concerning the liquidation of EFIM with a government appropriation of 9,000 billion lire to guarantee the payment of debts, many of which were with foreign financial institutions (after the agreement with the European Commission).[42] In 1992 a law was passed for the transformation of IRI, ENI and ENEL into joint-stock companies, and above all, the beginning of privatisation in both industrial enterprises and the large banks (Banca Commerciale and Credito Italiano) owned by IRI, the founder and still shareholder of Mediobanca, as well as the privatisation of the largest medium-term credit institution, Imi.[43]

As difficult and controversial a choice as it may be, Italy has clearly opted to move in the direction of an essential convergence and progressive integration with the rest of Europe. It is quite significant that this process has resulted in the decline of the universal bank on the economic scene, which was the instrument that permitted Italy to enter into what was then the small group of industrialised countries between the end of the nineteenth century and the beginning of the First World War. Its decline, which lasted sixty years, corresponded to a long period of Italian capitalism in which the public and private players in the economy had alternated in the role of key player. But they often made their own rules (such as unsecured public financing) for a game that could be played only in their own backyard. The return of the universal bank is occurring in an era when rules are written and observed for a much larger group of players, many of whom do not speak Italian, but can freely enter into the Italy's backyard.[44]

The limits of the strength – or of the apparent victory – of the private over the public are very clear in the 1990s. Italy succeeded with its big privatisation process, probably the most extensive project of its kind in the western world.[45] Nevertheless that process has shown that some features of the Italian capitalism are very deeply rooted and very difficult to modify: 1) the very high concentration of economic power in very restricted groups;[46] 2) the very low availability of the small and middle size firms to open themselves to the external business world through the access to the stock exchange. And this is a paradox, while all the previous constraints to the private investment in shares by the small investors seem to have disappeared, considering the increasingly low return on state bonds in the last 2–3 years.

Anyone believing, some years ago, that privatisation would have opened a new phase in the history of Italian capitalism, today seems to have changed his mind. The discussion on the concentration of power by the new shareholders of Italian Telecom, when it was privatised in February 1998 with an immense power held by the Fiat group is a classic and only the most recent example.[47] But one year later that pessimistic impression seems to belong to a very far past. There are rather optimistic opinions that the very recent success (May 1999) of the bid launched by Olivetti on Italian Telecom (historically the most expensive in Europe) may represent a turning point in the history of Italian capitalism.[48] But too many (supposed) turnings points are really what they purport to be.

On the other hand much is still to do really until 'the mission' of the state in the economy can be considered closed. A large part of the banking system has not yet been privatised, including the very rich and powerful savings banks. The transport sector (airways and railways) is still in public hands, as is the public utilities sector, but nobody can really be sure that these sectors will not very rapidly change their owners before the pendulum between public and private swings again towards the former.

NOTES

1. G. Toniolo, *L'economia dell'Italia fascista* (Bari, 1980), p. 268.
2. L. Avagliano, *Stato e imprenditori in Italia. Le origini dell'IRI* (Salerno, 1980), B. Bottiglieri, *Stet. Stretegia e struttura delle telecomunicazioni* (Milan, 1987), E. Cianci, *Nascita dello Stato imprenditore* (Milan, 1977).
3. B. Bottiglieri, 'L'industria elettrica dalla guerra agli anni del 'miracolo economico', in V. Castronovo (ed.), *Storia dell'industria elettrica in Italia 4. Dal dopoguerra alla nazionalizzazione 1945–62.* (Rome, 1994), M. Doria, 'Note sull'industria meccanica nella Ricostruzione', *Rivista di Storia Economica*, n. 1, 1987, L. Maugeri, *L'arma del petrolio. Questione petrolifera globale, guerra fredda e politica italiana nella vicenda di Enrico Mattei* (Florence, 1994), N. Perrone, *Obiettivo Mattei. Petrolio, Stati Uniti e politica dell'Eni* (Rome, 1994).
4. R. Ranieri, 'The Marshall Plan and the reconstruction of the Italian steel industry (1947–1954)', in *Le Plan Marshall et le relèvement économique de l'Europe* (Paris, 1993), pp. 367–83.
5. T. Fanfani, 'Per una storia della cantieristica in Italia dallo "Squero di san Marco" all'Italcantieri', *L'Industria*, 1988, n. 2.
6. Sicca and Izzo, 'La SME di Giuseppe Cenzato', in V. Castronovo (ed.), *Storia dell'industria elettrica in Italia, 4. Dal dopoguerra alla nazionalizzazione. 1945–1962* (Rome, 1994).
7. L. Maugeri, *L'arma del petrolio*; L. Segreto, 'Gli investimenti americani in Italia (1945–1963)' in *Studi Storici*, 37 (1996), pp. 273–316, D. Yergin, *The prize. The epic quest for oil, money and power* (New York-London, 1991).
8. P. Saraceno, *Il sistema delle imprese a partecipazione statale nell'esperinza italiana* (Milan, 1975), F. Barca and S. Trento, 'La parabola delle partecipazioni statali: una missione tradita', in F. Barca, (ed.), *Storia del capitalismo italiano dal dopoguerra a oggi* (Rome, 1997), pp. 186–236, here: pp. 209–14.
9. Magini, *L'Italia e il petrolio tra storia e cronologia* (Milan, 1976); L. Maugeri, *L'arma del petrolio* and L. Segreto, 'Gli investimenti americani in Italia'.
10. B. Amoroso and J. Olsen, *Lo stato imprenditore* (Bari, 1978), pp. 81–2.
11. M. Balconi, *La siderurgia italiana (1945–1990). Tra controllo pubblico e incentivi di mercato* (Bologna, 1991), pp. 129–54.
12. G. Bruno, 'Le imprese industriali nel processo di sviluppo', in *Storia dell'Italia Repubblicana*, vol. II.1 (Turin, 1995), pp. 355–420, here pp. 402–4 and Barca-Trento, 'La parabola delle partecipazioni statali', p. 213.
13. Bruno, 'Le imprese industriali nel processo di sviluppo', pp. 405–6.
14. Camera dei Deputati- Segretariato generale, *L'indirizzo e il controllo del Parlamento sulle partecipazioni statali, Indagine conoscitiva della V Commissione permanente (Bilancio e programmazione – partecipazioni statali)*, Comitato Partecipazioni statali, n. 21 (Rome, 1976), p. 187 and G. L. Osti, *L'industria di Stato dall'ascesa al degrado. Trent'anni nel gruppo Finsider, conversazioni con R. Ranieri* (Bologna, 1991), pp. 268–70.
15. V. Castronovo, *Storia economica d'Italia. Dall'Ottocento ai giorni nostri* (Turin, 1995), pp. 409–46.

16. P. Tordi and S. Bemporad, *Tanto paga Pantalone. La storia del caso EFIM* (Rome, 1995), pp. 21–2.

17. Bruno, *Le imprese industriali nel processo di sviluppo*, pp. 414–18; ISTAT, *Summario di statistiche storiche 1861–1957* (Rome, 1957) and N. Rossi, A. Segreto, G. Toniolo, 'I conti economia dell' Italia. Una ricostruzione statistica, 1890–1990', *Rivista di storia economica*, 1993, n. 1.

18. B. Bottiglieri, 'Una grande impresa chimica tra stato e mercato: la Montecatini negli anni '50', in F. Amatori-B. Bezza (eds.), *Montecatini 1888–1966. Capitoli di storia di una grande impresa* (Bologna, 1990), pp. 309–55, here pp. 349–55 and G. Sapelli, 'La Edison di Giorgio Valerio', in V. Castronovo (ed.), Storia dell'industria elettrica in Italia, vol. 4, pp. 519–45, here pp. 534–42.

19. L. Segreto, 'Models of Control of the Italian capitalism from the mixed bank to Mediobanca (1894–1993)', *Business and Economic History*, vol. 27, n. 1, (1997).

20. G. Piluso, 'Lo speculatore, i banchieri e lo stato: la Bastogi da Max Bondi ad Alberto Beneduce', *Annali di storia dell'impresa*, 7 (1991), pp. 386–91.

21. S. Battilossi, 'L'eredità della banca mista. Sistema creditizio, finanziamento industriale e ruolo strategico di Mediobanca 1946–1956', *Italia Contemporanea*, (December 1991), n. 185, pp. 627–53, N. Colajanni, *Il capitalismo senza capitale. La storia di Mediobanca* (Milan, 1991) and Segreto, *Models of Control*.

22. Battilossi, 'L'eredità della banca mista', pp. 646–47, F. Tamburini, *Un siciliano a Milano* (Milan, 1992), pp. 95–119 and M. De Cecco-G. Ferri, *Le banche d'affari in Italia* (Bologna, 1996), p. 41.

23. G. Bruno and L. Segreto, 'Finanza e industria in Italia (1963–1995)', in *Storia dell'Italia Repubblicana*, vol. III.1 (Turin, 1996), p. 511–15, G. Carli, *Cinquant'anni di vita italiana, in collaborazione con Paolo Peluffo* (Rome-Bari, 1993), pp. 269–70 and G. Mori, 'La nazionalizzazione in Italia: il dibattito politico-economico', in *La nazionalizzazione dell'energia elettrica. L'esperienza italiana e di altri paesi europei* (Rome-Bari, 1989), pp. 91–115.

24. A. Marchi and R. Marchionatti, *Montedison 1966–1989. L'evoluzione di una grande impresa al confine tra pubblico e privato* (Milan, 1992), pp. 25–38 and Bruno and Segreto, *Finanza e industria in Italia*, pp. 511–15.

25. E. Scalfari and G. Turani, *Razza padrona. Storia della borghesia di stato* (Milan, 1974).

26. L. Sicca, *Strategia d'impresa. La formazione di un gruppo italiano: la Sme* (Milan, 1987), pp. 16–30.

27. G. Piantoni, *La successione in azienda. Continuità dell'impresa e ricambio generazionale* (Milan, 1990).

28. G. Bruno and L. Segreto, *Finanza e industria in Italia*, pp. 530–37, G. Gualerni, *Storia dell'Italia industriale. dall'Unità alla seconda repubblica* (Milan, 1994), pp. 225–8.

29. Bruno and Segreto, *Finanza e industria in Italia*, pp. 574–8 and E. Pontarollo, 'Italy: effects of substituting political objectives for business goals', in B. Hindley (ed.), *State investment companies in Western Europe* (London, 1983), pp. 50–55.

30. F. Amatori and F. Brioschi, 'Le grandi imprese private: famiglie e coalizioni',

in F. Barca (ed.), *Storia del capitalismo italiano dal dopoguerra a oggi* (Rome, 1997), pp. 127–30, Marchi and Marchionatti, *Montedison 1966–1989*, pp. 48–56 and Tamburini, *Un siciliano a Milanese*, pp. 169–74.

31. L. Pennacchi (ed.), *Il sistema delle partecipazioni statali*, (Bari, 1980), G. Tagliabue, Investimenti delle imprese a partecipazione statale. Un'analisi settoriale, in *Economia pubblica*, V (1975), n. 11–12 and C. Virno, *L'azione anticongiunturale e antidepressiva delle Partecipazioni statali dal 1967 al 1977*, (Milan, 1978).

32. *Pontarollo*, Italy, p. 32.

33. P. Bianchi, 'The IRI in Italy: strategic role and political costraints', *West European Politics*, 10 (1987) and F. Grassini, 'The Italian enterprise: the political costraints', in R. Veron and Y. Aharoni (eds.), *State-owned enterprises in Western Economies* (Beckenham, 1981), pp. 70–84.

34. G. Pent Fornengo, 'Le politiche di ristrutturazione e salvataggio', in F. Momigliano (ed.), *Le leggi della politica industriale in Italia* (Bologna, 1986).

35. Marchi and Marchionatti, *Montedison 1966–1989*, pp. 160–66; Tamburini, *Un siciliano a Milano*, pp. 206–10; and G. Galli, *Il padrone dei padroni. Enrico Cuccia, il potere di Mediobanca e il capitalismo italiano* (Milan, 1995), pp. 144–5.

36. S. Cingolani, *Le grandi famiglie del capitalismo italiano* (Rome-Bari, 1990).

37. Bruno and Segreto, *Finanza e industria in Italia*, pp. 680–85.

38. Bruno and Segreto, *Finanza e industria in Italia*, pp. 664–9; M. Magatti, *Corruzione politica e società italiana* (Bologna, 1996) and *Tribunale penale di Milano, V Sezione penale, La maxitangente Enimont* (Milan,1997).

39. M. Giorgi Ronchi, 'Addio al sogno della grande chimica', *Espansione*, (November 1994).

40. P. Guerrieri and S. Manzocchi-P. Padoan, 'L'Italia e il mercato interno europeo: tra convergenza e polarizzazione', in F. R. Pizzuti, *L'economia italiana dagli anni Settanta agli anni Novanta* (Milan, 1994).

41. S. Cassese, *La nuova costituzione economica* (Rome-Bari, 1995), pp. 186–7.

42. Tordi and Bemporad, *Tanto paga Pantalone*.

43. G. Corsetti and G. M. Rey, 'Le privatizzazioni', in F. R. Pizzuti, *L'economia italiana dagli anni Settanta agli anni Novanta* (Milan, 1994); A. Macchiati, *Privatizzazioni tra economie e politica* (Rome, 1996) and F. Cavazzuti, *Privatizzazioni, imprenditori e mercati* (Bologna, 1996).

44. Bruno and Segreto, *Finanza e indutria in Italia*, pp. 509–11 and A. Predieri, *Il potere della banca centrale: isola o modello* (Florence, 1996).

45. OCSE, *Economic Survey of Italy 1995* (Paris 1995).

46. S. Bragantini, *Capitalismo all'italiana. Come i furbi comandano con i soldi degli ingenui* (Milan, 1996).

47. M. Esposito, 'Telecom, Il nuovo ordine dei privati', *La Repubblica*, (20 February 1998); M. Panara, 'Il 'golpe' del nocciolino duro', *La Repubblica*, (20 February 1998) and E. Marro, 'Prodi difende le privatizzazioni', *Corriere della Sera*, (21 February 1998).

48. R. Gianola, 'La vittoria di Olivetti conquistata Telecom', *La Repubblica*, (22 May 1999).

Nation States as Providers of Organisational Capability: French Industry Overseas, 1950–65

Ludovic Cailluet
Ecole supérieure universitaire de gestion (ESUG-IAE),
*University of Toulouse**

Continuing the seminal work of Chandler several historians have contributed to the understanding of the multiple ways taken by European large business firms in the twentieth century to create organisational capabilities.[1] France has often been absent from that analysis for various reasons, including the lack of sufficient research on large businesses. As a consequence, to date, there is still no general business history of the country. Interestingly enough, the long-term relationship between the state and industry since the First World War has been fully covered, but authors rarely refer to the managerial performance of firms.[2] Nevertheless, in a recent contribution, Fridenson has attempted to define some major patterns of French managerial culture.[3] He has emphasised the role of the state in education and the selection of the senior management of large firms. However, connections with government agencies, the recruitment of ex-civil servants and the acquisition of knowledge and skills from the public service have not been empirically studied in themselves. In addition, the international activities of French multinational enterprises (MNEs) after the Second World War still remains a barely explored topic.[4] Therefore, in the context of overseas operations, an analysis of the MNE's peculiar relations with the state as a competitive asset seems an original field for business historians.

The intent of the following article is to analyse the use of 'influence networks' in a dynamic perspective. Since the end of the Second World War, French corporations have moved from a classical use of alumni or networks of former civil servants to a more diversified pattern of business connections. In International Joint Venture operations (IJVs), they have taken advantage of opportunities for establishing connections with both public service and private sector partners. In such a process, acquaintances with cartel colleagues, bankers and consultants have been very effective.[5] Why have the overseas operations of large French industrial corporations in the post-1945 period been chosen to study that aspect of their national corporate culture? Because those largely responsible for developing the sophisticated and specific management skills concerned were individuals educated and trained within the public services. Surprisingly to some extent, the article shows how former French civil servants were successful, over all, in running IJVs, enjoying fruitful co-operation with non-French partners of radically differing backgrounds.

Furthermore, an efficient – albeit informal – French model of state–industry support existed independently of the government's explicit industrial policies. In this respect the state has provided valuable assets for some major firms. On the other hand, direct intervention on the part of the French government has also been crucial to the success of private corporations abroad. Success was often achieved thanks to strong and enduring links or acquaintances with former government departmental staff ('cabinet' members) employed by such enterprises. In this regard, the case of Pechiney, a public company producing aluminium and chemicals, is highly significant in the period 1950–65.

This research is based on the confidential archives of the Pechiney company in Paris, and on interviews with former executives of the same firm and its subsidiaries. Secondary material has also been used, especially in the last section, in particular Grinberg and Mioche's commissioned history of Aluminium de Grèce (ADG).[6]

As it is essential to understand the supposed uniqueness of the French case, the first section of the article provides a brief historical overview of government–industry relationships in France. This section considers the period starting with the two World Wars and focuses upon both the education system and the multiple bridges constructed between state and industry. At the same time, the evolutionary nature of the role of the state in French business practice is outlined. The following sections provide empirical case studies of two of Pechiney's overseas operations between 1950 and 1965. Both projects involved international associations and the mobilisation of various professional and personal networks, as well as the direct intervention of the French government.

The establishment of the Compagnie Internationale pour la Production de l'Alumine (FRIA) illustrates how the company used classic networks of civil servants to successfully erect, and later to operate, a giant alumina processing plant in French Guinea in the mid 1950s. The second case study is Aluminium de Grèce, an aluminium integrated reduction facility set up in Greece during the early 1960s. On this occasion, Pechiney used its government links to get the French government to put pressure on its Greek counterpart in order to facilitate the company's operations.

A LONG STANDING TRADITION: FRENCH STATE AND INDUSTRY
RELATIONSHIP

Government–industry relationships have thrived in French history in two
different ways: (1) direct action through regulation or state-ownership; (2)
the organisation of higher education and the selection of a national élite.
Regarding national industrial policy and direct intervention, Colbert is
considered to be the inventor of the so-called 'administrative monarchy'.
As a Minister of State he established in the 1660s what was to become a
long-standing tradition of direct intervention and of state-owned (or supported) industries accompanied by a set of royal manufactures. Three
centuries later, the ideology of French politics was dominated by the
Liberal order. In the 1890s the concept of state–industrial policy invented
by Colbert was therefore almost forgotten. Nevertheless, as a reaction to
the two World Wars, the state–industry relationship underwent a major
renewal, and, as a result, an almost planned economy existed between the
1940s and the 1960s. It was reinforced by the nationalisation of large
parts of the financial and industrial sectors of the economy.[7]

Such a strong tradition of intervention deeply influenced the structure,
and furthermore the managerial patterns, of French business. Indeed, even
during the liberal years of the nineteenth century, the state was influential
in a different manner. In the Revolutionary and the Napoleonic eras
(1789–1815), an efficient education system was established. Some of the
superior schools created in this period to train and educate the administrative and technical elite of the country rapidly came to be known as 'Grandes
Écoles'. Amongst the most prestigious was the military École Polytechnique.
Also called 'X', this famous school was created in 1794 as an artillery
officers' academy. To enter the school the future 'polytechnicians' had to
pass a nationwide examination dominated by mathematics. This thorough
selection process established the institution as one of the most elite in the
country. The egalitarian principle of entry exams created a class of scien-
tists and technicians theoretically based on the meritocratic principle. In
this way, during the nineteenth century, France gradually entrusted the
state with the selection and training of her technical and managerial élite.[8]

The system thus produced well-trained engineers who at first joined the
forces (artillery, engineers and signal corps). Polytechnicians also joined
the civil service through its technical departments ('corps techniques') – to
quote but the most influential – mines (corps des mines) and public works
(corps des ponts et chaussées). From the second half of the nineteenth
century, and accompanying the development of large firms during the
'second industrialisation', many civil servants and officers left the army,
public service and government in favour of business enterprises. From the
1880s onwards, private sector salaries provided a strong incentive for civil
servants to leave a public service career full of constraints. To give but one

example: in 1905, 75 per cent of the École Polytechnique graduates were working within the private sector, generally in large enterprises. After the First World War, it was customary, at least for the large, non-family owned business enterprises, to recruit their executives from the Grandes Écoles.

The intensification of state intervention from the late 1930s led on to a broader use of interpersonal relationships linking politicians or government officials to business executives. These 'typical' networks were operating mainly through informal professional or alumni networks. Pechiney (then known as Alais, Froges et Camargue) frequently used its directors' personal connections in the period. In addition, some senior politicians were elected members of the board. The role of these individuals was to inform the board about new regulation projects and government procurement policy, and, where possible, to influence it directly. They occasionally sat side by side with directors who had been their junior advisors as government staff in an early stage of their career. Albert Mahieu, a member of the board from 1926 to his death in 1944 was a senator and later a Minister of State. His colleague from 1933, Eugène Mauclère, was a former armaments general comptroller under whose command, during the First World War, had worked Louis Marlio, vice-president and director of Pechiney.[9]

Amongst internal directors and polytechnicians of the company, Marlio enjoyed a special position. Born in 1878, this engineer was a graduate from the École Polytechnique and a member of the elite corps of the 'ponts et chaussées'. From 1909 to 1914, he joined the council of state (conseil d'État) and participated in government work as a technical advisor for various ministers. Eventually he became Principal Private Secretary to E. Millerand, then Minister of Public Works, later Minister of War (1914–15) and President of the Republic (1920–4). During that period Marlio obviously built up high-level connections in the state apparatus and also within industrial circles. His administrative position involved the monitoring of various issues, including the regulation of hydro-power facilities.[10]

This domain represented a core area of Pechiney's activities as hydro-power producer and of energy consumer. Marlio therefore had the opportunity of meeting the most senior officers and several of the company's shareholders who themselves were interested in electricity questions. Thanks to the support of the latter, who were mostly polytechnique alumni and retired members of the 'ponts et chaussées' corps, in 1917, Marlio was appointed director of the company. A. Badin, CEO of Pechiney, ensured that he was brought back from the front where he was serving as an officer. This recruitment strategy was overtly designed to secure reliable connections with government networks at a time of strong state influence on the economy.[11]

Promoted managing director (administrateur-délégué) after the death of Badin in early 1917, Marlio repeatedly used his acquaintances with ministers and top-ranking civil servants in the course of the inter-war period. Amongst the company's letter books of the period lies evidence of the quality of his social influence. Writing to senior officials, Marlio used the form of address 'cher ministre et ami' (dear minister and friend). When writing to an alumnus of the École Polytechnique, he would start with the traditional formula 'cher camarade' (dear comrade), rather casual in any other circumstances. Such social ability and proximity were crucial in debates with top government officials whenever problems occurred. It has to be noted that Marlio's connections were well placed in French and international business circles, as well as in the academic world.[12]

At a lower managerial level, directors frequently negotiated with long-term civil servant acquaintances since many of the ministry's technical or economic directorates were held by graduates of the same Grandes Écoles. This phenomenon was reinforced from the First World War on, as it had become more common for industrialists to work with the public administration and the Army. For a company operating in strongly regulated areas such as mines or hydro-power facilities it was essential to maintain a permanent relationship with administration officials. From 1937, the aluminium domestic price was fixed by government decree. As a consequence, Pechiney's executives made more frequent visits to the ministerial departments in charge. During the German Occupation, the Vichy regime established a set of control instruments giving the state 'unprecedented powers to intervene in the economy'.[13] Pechiney's management had then to cope with the central office for allocating industrial products and other services of the powerful Ministry of Industrial Production (Ministère de la Production Industrielle). After the Liberation, the creation of the Commissariat au Plan (the planning agency) was symptomatic of a new stage in the state's intervention in the economy, and therefore saw a renewal of connections between industry and government agencies. Top civil servants, who were not engineers, but who had a law or political science background, began to enter large business enterprises in the late 1940s.

Following a trend common to many large corporations, the senior management of the Pechiney Company between 1950 and 1970 consisted mostly of ex-civil servants with a majority of École Polytechnique graduates (see Table 1). Nonetheless, it was not only for the networking potential that most of the firm's top management came from public service backgrounds. In French industry, graduates from the École Polytechnique and the 'Corps des Mines', usually the top ten of a class of polytechnicians, were justly considered to be the most talented engineers of their generation. The fact that they also belonged to a very effective network of alumni was almost incidental to their technical competence.

Nevertheless, when, after the Second World War, corporations came to face new environments they sometimes had to reinforce 'classical' net-

Table 1: Educational/Professional backgrounds of Pechiney's top management (rank of 'directeur de la compagnie'), 1950–70

Name	Education and/or Public Service origin	Previous Position ('Pechiney' means that the person was hired as a beginner)
Bartholin (Pierre)	Law/Political science	Pechiney
Bès de Berc (Olivier)	X-Mines	Civil Service technical corp
Boulongne (Henry de)	X	Army
Chaintreuil (Jean)	X-Génie maritime	Navy Engineers Corp
Desazars de Montgaillard	Ecole Nationale d'Administration	Government Staff
Dumas (André)	École Centrale	Pechiney
Dupin (Jean)	X-Ponts et chaussées	Unknown
Guinet (Paul)	X-Génie	Engineers Corp Officer
Gutmann (Francis)	Law/Political science	Government Staff
Jacomet (André)	Conseil d'État	Government Staff
Jean (Paul)	X-Mines	Unknown
Jouven (Pierre)	X-Mines	Civil Service technical corp
Jullien (Louis)	X-Artillerie	Army Officer
Lantenois (Roger)	X	Colonial technical corp
Marchandise (Jacques)	Conseil d'État	Government Staff
Masselin (Jacques)	X	Pechiney
Matter (Jean)	X	Pechiney
Moundlic (Jean)	École Centrale	Pechiney
Normand (Georges)	X	Other company
Ribadeau-Dumas (Jacques)	Law	Pechiney
Serpette (Maurice)	X-Ponts et chaussées	Civil Service technical corp
Thomas (Philippe)	X-Inspection des finances	Government Staff
Vitry (Raoul de)	X-Mines	Civil Service technical corp

X = graduate from the École Polytechnique
X - Artillerie, Génie, Ponts et chaussées, Mines, Inspection des finances = École Polytechnique + one of its so-called 'application' school (specialisation course)
Conseil d'État = Council of state
École Centrale = engineer school (civilian)

Source: Archives Pechiney.

works with 'alternative' ones. From the early 1950s Pechiney sought to find new sources of energy and raw material overseas. Such capital-intensive operations required funds, and therefore foreign partners, since France was suffering from a shortage of hard currency. This was the main motivation for French businesses to establish international industrial and financial joint-ventures. To gain access to reliable industrial partners, Pechiney exploited its long-standing international relationships with aluminium and chemicals industrialists. These connections had endured from the beginning of the century and were usually formalised through international cartels. To secure a foreign financial partnership, the company relied on bankers, most of them North Americans.[14] Such 'alternative' connections implied the payment of fees. The transaction cost compared with the 'classical' public service networks was obviously higher but the 'classical' networks were not able to provide international links at that time. Though costly, 'alternative networks' operated simultaneously with public service ones and were essential to the success of the Guinean aluminium plant of FRIA in Guinea.

Later on, particularly after the return to power of General de Gaulle in 1958, the international economy became a central issue in French politics. From a Gaullist perspective the goal of economic growth was not to improve French living standards but to restore France's leading international position. The national independence policy therefore led the government to directly support large French enterprises abroad. Continuing to function as a provider of élites, through various government agencies, the state also became a real actor in the achievement of private industries' international projects.[15]

As a consequence, the nature of the relationship between industrialist and state changed. Maintaining strong interpersonal connections with government agencies had actually reduced transaction costs for Pechiney in the pre-1945 period. In the following years, connections continued to decrease this cost in the majority of cases. Yet, in two main ways, from the 1950s, these strong connections began, on occasion, to have a contrary effect. First, the almost exclusive recruitment of former civil servants influenced the business and corporate culture of the company with some negative side effects. Second, as the government started to insist on its own agenda in international economics, the firm had to answer to stronger pressure to act in accordance with their wishes. Government agencies were supportive, but were at the same time formally or informally directing the firm's strategy. In this respect, the 1950s and 1960s mark a new phase in the relationship between the French state and industry.

LA COMPAGNIE INTERNATIONALE POUR LA PRODUCTION DE
L'ALUMINE: FRIA, 1956

In the 1950s, world aluminium production increased at a fast pace for
several reasons, and despite the huge war stocks of the metal, by 1948
there was clearly an excess demand in the US market for aluminium. This
was a consequence of Cold War defence spending together with the growing use of aluminium in a wide range of consumer products. Automobile
manufacturers had started in the post-Second World War period to switch
from copper or iron to aluminium components and considering the volumes involved in mass production, this had a tremendous effect on aluminium sales. Moreover, the foreign policy of the USA and its military
expression boosted aluminium consumption in the 1950s. From the beginning of the Korean War, the American defence industry's needs for aluminium grew dramatically. Fearing future supply problems, the US Office
of Defense Mobilisation consequently called for an expansion programme
supported by accelerated amortisation. It is hardly a surprise, then, to
observe that the Aluminum Company of America (ALCOA) multiplied its
output by 140 per cent between 1950 and 1955.[16] Confident about the
long-term growth forecast, most of the other world producers followed
the American example and erected new reduction plants. As a consequence
of their increasing aluminium reduction output, producers had to secure a
reliable supply-chain for alumina.[17]

On account of the nationalisation of electricity in France in 1946 and the
large quantity of power involved in the aluminium reduction process, Pechiney
had no choice but to develop its reduction capacities overseas. Furthermore,
its mainland bauxite reserves were declining. As a result, Pechiney initiated
several projects in what was then French West Africa. Since 1942, company
geologists had been exploring mining opportunities in Senegal, Morocco
and Guinea as well as surveying the hydraulic resources of the Belgian
Congo and Cameroon. At the beginning of the 1950s, independence for the
countries of the so-called 'Union Française' was considered to be neither an
issue nor a threat. Therein, industrialists were very confident about the
opportunities for industrial development in Africa.

With its promising water-flow and river networks, as well as bauxite
deposits, Guinea was eventually chosen for the building of a new alumina
complex. The project was enormous in contemporary terms: the target set
was an impressive annual output of 700,000 tons of alumina to be
obtained through the processing of the nearby Boké bauxite mine's ore.
The project implied not only the construction of a plant, but also the
development of adjacent facilities: roads, railway to the sea, a harbour, a
power station and lines. Furthermore, the construction of a town to house
a population of 30,000 local people, nearby territories immigrants and
French expatriates was planned.[18]

Unsurprisingly given the planned operation's size, the 'Compagnie internationale pour la production de l'alumine' was an imaginative organisation. Incorporated in 1956, the firm was an IJV between European and American aluminium and chemicals corporations. Two French aluminium producers, Pechiney and Ugine, combined to build the works and later to conduct local operations. Their industrial partners were Montecatini (Italy) and Olin Mathieson (USA), joined a few years later as junior partners by the British Aluminium Company Ltd (United Kingdom) and Vereinigte Aluminium Werke (Germany). Since FRIA was a co-operative operation by nature, every associate was supposed to take its part in the production or pay for it.

The financing of the project was nonetheless novel given French standards of the time. It involved a mix of French and International public bodies and private financiers. The colonial authority was represented by its financial offshoot: the 'Caisse Centrale de la France d'Outremer', a formally autonomous public entity. In addition, there was the World Bank, along with private sector investors amongst whom were American Insurance companies.[19] These ties to North American sources of funding were essential in a period of dollar shortage in Europe. Pechiney, even when allied with French partners, could not have found sufficient dollars to purchase the requisite material and machinery.

As the 'classical' alumni network was not able to provide the necessary international connections, Pechiney's CEO Raoul de Vitry used his own personal network. He contacted a close friend of French origin, the merchant banker André Meyer head of Lazard Brothers in New York.[20] The latter introduced De Vitry and Pierre Bartholin, his senior finance officer, to influential individuals in New York such as the future US Ambassador Félix Rohatyn. Lazard Brothers eventually arranged the negotiation with the American partners and later represented their interests in FRIA. On the other hand, convincing aluminium industrialists was not too difficult since the profession has been characterised from the late nineteenth century by international cartelisation. Long-term connections still existed between European and American aluminium ingot producers.

As soon as the project was conceived in 1951–54, Pechiney had to think about a specific deployment of personnel. By tradition, since its foundation in the mid-nineteenth century, the company had recruited its managers amongst chemical engineers and, from the 1900s onwards, selected graduates from the École Polytechnique. The top management was exclusively formed of engineers. The transformation of the French business environment, i.e. a more proactive government in economic matters, prompted a change in Pechiney's recruitment strategies. The special and sophisticated legal structure of FRIA, and the sensitive political nature of its location in a colony, called for the engagement of politically skilled senior civil servants. In addition, Pechiney executives had to face the fact that it was only amongst such specialists that men could be found with experience of monitoring large-scale African industrial ventures.

The previous public service career of the future head of FRIA and later the African and Greek department of Pechiney was very significant in this respect. Jacques Marchandise's professional track-record perfectly matched Pechiney's requirement for an individual with the ability to understand and manage high-level negotiations with both international partners and public authorities. Born in 1918, Marchandise was a graduate of one of the Grandes Écoles (Sciences Politiques) and an auditor in the Council of State (Conseil d'État). An ex-member of the Gaullist Resistance, he quickly became an expert in colonial questions in the administration. From 1948 to 1952, he worked at the Caisse Centrale de la France d'Outremer on the colonial aspects of the Marshall Plan programme. He later joined the former Ministry of the Colonies now named the Ministry of the 'Overseas France'. During discussions on Pechiney's African industrial projects, he met for the first time Raoul de Vitry and Jean Matter, CEO and managing director of the company. Two years later he was appointed advisor to the Prime Minister (Président du Conseil) Pierre Mendès-France, the highest position he attained in government. In February 1955, as a result of Mendès-France's fall, Marchandise became general secretary of the Overseas Territories Mine Office (Bureau Minier de la France d'Outremer).

Besides his high profile and government connections, Marchandise was hired in 1954 by Pechiney because he happened to be an expert in colonial law and mining questions. Following a long-established tradition he did not immediately resign from the administration but took leave of absence to start Pechiney's Guinean subsidiary. His assigned role was, on one hand, to negotiate with the French central and local authorities at a political level, and on the other, to recruit a small team of specialists to run the FRIA project. Although there were many talented technicians amongst the company's own staff, specific skills in key positions were needed in Africa. For every challenge faced, Marchandise tried to find the proper matching profile from the environment he knew: that of public administration. As it was difficult to find French managers with sufficient experience in international negotiation, or with foreign language and law qualifications, a young member of the diplomatic corps with an experience of government departmental staff teamwork, Francis Gutmann, was chosen. Gutmann had participated in the early 1950s in diverse international negotiations on behalf of the French government. A legal advisor by training, Gutmann was nonetheless able to speak English properly, a rare quality amongst French managers of his time.

As regards the technical side, the engineer in charge of the construction was a young polytechnician, Jacques Bocquentin. He had started his career at Pechiney, training in the company's plants during the war. Nevertheless, to manage the construction of the harbour, the railway and the plant itself, the company recruited several engineers and Army officers from diverse colonial services. Their leadership, experience of Africa and general technical training were clear qualifications. As local representatives of their government departments in the earlier stages of their careers, they were supposedly very well prepared to act independently in difficult conditions.

Roger Lantenois was one of them. A former serving officer and a distinguished member of the underground resistance during the war, he worked as head of the public works administration in the city of Dakar (Senegal) and was later promoted with responsibilities for the whole of French West Africa. Eventually hired by Pechiney, his role was to monitor the subcontractors on FRIA's works. His colleague Maurice Serpette, hired in 1959, was also a graduate from the École Polytechnique and a member of the 'ponts et chaussées' colonial corps which had previously organised major public works in West Africa and the Pacific Islands. These engineers carried on working in the same environments and even continued to work with the subcontractors with whom they had previously co-operated.[21]

At shop floor level, when the works began in mid-1957, many of the middle managers were ex-servicemen. The daily monitoring of the workforce was the specific responsibility of former colonial troop officers because of their knowledge of indigenous issues and their sensitivity to tribal tensions. By merit of his military experience, a former commander of an indigenous North African military unit named Roure, was, for instance, in charge of the camp.[22] His main role was to avoid or reduce violent conflict between Senegalese and Guinean workers.[23] In addition to these ethnic problems, political issues rapidly arose and Guinea appeared for a while to the French industrialists to be an unfortunate choice for a long-term investment. In the late 1950s, while on the road to independence, most of the French colonies remained in the so-called 'Union Française', envisioned as a Gallic version of the Commonwealth of Nations. However, personally opposed to General de Gaulle, President Sekou Touré decided to declare Guinea's complete independence in September 1958. Political tension increased immediately at FRIA's construction-site as workers' unions were deployed to deliver the new regime's anti-colonialist credo.[24] There then opened a new chapter in Pechiney's Guinean venture, with greater reliance being placed upon the local authorities than upon the French administration.

As a whole, at least during its first months, the management of the Guinean venture partly replicated the colonial administration, even if Bocquentin, the man in charge of the works, had no previous connection with the old colonial administrative system. It is therefore clear that civil service culture and methods had a deep influence on the destiny of FRIA.

On the positive side, skilled negotiators such as Marchandise and Gutmann were extremely useful, as were experienced colonial officers at an intermediate hierarchical level. On the other hand, such a specific corporate culture created problems, especially when confronted by opposing systems.

French legal specialists had to admit that the concept of the American mortgage was barely used in French commercial contracts. Such problems resulted in different legal systems, but also different cultures. French representatives were amazed by the '1000 pages contract' required by the American lawyers when they were used to more personal and less formal commercial 'gentlemen's agreements'.

At operational level, discrepancies between estimates and actual costs in public projects were considered typical of civil service engineers. To quote Marchandise: 'they did at FRIA as they had always done, they underestimated the costs. Because there had never been any *a posteriori* control nor any reprimand for such a mistake in the civil service.' Being mostly alumni or fellows of the same 'corps', it was difficult for other company managers to criticise the mistakes of their colleagues. The international partners, particularly the Americans, did so instead on behalf of Pechiney's executives. When the differences between estimates and cost reached nearly 30 per cent, the American partners judged it unacceptable. The lawyers urged the introduction of auditing procedures at FRIA and French engineers were forced to adopt a management accounting system to properly monitor the costs, despite the fact that they were supposed to be entirely in charge of the construction.[25]

The French public service system was extremely successful in selecting, educating and training gifted and well-connected specialists who later served in private companies. Its part was then crucial in the international success of some large corporations since outside government departments few French engineers with an effective African experience were available in the job market in the post-war decade. In most cases, the skill and experience of civil engineers and Army officers were perfectly adapted to the requirements of FRIA. Because Guinea was a colony with a powerful French administrative structure, it was also easier for civil servants to understand and use the environment for the benefit of the company.

From these individuals Pechiney gained new organisational capabilities, first of which was the ability to operate large and complex projects in a precarious environment. Surprisingly, the company 'benefited' also from the weakening of the civil service culture at the hands of the American partners of the FRIA project. If it had been a perfect provider of talented staff and public funding, the French state due to its fierce opposition to the regime of president Sekou Touré was eventually of no use to Pechiney in Guinea. It would not be the same when Pechiney started a new international joint venture in Greece during the next decade.

ALUMINIUM DE GRÈCE: 1959–66

The Aluminium de Grèce (ADG) project started in 1959 following a Greek government initiative backed by the USA. As part of its foreign policy, the latter had financed a major hydraulic dam on the river Acheloos and was pressing for national industrial development. Meanwhile, Greece was applying for an association with, and later full membership, of the Common Market; and this claim was supported by the French government. As a consequence, looking for an energy consumer with long-term development aims, the Greek government contacted Pechiney in late 1959. The French company created a national industry and become the first electricity consumer of Greece with a consumption forecast of a third of the national production in 1960! The negotiations were protracted and, while ADG was incorporated in 1961, the plant's operations did not commence for another five years.

From a very early stage, both governments were closely involved in the venture. The French government participated in the financial side since COFACE and HERMES, the French and German export insurance agencies, secured loans of up to $59 million. $130 million of the project were raised from various international lenders: the European Investment Bank, the Crédit Suisse, the National Bank of Greece, the Crédit Foncier de Grèce and the Greek agency for industrial development (ETBA).

Due to operational and financial constraints similar to FRIA's, ADG was established as an IJV from the outset. The former head of the Guinean joint venture, Marchandise, was made managing director of the new Greek subsidiary. Following the same procedure established for FRIA, Pechiney was to run the construction and later to operate the plant on behalf of its associates. The industrial project was very original as reduction facilities were unusually integrated, with the bauxite mine, the alumina processing plant, the reduction smelter and the shipping facilities almost in the same location. The scale of the project was impressive: in addition to the construction of the two plants mentioned above, infrastructure comparable to FRIA's was also planned. The total budget of the scheme was estimated at $75 million (1960), but the total cost was actually $140 million (1967).

The environment was nevertheless rather different. Greece was a European country that had enjoyed, since the end of its 1946–49 civil war, a supposedly stable political climate. On the other hand, there was no significant national industry and therefore no domestic market for ADG's future output. That is why, besides the financial burden, the operation had to be an association of producers looking for extra European aluminium ingot-supply. As for the FRIA venture, the strategy of Pechiney was to generate a dynamic of integration among the international producers. The rationale beyond this strategy of co-operation was to make the French company's technology the global industry standard. Operating the aluminium production joint ventures, Pechiney maintained its status as technological leader and was able to sell its knowledge to its competitors.

The central role of both governments and the international nature of the agreement led to a meeting of radically different partners. The Greek government had insisted on the presence of local financial partners. This was reckoned to be useful for covering some of those expenses that needed to be paid in drachmas. As a result of this condition, the board was a diverse one. The aluminium producers involved were Pechiney, associated with Ugine and Reynolds Corporation (USA), since after some initial interest, Vereinigte Aluminium Werke (VAW) from Germany had quickly withdrawn. The Greek state itself was represented by delegates of two public agencies OBA (the Greek Industrial Development Agency) and OXOA (later to become ETBA, a public financial body) and DEH (the National Electricity Company).

New to the Greek environment, Pechiney had recruited as general secretary a specialist in European affairs, J. Poincaré, who was a former principal private secretary (chef de cabinet) of the Coal and Steel European Community. Still, the French had to find information on a possible local partnership. For that, the company's connection with the French public service was inoperable. Marchandise used an alternative private network and hired COMPADEC, a consultancy run by a graduate of the École Polytechnique, J. Goutail. The firm specialised in the establishment of companies in the Balkan region and Southern Europe. It had advised the aluminium producer in Yugoslavia in the mid-1950s on a smaller-scale project. In the early stage of ADG's creation, Goutail was even considered as a partner and elected a member of the board. He advised Pechiney to appoint to the board the adventurous financier Stavros Niarchos, whose ties with the Greek Royal family, the court and the cabinet were thought to be crucial to the success of a Greek project. This turned out not to be the case and it cost Pechiney a considerable sum to buy back Niarchos's shares some months later. Then, Goutail was asked to leave ADG when Pechiney discovered that he was using his knowledge of operations to advise Reynolds Metals to establish a competing plant in Norway. As the interests of the partners were clearly antagonistic, the management of the project at board-level was extremely sensitive. The changes in the distribution of shares, shown in Table 2, illustrates the increasing role played by Pechiney and the Greek government in this venture. The story of COMPADEC and Niarchos showed that the use of 'alternative' networks could be extremely costly and potentially disastrous in a new environment.

As the corporation in charge of organising the construction Pechiney experienced serious administrative problems during the same period. From the first months of their activities in Greece, the French industrialists faced

Table 2: Distribution (in per cent) of Aluminium of Greece's ordinary shares in 1962 and 1970

Major Shareholders	1962	1970
Hellenic Metals (S. Niarchos)	21	
Reynolds	17	
ETBA (Greek State)	12	10.8
SFDAG (Pechiney+Ugine)	50	45
Pechiney		31.3
Ugine		2.9
Others		10
Total	100	100

Source: P. Mioche and I. Grinberg, *Aluminium de Grèce* (Grenoble, 1997).

numerous bureaucratic problems. For instance, it took Pechiney sixteen months to get official permits to buy the land, despite the official support of the Greek government. In addition, in the following years ADG became implicated in Greek politics. Energy price was a key issue in Pechiney's decision to install the smelter in Greece, as it represented 25 per cent of the production cost of aluminium. The first motivation of the Karamanlis government was to find a consumer for the electricity of the Acheloos dam. But, with the opposition attacking the deal as 'neo-colonialist', the energy agreement between ADG and the Greek government was quickly seen to be too advantageous to the foreign multinational.[26] The 1964 Greek general election saw the defeat of the Karamanlis cabinet. The new leader of the country, Georges Papandreou, and his minister Iannis Zigdis, immediately called a meeting with the executives of ADG and stated that the contract was to be re-negotiated. The French government was informed immediately by Pechiney. Indeed, through its export insurance agency the COFACE, the French government was directly involved. Nearly $59 million of loans was covered by COFACE and its German counterpart HERMES.

In the following stages, links between industry and state were clearly crucial. P. Jouven, then managing director of Pechiney, himself a former civil servant in the 'corps des Mines', personally intervened. Along with Marchandise, they secured access to both the highest level of the Foreign office ministry and the presidency of the Republic because this was a matter of national foreign policy. Paris was then backing Athens in her efforts to have Greece's external debt reduced. French diplomats had been very pro-active in recent years lobbying, amongst other international institutions, the Organization for Economic Co-operation and Development

(OECD) and the European Bank. As a response to the Greek threat to re-negotiate ADG's electricity contract, France immediately stopped her campaign in favour of Greece and let it be known to the Greek cabinet. As a result, a few weeks later, Papandreou issued a declaration emphasising the fact that it was essential for Greece to maintain a harmonious relationship with France. Minister Zigdis resigned, and the energy contract between DEH and ADG was eventually ratified.

In this case, there was a direct intervention by the French authorities imposing financial pressure on the Greek government. Considering themselves a partner, they also exerted influence on the French side. To fulfil a treaty between France and Germany, and as a condition for obtaining the backing of the COFACE for its loans, Aluminium de Grèce had to purchase a large amount of its machinery in Germany. If two suppliers were to offer the same cost, Pechiney had no choice but to favour the German one even though its engineering department was far from pleased by such decisions.[27] On the whole, the influence of the French governments between 1961 to 1973 was extremely positive, with COFACE agreeing throughout to guarantee additional loans till the completion of the plants.

From the early 1950s and Pechiney's Guinean operations, the French government's attitude towards supporting private firms altered dramatically. From a vague commitment, Government agencies were increasingly urged to act as partners in industry by a Gaullist regime that considered economic policy as a part of national foreign policy. This proactive stance proved to be extremely helpful in accelerating conflict resolution.

CONCLUDING REMARKS

Three aspects characterise the evolution and the development of the relationship between state and industry in France, and its emergence as a basic element of both domestic and international industrial operations.

The State as a provider of skilled staff and administrative methods

From the turn of the twentieth century to the inter-war years, Pechiney recruited its executives from among the graduates of the École Polytechnique. Such an exclusive system of recruitment for top management positions reflects three patterns. First, based on the sciences – and especially mathematics – the École Polytechnique entry competition was the most prestigious and predictably attracted the most gifted secondary school pupils. Second, industrialists at that time considered production to be at the very heart of an industrial firm and, as a consequence, few disputed the entitlement of technicians to run businesses. Third, graduates of the Grandes Écoles and ex-members of the technical corps had access to precious information through their very strong alumni network. What did these state engineers bring to the firm in terms of organisational capabilities? In the case of Pechiney, they adapted military and administrative models to the structures and the administrative procedures of the company. By improving the communication and reporting systems they developed new methods to control distant facilities.[28] Regarding large industrial firms, the existence of an elite supplier devoted to the State emerges as one of the specific aspects of French business and management practice in the period covered by this article.

The State as a direct support

Except during the First World War,[29] the fact that these large firms were managed after 1900 by former civil servants cannot be considered as a simple response to attempts at state intervention. On the contrary, and from the late 1930s, large firms involved in the exploitation of so-called strategic materials, defence mobilisation plans or, later, in colonial ventures, had to develop political and administrative connections. That was the rationale behind the election to the board of leading politicians in the 1920s and 1930s and the later hiring of former ministerial department staff. After 1945, the recruitment of civil servants was planned at corporate level and executed as part of a specific industrial project. The new appointees were still 'generalist' managers but with specialised knowledge, e.g. colonial issues in the case of Guinea. That 'second generation' of former civil servants 'imported' essential organisational capabilities into domains unknown to the firm, such as international legal or political negotiation. After 1958, the international economy became a political issue for the Gaullist regime and, as a consequence, the government more actively supported the overseas operations of French industrialists. A new type of relation between state and industry appeared involving frequent direct government interference. These interventions, in the case of Pechiney in Greece, not only permitted successful financing, but also saved the project at a stage when it was threatened by internal political disputes. Therefore, in this case a close relationship with the State conferred an undeniable competitive advantage.

Alternative connections to complement state networks

The 'classical' state-related old-boy networks described above were not always sufficient to handle complex and innovative operations in barely known environments; although, in the French or imperial contexts, such connections greatly improved access to information at a relatively low cost. Nevertheless, the State was never considered by industrialists to be a monopoly provider of information: bankers, competitors, cartels and also consultants were employed.

Where and when 'classical' state networks were useless or ineffective, 'alternative networks' were instituted, often through the CEO's personal connections. In the case of Pechiney, the association with merchant bankers and foreign financiers greatly increased short-term transaction costs but they also provided long-term assets. When Pechiney started industrial operations in the United States in 1964, the company's experiences in Guinea and Greece, as well as its familiarity with American financial networks maintained since the ventures of the 1950s, were crucial to its success.[30]

Despite some cultural problems described earlier, and the explicit commitment of its executives to private enterprise,[31] close personal and organisational connections to the civil service and French government proved a real asset for the international operation of Pechiney in the post-1945 period. Exploiting a long-term tradition of state–industry relations, as well as alternative connections, the firm adapted its use of networks to transform its internal organisational capabilities and to enhance the effectiveness of its overseas operations.

NOTES

*   This article is based on research undertaken while a research fellow at the Centre for International Business History, University of Reading.

1.   A.D. Chandler Jnr, *Scale and Scope, the Dynamics of Industrial Capitalism* (Cambridge, Mass., 1990), p. 24.

2.   M. Lévy-Leboyer and J. C. Casanova (eds), *Entre l'État et le marché* (Paris, 1991), p. 332; J. Marseille, *Les performances des entreprises françaises au XXe siècle* (Paris, 1995).

3.   See P. Fridenson's contribution on France in A.D. Chandler Jnr, F. Amatori and T. Hikino, *Big Business and The Wealth of Nations* (Cambridge, 1997), pp. 207–45.

4.   A. Broder, 'L'industrie française et le marché mondial', in J. Marseille, *Les performances des entreprises françaises au XXe siècle* (Paris, 1995), p. 38.

5.   On the role of investment bankers Lazard Frères see C. Reich, *Financier: the Biography of André Meyer* (New York, 1983).

6.   I. Grinberg and Ph. Mioche, *Aluminium de Grèce, l'usine aux trois rivages* (Grenoble, 1997).

7.   On the role of J.B. Colbert and more generally the evolution of the state in France see G. Duby (ed.), *Histoire de la France* (Paris, 1986), vols 2 and 3; and for modern France see R. F. Kuisel, *Le capitalisme et l'État en France* (Paris, 1984), pp. 27–72.

8.   On the managerial pattern of modern France see M. Lévy-Leboyer, 'The Large Corporation in Modern France', in A.D. Chandler and H. Daems (eds), *Managerial Hierarchies: Comparative Perspectives on The Rise of Modern Industrial Enterprise* (Cambridge, Mass. and London, 1980), pp. 117–60; and F. Caron, *Histoire économique de la France* (Paris, 1995), p. 252. On the early hiring of polytechnicians by entrepreneurs see J. Lambert-Dansette, *Histoire de l'entreprise et des chefs d'entreprises en France: genèse du patronat, 1780–1880* (Paris, 1991). For an overview of the mod-

ern French managerial education system see D.J. Hickson (ed.), *Management in Western Europe* (Berlin, 1993).

9. L. Cailluet, *Stratégies, structures et pratiques de gestion de Pechiney des années 1880 à 1971* (forthcoming, Grenoble, 1999).

10. On the status and importance of engineers such as former scholars of the 'École Polytechnique' see C. Charle, *Les élites de la République (1880–1900)* (Paris, 1987) and J.P. Rioux, 'Ces élites qui nous gouvernent', *L'Histoire* 147 (1991), pp. 48–58.

11. P. Toussaint, *La Compagnie des produits chimiques et électrométallurgiques Alais, Froges et Camargue, première partie: les quatre sociétés constitutives.* Pechiney Archives 00–8–11247–9.

12. See H. Morsel, 'Louis Marlio : position idéologique et comportement politique d'un dirigeant d'une grande entreprise dans la première moitié du XXe siècle', *Cahiers d'histoire de l'aluminium*, 2 (1988).

13. F.M. Lynch, *France and the International Economy, From Vichy to the Treaty of Rome* (New York, London, 1997).

14. On the long term relationship of Pechiney with the USA see L. Cailluet's contribution to M. Kipping and O. Bjarnar (eds), *Americanisation of European Business* (London, 1998).

15. On General De Gaulle's economic vision see S. Bernstein, *La France de l'expansion* (Paris, 1989) pp. 220, 236–40.

16. On post-war capacity expansion see M.J. Peck, *Competition in the aluminum industry 1945–1958* (Cambridge, Mass., 1961), pp. 144–65.

17. In the period the aluminium production process was as follows: 4 to 5 tons of bauxite ore were needed to extract 2 tons of alumina; after reduction in a smelter, these 2 tons yielded one ton of primary aluminium.

18. The Boké mine itself was established as an international joint venture between European and American partners.

19. On the Caisse Centrale de la France d'Outremer see Lynch, *France and the International Economy* (London, 1997), p. 193.

20. On aluminium international cartels see F. Hachez, 'Le cartel international de l'aluminium du point de vue des sociétés françaises' in D. Barjot (ed.), *International cartels revisited: 1880–1980: relating to the history of business development and international economic order* (Cormelles, 1994).

21. That was the case of Dumez, a large public works corporation which had worked in colonial French Africa for decades; they were selected by Pechiney on the FRIA workings because of that experience but also because they were accustomed to working for foreign clients, especially the US Navy in North Africa since the Second World War.

22. During the colonial era, France trained and maintained various military units in Africa whose personnel was almost entirely composed of local soldiers (Senegalese Rifles, Moroccan Tabor, etc.). The French officers in charge of these special units were very often able to speak the local language and were occasionally used as local administrators. As a consequence, these men became very knowledgeable about ethnic and tribal questions. See *Revue Historique des Armées*.

23. On Bocquentin's experience of Guinea see J. Bocquentin, 'Problèmes de

relations entre Européens et Africains sur le chantier de Fria', *Cahiers d'Histoire de l'Aluminium* 15 (1994), pp. 78–101.

24. On the independence of French African colonies see G. Comte, 'L'afrique noire française accède à l'indépendance', *Le Monde* (1 April 1980).

25. Source: Interviews I. Grinberg/J. Marchandise, May 1990 and I. Grinberg/F. Gutmann, May 1988. Institut pour l'histoire de l'aluminium (Paris).

26. On the conditions attached to the negotiation see Mioche and Grinberg, op. cit., pp. 56–7.

27. The company's engineering services were not used by these German companies and Pechiney had a very bad experience with German engineering and a heavy machinery supplier. Despite complaining, the engineering services were told by Marchandise that they would have to follow company policy.

28. See L. Cailluet, 'Un exemple français d'acquisition de capacités organisationnelles: Alais, Froges et Camargue (AFC-Pechiney), d'une avant-guerre à l'autre', *Entreprises et Histoire* 13 (1996), pp. 115–27.

29. That has to be nuanced as the industrialists were often themselves in charge of the defence mobilisation during the war. Loucheur, Minister of Armaments, and his advisors Petsche and Mercier, were connected with private corporations (electricity, non-ferrous metals). They took the opportunity presented by the war to concentrate some of their industrial sectors.

30. Interview with J.P Altorfer, former executive of Pechiney's manufacturing operations in North America.

31. After the 1946 nationalisation of Pechiney's electrical production facilities, several executives of the company protested vigorously in the press.

Chosen Instruments:
The State and British Commercial Air
Transport since 1920[*]

Peter Lyth

Deutsches Museum, Munich

> The structure of world civil aviation
> has been fashioned by many forces,
> amongst which economic logic
> has played only a modest part.[1]

The international airline industry has been on a roller-coaster ride for much of its seventy-eight-year history. It has been up and down between meagre profits and devastating losses, and swept back and forth by oil crises, terrorism, and the fickle habits of the modern tourist. It has also had to bear the heavy hand of government. Indeed national governments have had a hard time keeping up with its antics and have more often than not adopted misguided aviation policies. Britain has been no exception to this tendency and has tried every kind of approach to its own air transport industry since the end of the First World War, from open competition to subsidised private monopoly and duopoly, to full nationalisation, to mixed duopoly and finally back again to an attenuated form of competition.

This article deals with the meandering course of British policy, and the relationship between the British flag-carrier and the state. It focuses on three aspects of that relationship: changing government policy on the subsidisation and ownership structure of the national airline; the link between that policy and the government's concern for the British aircraft industry; and the flag-carrier's operational performance. For explanatory convenience it is divided into three periods.

PRIVATE COMPANIES, PUBLIC SUBSIDIES, 1920–40

In the years between the end of the First World War and the foundation of Imperial Airways in 1924, civil aviation in Britain grew haphazardly. The importance of government subsidy to the industry had been recognised as early as 1917, but initially there was no political support for the idea that the state should assume financial responsibility for fledgling airlines. If commercial air transport was to fly, said Winston Churchill, it 'must fly by itself'.[2] The first international passenger-carrying service was opened in August 1919 by Air Transport & Travel (AT&T) between London and Paris. Handley Page Transport (HPT) began another Paris service about a week later, and a third British airline owned by the shipowners Instone joined the others in February 1920. Unfortunately few financial data have survived, but it is clear that these airlines were in difficulties from the outset and when two new French operators entered the cross-Channel market, they folded one after the other.[3] In 1922 the government reluctantly accepted the need for subsidy and began what was to be a long financial involvement in the industry. A grant of around £100,000 was awarded to Handley Page, Instone and Daimler Hire Co., on condition that they avoid competition with each other and develop separate routes in Europe. Passenger traffic across the Channel doubled in the next two years, but despite the subsidy the British airlines continued to lose money. With hopelessly uneconomic aircraft, their costs were prohibitively high and, in any case, with only a few intrepid passengers they were lucky to take off with their planes half full.[4]

With no prospect of unsubsidised air transport in sight, the government appointed a committee in January 1923 under the chairmanship of Sir Herbert Hambling to look into the future of British civil aviation. Hambling recommended that the existing airlines be merged to form a single company and that this 'chosen instrument' be the sole recipient of a state subsidy.[5] Hitherto 'the benefit of competition (had been) illusory', and until the industry became more nearly self-supporting, competition could not be 'relied upon to stimulate its development.'[6] At the end of March 1924 the new company – Imperial Airways – was founded, with the former railway executive, Sir Eric Geddes, as chairman. Monopoly replaced competition. Imperial's operating subsidy amounted to £1 million, to be paid in diminishing instalments over ten years. Thereafter it was hoped that the company would be self-supporting; however this proved unfounded and the subsidy was actually extended until 1939.

Why was the British government persuaded of the need to change policy and support the airline industry within just five years of its birth? This was largely, it seems, a result of the close relationship in its early years between civil and military aviation. Civil aviation quickly became a matter of concern to the state because of its perceived connection to national defence and prestige; the British view was that if the French were subsidising their airlines, Britain could not afford to be left behind. In addition the government was almost certainly influenced by what one expert has called the 'overweening enthusiasm' of the young industry's protagonists and by their claims of future profitability.[7]

After 1924, and particularly after 1929, Imperial Airways devoted itself, appropriately enough, to the task of building air mail and passenger links to the Empire. By the late 1930s its famous Short flying boats were a regular feature of life around the colonial outposts of India, Africa and Australia, although its all-British aircraft fleet had become notorious for its out-dated 'landplanes' (eg. the Handley Page HP42) while European competitors like KLM, Swissair and Lufthansa were flying modern American and German types. Imperial Airways was also neglecting the European network at a time of intensified national rivalries; in other words, the 'chosen instrument' was failing in its prestige role.[8] In the 1938 Cadman Report, the airline was criticised for disregarding the wider needs of national policy. Despite the earlier encouragement it had received for its development of colonial routes, it was seen as imperative that better services be established between London and the principal capitals of Europe.[9] The need for a more vigorous British presence on the Continent had been partly met by a second international carrier, British Airways Ltd., which had begun subsidised mail and passenger services to northern European destinations in 1936. However, in the wake of the Cadman Report, the decision was taken – remarkable for a Conservative government – to combine the two airlines and form a publicly-owned air corporation – British Overseas Airways Corporation (BOAC).[10]

The importance of the Cadman Report lies in its greater appreciation of the dynamics of international air transport and of Hambling's over-optimism regarding the extent of financial support that the industry required. It was clear that British flag-carriers could not succeed against foreign competition unless they were subsidised on a long-term basis. Had Cadman's recommendation to subsidise both Imperial and British Airways been accepted, then dual chosen instruments would have been created, not unlike the situation in the United States where in the 1930s four trunk operators established an oligopoly that was to dominate domestic air transport for the next forty years. However in Europe the market was smaller and single protected flag-carriers were preferred for international services; the British were following convention in deciding to pay the subsidy to a single, nationalised airline.

In terms of operational performance Imperial Airways was a qualified success. It was, after all, a private company which paid a dividend to its shareholders in almost every one of its sixteen years. The problem was that it paid its private dividend with the aid of an operating subsidy from the public purse, and this anomaly could not be sustained indefinitely. Seen against a background of intensified interest in the Empire, particularly after the abandonment of free trade in 1931 and the adoption of Imperial Preference at the Ottawa Conference, Imperial Airways did precisely what was asked of it – and did it rather well. In the space of a decade it extended its routes from the south coast of England to Cape Town and Sydney, and in the process built up the longest international network in the world. It was therefore a little unfair of critics in the late 1930s to say that it had been neglecting its duty in Europe.[11] However in its role as promoter of British civil aircraft – and it was required by the terms of its subsidy agreement to fly only British types – Imperial was less successful. But then its aircraft procurement was a direct consequence of its colonial route policy and that had been in accordance with the government's wishes. Unable to use landplanes across Africa and the Middle East, where airport construction was blocked by jungle or political impediments, it settled for flying boats and thus failed to provide the necessary stimulation to British manufacturers to build types comparable to the Douglas DC3 and Lockheed Electra.[12]

NATIONALISED MONOPOLIES, 1940–73

BOAC was intended to correct this situation. As a publicly-owned enterprise, the government would be able to supervise its operations and investment policy, and make sure that grants from the Treasury were well-spent. Unfortunately BOAC came into being in April 1940 – its timing could hardly have been worse. The skies over Britain were full of combat aircraft and the airline was immediately placed under the control of the Air Ministry. Normal business procedures were suspended and BOAC's task was reduced to ferrying men and supplies along whatever international routes were still safe from enemy action.[13]

It was not until the autumn of 1944 that the wartime coalition gave serious consideration to the future of BOAC and the new Minister of Civil Aviation, Viscount Swinton, assembled a plan which appeared as a White Paper in March 1945. This envisaged British civil aviation in the hands of several organisations with mixed ownership and significant participation by surface transport interests. BOAC was to remain state-owned but two new corporations, British European Airways (BEA) and British South American Airways (BSAA), would have mixed ownership of which the majority would be private.[14] The 1939/40 plan for a single corporation for all international services, with domestic aviation left to private independents, was now discarded and the dividing line moved so that European services were separated from other international flights. The Swinton Plan aimed to fulfil a number of tasks, which are worth mentioning because they had an enduring influence on post-war policy. Firstly it sought to secure unprofitable social services, by offering monopoly rights on profitable routes; asking the airline, in other words, to cross-subsidise.[15] Secondly it tried to stimulate management by setting up several flag-carriers, which nonetheless were to operate in separate regions, in a non-competitive relationship to each other. Thirdly it required the airlines, as far as possible, to fly British aircraft. And fourthly, it intended the airlines to 'operate as far as possible without subsidy'. The companies were to be chosen not simply because of their skill and experience, but because they were 'prepared to invest their own money without any Government guarantee'.[16]

The Swinton Plan was superseded by the electoral victory of the Labour party in the summer of 1945, but its structural provisions were largely retained in the 1946 Civil Aviation Act. In the debate on this bill, Labour re-stressed the need for subsidies, thus reversing the last of Swinton's four objectives, and abandoned the inclusion of private transport interests. However its intention to proceed with full nationalisation was quite uncontroversial, since the Conservatives had already used it with the creation of BOAC in 1940.[17] Labour's retention of Swinton's three-airline approach was justified by Sir Stafford Cripps, the former Minister of Aircraft Production, on the grounds that a *multiplicity of instruments* would enable the testing of 'different techniques' for civil air transport.[18] Labour's policy would ensure 'orderly, economic and efficient development of air transport', by not placing 'matters of great national importance' in the hands of a single managerial group.[19] In fact the three-airline approach was quickly reduced to a two-airline approach, as BSAA proved to be unfeasible after its Avro Tudor aircraft began crashing in 1948, and it was taken over by BOAC in 1949.

As one authority has remarked, in carrying out its post-war nationalisation plan Labour was 'quite clear on the issue of ownership but not at all clear about control'. Beyond the belief that essential industries and services were to be run by the state, little had been thought out.[20] Civil aviation was obviously not *essential* in the sense that rail transport or the coal industry were; moreover airlines are not natural monopolies like power generation or the railways – so why bother to nationalise? Why not simply *control* the industry, much as the pre-war governments had controlled Imperial Airways? The answer would seem to be a mixture of ideological consistency and the recognition by Labour that air transport was strategically important, in other words, it competed with foreign firms.[21] There seems to be no evidence that Labour considered that the most *interventionist* issues inherited from Swinton, ie. the 'fly-British' policy on aircraft procurement and the maintenance of *social* air services, would be better handled by a state-owned enterprise. However in practice it *was* these two policies that required the most frequent Ministerial involvement in the affairs of BOAC and BEA; it is reasonably safe to say that state-ownership and the politicisation of these two airlines facilitated their implementation. As one of the chroniclers of the nationalisation programme once noted, BOAC could not buy the American aircraft (which it wanted) without other aspects of the national interest being considered, eg. the effect of the purchase on the British aircraft industry and the balance of payments. Thus the decision became political, and political control is easier to exercise over a public corporation than a private one.[22]

Having created the air corporations, it was comparatively easy for the government to attach further elements of its political agenda. The most obvious was its commitment to full employment. One writer reckoned in the late 1940s that there was a tendency to replace the 'excessive leanness' of Imperial Airways and British Airways with an 'excessive fatness' at BOAC.[23] It is undoubtedly true that BOAC was overstaffed for much of its history, but did the corporations need to be labour-efficient when they were serving other aims? It is more useful to see BOAC and BEA as chosen instruments within the broad realm of British civil aviation policy. Their twenty-seven-year history was characterised by two features which were in many ways more important than their state-ownership and which they shared with most other European flag-carriers. The first was their monopoly status and the second, flowing very much from the first, was the high degree of protection they enjoyed from the government and through their membership of the international airline cartel, IATA. Monopoly of international passenger services out of Britain was important because it afforded the airlines the means to cross-subsidise loss-making services and compensated them for buying less efficient British aircraft; indeed by the end of the 1950s, the chairmen of BOAC and BEA were making the maintenance of their monopoly privileges the *quid pro quo* for their continued support for the British aircraft industry.

BOAC had continuous problems with aircraft procurement, of which the Comet crashes of 1953/54 were the ultimate low point. Britain had actually begun to produce adequate commercial landplanes in 1939 – the elegant de Havilland DH91 being the best example – but then it had been obliged to abandon the field for the duration of the war. By 1945 it was far behind the Americans, although 'flying British' remained an article of faith, even for the Labour government. BOAC was allowed to buy some American aircraft (i.e. Lockheed Constellation, Boeing Stratocruiser and Douglas DC7C), but only as a stopgap measure and on the understanding that they would be replaced with British long-range aircraft as soon as the latter were available. This proved to be a long and disappointing experience, and government insistence on helping the British industry was only relinquished in the mid-1960s after the introduction of the Vickers VC10. BEA had less trouble than BOAC with its British aircraft in the 1950s and actually sponsored the single most successful British airliner – the Vickers Viscount. However in the 1960s it suffered the consequences of endemic overtailoring,[24] had a unsatisfactory record with its Hawker Siddeley Trident jets, and by the end of the decade was ready to buy American.[25]

Neither BOAC nor BEA made any profits in the early years and between 1946 and 1952 BOAC received about £35 million in Treasury grants, while BEA received about £16 million in the years until 1955.[26] Thereafter they operated without direct subsidies although they continued to receive investment grants. In the boom years of the mid-1960s, both airlines came into profit, but a new development threatened their future. As the international air transport industry expanded, their monopoly was challenged. As early as 1952 the incoming Conservative government had made a token gesture to greater competition and allowed applications for new services from independent airlines to be heard by the Air Transport Advisory Council (ATAC). However, at this stage no one in the government wanted to dismantle or privatise the air corporations, who were assured that their scheduled routes would not be opened to competition. In 1960 a statutory change threatened to deprive them of their exclusive rights to scheduled services and the ATAC was replaced with the more vigourous Air Transport Licensing Board (ATLB). Still, any erosion of BOAC and BEA's monopolies was limited and new applicants for air routes had to prove that their projected service would not cause 'material diversion of traffic from any air transport service which is being, or is about to be provided.'[27]

It was neither politics nor legislation which threatened BOAC and BEA, but the market, the consumer society and a new breed of independent airlines specialising in cheap flights and inclusive tours.[28] Two trends were developing among British independent airlines: non-scheduled operators specialising in charter inclusive tour services, e.g. Britannia Airways, and bigger carriers, often backed by shipping interests which were anxious to diversify, e.g. British United Airways (BUA) and Caledonian Airways. By the end of the 1960s the latter two airlines were large enough to be a major concern to BOAC. They were buying jet aircraft like the Boeing 707 or the Vickers VC10, or acquiring – at bargain prices – large turbo-prop aircraft such as the Bristol Britannia which BOAC had struggled to develop at great cost in the 1950s. Both the air corporations felt threatened, as a cursory reading of their annual reports from the period reveals. BEA was worried about the fast-growing European tourist industry which was fundamentally changing the air transport market. '... there is no doubt that the habit of holiday-making abroad by air is here to stay.' noted BEA in 1968. 'As each year goes by more and more people are on the move all over Europe.'

Inclusive tours grew fast because they provided cheap and convenient air travel – a concept which had not been part of BEA's policy brief in the late 1940s. Initially BEA tried to strangle the newcomers with legislation to restrict the issue of their operating licences, but in 1965 a Labour Minister, Roy Jenkins, opened up the inclusive tour market to new tour operators and BEA's share of the British holiday market fell. Unable to hide any longer behind its monopoly protection, and rid of its obligation to be a captive customer for the British aircraft industry, BEA began to adapt – launching its own charter airline and even going into the hotel business in 1968.[29] A similiar situation emerged at BOAC, although there the major threat was from trans-Atlantic charter operators such as Caledonian and Laker Airways.

The state of the British air transport industry was thus in flux as the 1960s drew to a close. The two state-owned flag-carriers, BOAC and BEA, still dominated the industry, thanks to their monopoly privileges and the high, fixed fare levels they were able to charge as long-standing IATA members. But their market situation had changed with the lapsing of post-war policy; above all, with the abandonment of the fly British provision, the two airlines could now look for the best aircraft (i.e. American or, possibly, European). The only major British civil aircraft project still under way in the late-1960s was the Anglo-French supersonic Concorde and that was a high-level prestige project shared between governments, rather than the solution to an airline procurement problem. (It is noteworthy that neither of the flag-carriers involved – BOAC and Air France – wanted the aircraft).

It was at this juncture that the Labour government launched a major enquiry into the air transport industry led by Sir Ronald Edwards, the first such study since the 1938 Cadman Report. The Edwards Report was published in 1969 and while it made no major criticism of BOAC and BEA's performance, and favoured their continued public ownership, it did recommend changes. The most important of these were the creation of a so-called 'second force' airline in the private sector and a joint holdings board to oversee the future development of BOAC and BEA.[30] These proposals were accepted by the new Conservative government and put into effect in the 1971 Civil Aviation Act, which set up the Civil Aviation Authority (CAA) in place of the ATLB, cleared the way for the merger of BUA and Caledonian into British Caledonian Airways (BCal) and the new airline's recognition as the *second force*, and established the British Airways Board. Although Edwards did not envisage BOAC and BEA losing their separate identities, a process of amalgamation was now irreversibly in train. The multiplicity of instruments favoured by Stafford Cripps in 1946 was to be replaced with a single flag-carrier, and a genuine, if limited, form of competition in the *second force*. Another of Edwards's conclusions is also noteworthy. It was the strong condemnation of long-term cross-subsidisation of one route by another and the recommendation that no air services should be provided at fares below cost.[31] Although the Report's authors may not have intended it, this challenged the last major justification for the air corporations' monopoly, i.e. that they should use the easy profits from their international services to pay for their loss-making domestic and political routes.

DEREGULATION AND PRIVATISATION, 1973–90

The British Airways Group was established in September 1972 and brought together the top management of BEA and BOAC. Then in early 1973 the British Airways Board recommended the full merger of BOAC and BEA, under the name British Airways (BA), from 1 April 1974. The new airline had the most comprehensive route network in the world and the biggest international fleet, but it also began life in a difficult decade for European flag-carriers. The 1950s and 1960s had been a golden age of growth and low inflation – and a boom time (particularly in the 1960s) for passenger air travel. The 1973 oil shock and the recession which followed it, slowed the growth rate and brought new burdens including sharply rising fuel costs. It was not the best time to launch a new airline, although it was less disastrous than the launch of BOAC in 1940. In fact a merger between the two airlines had been mooted on several occasions over the previous twenty years, on the grounds that a pooling of resources and know-how would benefit both carriers, and in the 1960s there had been a strong general trend towards industrial concentration in the British economy.

If, however, rationalisation and a pooling of resources had been promised before, they were wholly absent in 1973 merger. From the outset BA had a huge staff, as well as a recent history of labour disputes, and it now showed a distinct unwillingness to tackle problems in the labour force. Indeed one of the first actions of the merged management was to 'give an undertaking to our 48,000 staff in the UK that they would not suffer lack of continuity or security of employment as a direct result of the merger.'[32] It was hoped that BOAC and BEA's respective problems would be solved without redundancies through the mere fact of fusion; the labour-saving rationalisation which might have flowed from it, was disregarded. The government, having blessed the marriage, also showed itself disinclined to force the new airline to streamline its structure. By 1975 it was clear that the Labour government's policy sought primarily to protect BA and the jobs it provided, and its continued position as a state monopoly was defended by the Minister (Peter Shore) against the challenge and pretensions of Freddie Laker's new Skytrain, as well as the *second force*, BCal, which was not allowed to expand in any significant way into BA's sphere of operations.[33]

Throughout the decade BA's productivity growth remained low, while passenger numbers rose at a pedestrian pace, actually falling in 1978. One of the causes of this was the wide variety of aircraft in its fleet and the high operating costs of its remaining British types, i.e. the Trident, Super VC10 and BAC 1–11. The effects of the earlier Buy British policy still impacted on the flag-carrier's accounts and BA's management admitted that the American aircraft which it had acquired were more economical on fuel, more productive and more reliable.[34] When one compares BA's performance with that of the best US airlines at the time one sees the distance that the 'chosen instrument' would have to cover in order to turn itself into an 'efficient' airline. In 1977 Delta Airlines carried over twice as many passengers as BA (30.7 million against 13.3 million) with little more than half the number of staff (31,000 against 56,000) and the same number of aircraft. Moreover Delta's maintenance productivity was four to five times greater than BA's, proof that the engineering problems that had plagued BOAC and BEA had still not been resolved.[35] In its defence BA claimed in a study for the CAA that its high costs derived from the nature of European air travel, i.e. higher fuel costs and landing fees, night jet bans and the demands of multi-market advertising.[36] Nonetheless it performed poorly even in comparison with other European airlines and in 1978 BA had the lowest output from a sample of ten American and European carriers.[37]

BA's performance in the 1970s reflects the nature of the BOAC-BEA merger as a political rather than economic move. The airline acquired a new livery but it remained a state-owned flag-carrier in the 1950s mould, without acquiring the more commercial workplace culture which would have been necessary to bring it up to the operating standards of its American rivals. Instead of improving its service in the competitive atmosphere of the 1970s, it relied on the government and IATA – weapons of the past – to block and cripple its British rivals. By 1980 BA had a reputation among international airline passengers for poor service and the jibe that BA stood for 'bloody awful' was an indication of how badly its image was tarnished. When BA eliminated the word 'airways' altogether from its name on aircraft and tickets, it seemed to symbolise its failure.

'Stunned travellers', suggested *The Economist*, 'to whom it had not occurred that BA's big problem was its name, are now well primed to look for more change from the airline: lower prices, punctual flights, cleaner planes, polite and helpful service ...'[38]

Change *did* come to BA, as to many other sections of the British economy, with the election of a new Conservative government under Margaret Thatcher in 1979. An important part of her programme was the privatisation of nationalised industries and BA was among the targets. But could this overweight airline be made efficient enough to fly for private investors? Admittedly some steps had already been taken to improve its results. For example, a financing deal with the government had relieved BA of the depreciation costs associated with the Concorde, and attempts to force it into accepting any more major British aircraft had been resisted (Boeing 757s were ordered in 1978 to replace the aging Trident 3s). However, could the productivity level among its strike-prone labour force be raised, and above all, could it be made attractive to passengers again?[39] In July 1979 plans were announced to privatise part of BA, based on a model similar to the oil company, BP. But within a year the airline industry had gone into one of its periodic nosedives and BA's profits crashed. With sharply rising fuel costs and declining traffic growth, the airline was knocked off its privatisation course. Plans to replace half of its ageing fleet were delayed, cuts in the labour force abandoned and privatisation put on hold by the chairman, Sir Ross Stainton. In the spring of 1981 BA was heading for a monumental loss and seeking extra government funds – it seemed to be back where BOAC had been twenty years before.

This was the background to the search by the government for a new BA chairman. The successful candidate needed to be an outsider and someone who could take the unpalatable decisions necessary to get BA into shape for privatisation. By the end of 1980 the choice had fallen on Sir John King, a former ball-bearing manufacturer and a self-made millionaire. Having been made a peer by Mrs Thatcher, Lord King launched a bloody revolution at the airline, and attitudes which had typified its management since the Second World War were purged. Massive job cuts were announced, the blow softened by an equally massive compensation scheme for those hit by redundancy. Applying the simple criteria of whether or not they made profits, King closed routes, maintenance stations and staff training colleges, as well as BA's all-cargo services. The trade unions, conscious of the airline's losses and tempted by the generous compensation package, acquiesced. Moreover BA's senior management was not spared the axe and 50 out of 240 managers were unceremoniously packed off to early retirement.[40] In 1983 Colin Marshall, a former executive of the American car rental firm Avis and therefore another outsider, became BA's chief executive. It was Marshall who set about repairing BA's customer image by shifting the central focus of the airline's purpose from policy fulfilment as a state-owned air transport undertaking, to commercial success as a full-blown service industry. Particular effort was made to recapture the high-revenue business travellers who had deserted BA by the planeload in the 1970s. And to assure passengers that a different spirit ruled, BA was re-launched as 'the world's favourite airline' with the help of the high-flying advertising agency Saatchi & Saatchi. By 1983 close to 20,000 staff had been shed and £200 million spent on redundancy payments. Loss-making domestic routes, which had plagued the airline for so long, were now gladly handed over to independent competitors such as British Midland. At the end of 1983 the decision was taken to sell 100 per cent of the airline and use the money (£800 million) to pay off that part of BA's debt which was owed to private banks. After reporting record profits in 1984 and 1985, BA shares were finally floated on the London Stock Exchange in February 1987. It proved to be a good investment and in 1988 Britain's newly privatised flag-carrier was the world's most profitable airline.[41]

The story of BA's recovery, sketched here in the briefest outline, was not surprisingly trumpeted by the Conservative government in the late 1980s.

However it needs to be treated with some caution and put into the broader context of Britain's civil aviation policy. It should be remembered that British policy in the years between 1945 and 1980 stressed orderly growth in the airline industry. BOAC, BEA and BA may have paid lip-service to the idea of competition (e.g. BCal), but in practice the only rivals they tolerated were designated foreign flag-carriers with whom they served common routes under a regime of strict capacity and price controls. They were innovative in the field of creative fares when faced with the challenge from non-scheduled carriers such as Britannia, but they remained high-cost supporters of the IATA cartel and of the international regulatory system worked out at Chicago (1944) and Bermuda (1946).[42] As state-owned enterprises they relied on their government to protect them from market forces in return for fulfilling certain non-commercial roles. The essence of the Thatcher initiative in air transport was to more or less end this regime and therefore it should be seen as a policy change equal in importance to those of 1924 and 1940. But it was not achieved without compromise, and probably would not have been achieved at all had a true revolution in the airline industry not been taking place on the other side of the Atlantic – deregulation.

The deregulation of American domestic airlines after 1978 launched shock waves in the industry which quickly reached Europe. Europe's response was slow and measured, although twenty years later the deregulatory trend seems irreversible. Europe was forced to react, particularly to the operational innovations which deregulation brought in its train, eg. hub-and-spoke networks, computer reservation systems (CRS) and frequent-flyer programmes, and it divided itself between those countries which more or less embraced deregulation (Britain, the Netherlands, Scandinavia and to some extent Germany), and those which resisted it and raised further the protective walls around their state-owned flag-carriers (France, Italy, Spain, Greece and Portugal).[43] The coincidence of American deregulation and the Thatcherite changes of the early 1980s is key to understanding BA's privatisation. Thatcher came to power dedicated to the idea of greater competition in industry and greater reliance on market forces; in theory at least, the privatisation of major nationalised industries like BA was to flow naturally from this position. American deregulation provided a successful model and ideological support for its implementation in the airline industry. A privately-owned BA would sink or swim in the market and relieve the British Treasury of any further need to support the flag-carrier. It would be the end, not only of subsidies, but of any preferential treatment for the flag-carrier. However, there was a problem with which the government wrestled for a number of years and this was the practical one of how to reconcile privatisation with greater competition in the industry. Too much competition and BA's successful sale to private investors would be endangered, too little and Thatcher's ideological crusade would be revealed as a fraud. The compromise which the government settled on was to sponsor greater competition in Europe, where state-owned flag-carriers like Air France could be harangued for their subsidies and collusion, while supporting the bilateral status quo on the North Atlantic. The compromise protected BA's most profitable routes from the appetites of the new US mega-carriers like American Airlines, United and Delta, and appeased BA's future investors in the process.[44]

It was quite a hard balancing act to perform. The first step was the achievement of a deregulated regime with the like-minded Netherlands in June 1984, allowing multiple designation and substantial fare reductions on the route between London and Amsterdam.[45] However the CAA's 1984 report recommending more competition for BA and the transfer of BA routes to BCal, was rejected by the government.[46] BCal wanted more routes, particularly in Europe and the Far East, but an alliance of BA and the Treasury blocked the recommendation on the grounds that nothing should be allowed to jeopardise BA's privatisation. Unable to grow and in serious financial difficulties, BCal now lay open to a take-over bid by BA and this eventually happened in 1988.[47] The merger was investigated by the Monopolies Commission, but the recently privatised BA now managed to convince the government that swallowing the 'second force' was necessary to stand up to the Americans.[48] Interestingly, the alternative fate for BCal had been a take-over by the Scandinavian carrier SAS and that option was defeated by BA's jingoistic assertion that the airline could not be allowed to fall into foreign hands – so much for the free play of market forces under Mrs.Thatcher! The classic example of BA's uncompetitive behaviour in the years leading up to its privatisation was its predatory tactics in dealing with Laker's Skytrain which led, in collusion with BA's allies, to Laker's bankruptcy in 1982. 'They are running their flights on my routes at a loss to put me out of business', he said bitterly.[49] And whatever the truth of this it is a curious fact that BA's transatlantic fares rose quickly after Skytrain's crash. The subsequent court case against BA delayed its privatisation, probably by up to two years. BA initially scorned Laker when he took action under American anti-trust law, but as the case dragged on and BA faced both civil and criminal investigations, as well as having to endure a considerable amount of adverse publicity, it changed its mind and in 1985 it reached an out-of-court settlement with Laker, aided by a high-level intervention on its behalf by Mrs.Thatcher with US President Ronald Reagan.

CONCLUSION

Judged by the airline's subsequent profitability and growth, BA's privatisation was an undoubted success. However it hardly conformed to the

Thatcher government's stated aim of achieving wider share ownership in Britain and its share price was almost certainly too low (judged by the over-subscription rate), which means that, as a state-owned enterprise, it was sold off at the taxpayers' expense.[50] Its success in the last decade has been due to the basic managerial restructuring and reorientation that has taken place; by contrast the massive payroll cuts of 1982–83, for which Lord King became renowned, could not have sustained a long-term improvement in the airline's performance. One important observation to make about the BA privatisation is that the airline did not become efficient on its own, through competition. Indeed, as we have seen, the Thatcher government's policy on competition was ambiguous to say the least. Rather, BA was driven to efficiency by the government for the purpose of facilitating a successful privatisation.[51]

What kind of undertaking was BA in 1990? How did it differ from the airline which had been nationalised 50 years before? Was it in any way comparable to the last privately-owned British flag-carrier, Imperial Airways? On the last point it is noteworthy that the privatised BA has paid as much attention to its shareholders' interests as did Imperial Airways, the difference being, of course, that BA has not paid its dividends out of state subsidies. In other ways the privatised BA differs radically from its predecessors. Firstly, it has more or less abandoned British aircraft – or at least British airframes. Both Imperial Airways and BOAC/BEA were obliged by their founding statutes to use British-built aircraft and engines as far as possible, and for twenty years after 1945 enormous sums were spent by both the airlines and the government on introducing British airliners into service. This policy was already moribund in the 1970s, although Britain's participation (to varying degrees) in the Concorde and Airbus projects, meant that there would always be pressure on a state-owned flag-carrier to buy British, or partly British aircraft, in order to support skilled employment in the domestic aircraft industry. Privatisation cut away the logic of the policy, so that 'Buy British' was dead in spirit as well as deed. By the end of the 1980s BA had become Boeing's best international customer and was reaping the rewards for standardising its fleet on a single (American) manufacturer. It is interesting, however, to note that even a privatised flag-carrier was supposed to take note of the national interest and when BA announced plans to use General Electric (GE) engines on some of its aircraft, in preference to the products of the (similarly privatised) national champion Rolls Royce, there was protest from both sides of the House of Commons.

Secondly, there is the question of monopoly, which in the final analysis has proved to be a more important factor in the flag-carrier's history, than its ownership. In a sense the history of British civil aviation has been the history of government policy vacillation – or at least movement back and forth – between competition and monopoly. It seems that whenever the government's instincts favoured competition, practical considerations brought it back to monopoly, both 1924 and 1939 show this change after a period of experiment with competition. In the post-war era, the nationalised flag-carriers were granted monopoly rights on scheduled services in return for carrying out certain policy objectives, but the instincts of governments (Labour no less than Conservative) brought them back repeatedly to the question of how greater competition could be fostered. The Edwards Report and the 'second force' recommendation was a clear and official sign of this instinct at work. After the late 1970s, when the Labour government found itself increasingly on the defensive, protecting BA's monopoly from entrepreneurial upstarts like Freddie Laker, it was easy for Margaret Thatcher to proclaim the return of competition to the airline industry, even if, for practical reasons, she was obliged to perpetuate (in fact, strengthen) BA's international monopoly in order to ensure the success of her other favourite policy objective – privatisation. Thus when BA passed into private ownership in 1987, it did so as a giant in the industry, freed of its debts by a government write-off and ready to engulf smaller competitors like BCal. Only the appearance of another entrepreneur (Richard Branson) and his Virgin Atlantic airline has prevented BA from achieving a total long-haul monopoly. Ironically (or perhaps typically?), the government which liked to be known for its dedication to free markets and competition, obstructed them for most of the 1980s in the British airline industry in order to allow the creation of a profitable private monopoly.

NOTES

*   This article began life as a contribution to a joint ASSI/BHU Conference on 'British and Italian Public Sector Performance in Comparative Perspective' at San Miniato, Italy, in October 1997.
1.   *British Air Transport in the Seventies. Report of the Committee of Enquiry into Civil Air Transport* (the Edwards Report), HMSO, May 1969, I, para. 13.
2.   The Civil Aerial Transport Committee [Cd 9218, 1918] recommended government support. Churchill was Secretary of State for War and Air until 1921. *House of Commons debates*, 5th series, vol. 126, 11 March 1920, c.1622.
3.   H.J. Dyos and D.H. Aldcroft, *British Transport. An Economic Survey from the Seventeenth Century to the Twentieth* (Harmondsworth, 1974), p. 403.
4.   See Eric Birkhead, 'The Financial Failure of British Air Transport Companies 1919–1924', *Journal of Transport History*, 4, no. 3, 1960.
5.   Civil Air Transport Subsidies Committee. Report on Government Financial Assistance to Civil Air Transport Companies, *Hambling Report*, Cmd 1811, 1923. Also *Formation of Imperial Air Transport Co. Ltd*, Cmd 2010, 1923.

6. Sir Henry Self, 'The Status of Civil Aviation in 1946', *Flight Magazine* 3 (October 1946).

7. P.W. Brooks, 'The Development of Air Transport', *Journal of Transport Economics and Policy*, no. 1 (1967), p. 164.

8. For a history of Imperial Airways, see Robin Higham, *Britain's Imperial Air Routes, 1918 to 1939* (London, 1960).

9. *Report of the Committee of Inquiry into Civil Aviation*, (the Cadman Report), Air Ministry, 1938, Cmd 5685; 13, para. 34.

10. For a history of British Airways, see Robin Higham, 'British Airways Ltd, 1935–1940', *Journal of Transport History* 4, no. 2 (1959), pp. 113–23.

11. See Peter J. Lyth, 'The changing role of government in British civil air transport, 1919–1940', in Robert Millward and John Singleton (eds), *The Political Economy of Nationalisation in Britain, 1920–1950* (Cambridge, 1995), pp. 74–80.

12. Peter Fearon, 'The British airframe industry and the state, 1918–1935', *Economic History Review* 27, no. 2, pp. 249–51. Neville Chamberlain was obliged to fly in an Electra (belonging to British Airways) to see Hitler in 1938.

13. Winston Bray, *The History of BOAC, 1939–1974* (London, 1975), pp. 19–22.

14. *British Air Transport*, Cmnd 6605, HMSO, March 1945.

15. Swinton's Memorandum to the Cabinet, Lord President's Committee, LP[45]101, 10.5.1945, Public Record Office, Kew, AVIA.2/2760.

16. *British Air Transport*, para. 23.

17. William Ashworth, *The State in Business 1945 to the mid-1980s* (London, 1991), p. 22; also Sir Norman Chester, *The Nationalisation of British Industry, 1945–1951* (London, 1975), p. 38.

18. Sir Stafford Cripps, *Cabinet Papers*, PRO. CAB 129/CP(46)37.

19. Winster, Minister of Civil Aviation, *Cabinet Papers*, 12.1.1946, PRO. CAB.129/CP[46]37.

20. Alec Cairncross, *Years of Recovery: British Economic Policy 1945–1951* (London, 1985), p. 464.

21. See for example Yair Aharoni, *The Evolution and Management of State Owned Enterprises* (Cambridge, Mass., 1986), p. 42.

22. William A. Robson, *Nationalized Industry and Public Ownership* (London, 1960), pp. 427–9.

23. J.W.S. Brancker, The Effect of Nationalisation on Air Transport, *Journal of the Institute of Transport* (May 1949), p. 111.

24. The aircraft were so 'tailor-made' to the requirements of BOAC and BEA that any overseas sale potential was ruined. The overtailoring was endemic because there was a deep-rooted perception among the state-owned British airlines that they could only operate successfully with aircraft made to their particular requirements. This was proved incorrect by the American manufacturers Boeing and Douglas who made aircraft with general appeal and the airlines (including eventually BOAC and BEA) who operated them found they made more money with these craft than with the 'tailor-made' types.

25. See Peter J. Lyth, 'A Multiplicity of Instruments: The 1946 Decision to create

a separate British European Airline', *Journal of Transport History*, 3rd series, 12 no. 2, (1990), p. 13–15. Also valuable is Keith Hayward, *Government and British Aerospace* (Manchester, 1983).

26. The BOAC figures include grants paid before the 1946 Act and subsidies to BSAA, *BOAC & BEA Annual Reports & Accounts*.

27. *Civil Aviation (Licensing) Act*, HMSO, 1960, s.2 (2).

28. Peter J. Lyth and Marc L. Dierikx, 'From Privilege to Popularity: the Growth of Leisure Air Travel', *Journal of Transport History* 15, no. 2, (September 1994).

29. Civil Air Transport Inquiry – Submission by BEA, Edwards Committee, *BEA and the Holiday Maker* (1968), Royal Air Force Museum, Hendon, Box 341.

30. *Edwards Report*, pp. 257–67.

31. *Edwards Report*, para. 12.

32. D.L. Nicolson, 'British Airways in the Eighties', *Journal of the Institute of Transport* 84, (May 1974). Nicolson was the first chairman of the British Airways Board.

33. 'Airlines: No to Enterprise', *Economist* (2 August 1975), pp. 81–2; 'Airlines: Shoring up BA', ibid. (14 February 1976), p. 100. See also the *White Paper,* Cmnd 6400, HMSO, February 1976.

34. See Richard Pryke, *The Nationalised Industries: Policies and Performance since 1968* (Oxford, 1981), pp. 132–3.

35. Air Transport Users Committee, *European Air Fares*, Civil Aviation Authority (CAA), (1979), Table B, p. 9.

36. British Airways, *Civil Air Transport in Europe*, document prepared for the CAA, January 1977.

37. European Air Fares, Air Transport Users Committee, (CAA), 1978.

38. 'Delete 'airways' delete' *Economist* (28 June 1980), p. 76.

39. Duncan Campbell-Smith, *The British Airways Story: Struggle for Take Off* (Sevenoaks, 1986), p. 10.

40. 'Chopping heads off', *Economist* (16 June 1983).

41. 'Bottom Lines: British Airways', *Economist* (28 May 1988), p. 77. The share issue was oversubscribed slightly under ten times.

42. International Civil Aviation Conference, Chicago, 7 December 1944, Final Act & Appendices, I-N, HMSO, Cmd 6614, London.

43. See Peter Lyth, 'Experiencing Turbulence: Regulation and Deregulation in the international air transport industry, 1930–1990', James McConville, *Transport Regulation Matters* (London, 1997), pp. 166–71. Also valuable is David Sawers, 'Competition in the Air: What Europe can Learn from the USA' (London, 1987), and George Williams, *The Airline Industry and the Impact of Deregulation* (Aldershot, 1993).

44. See Kyohei Shibata, *Privatisation of British Airways: Its Management and Politics, 1982–1987*, EUI Working Paper EPU 93/9, Florence, 1994, esp. pp. 52–3.

45. *Economist* (6 October 1984), 'In the wings with a prayer'.

46. CAA, *Airline Competition Policy*, CAP 500, (London, 1984).

47. See M. Cronshaw & D. Thompson, 'Competitive advantage in European

aviation – or whatever happened to BCal?', *Fiscal Studies*, 12, (1991), pp. 44–66.

48. Monopolies & Mergers Commission, *Report on the proposed merger: British Airways plc and British Caledonian Group plc*, November 1987, HMSO, Cmd 247.

49. Martyn Gregory, *Dirty Tricks* (London, 1994), p. 35.

50. The large number of small investors who received allotted shares in BA in February 1987 was quickly reduced in a wave of profit-taking as their shares passed to institutional investors. Shibata, *Privatisation*, p. 75.

51. A rather similar process seems to have taken place with Rolls Royce before its privatisation. Keith Hayward, *The British Aircraft Industry* (Manchester, 1989), p. 161.

Learning from Italy? The British Public Sector and IRI*

Jim Tomlinson

Brunel University

In the 1960s and early 1970s a number of authors in Britain drew on the Instituto per la Ricostruzione Industriale (IRI) as an example of how Britain should attempt to build new publicly-owned enterprise structures. Such advocacy found considerable resonance in British politics in this period, and the IRI example had some impact on the debates surrounding the creation of both the Industrial Reorganisation Corporation in the 1960s and the National Enterprise Board in the 1970s. This interest in the IRI stemmed from two major features of contemporary public policy debate in Britain. First was the disillusion with the 'classic' form of nationalisation as practised on a large scale by the post-war Attlee government. The second was the growing sense of 'economic decline', for which new forms of public enterprise were seen by some as a solution. This paper looks at the way IRI was taken up in British discussion of these issues, and the attempts to copy at least some features of IRI in new institutions.

PUBLIC OWNERSHIP IN BRITAIN

After the nationalisations of 1945–51 the British public sector extended to approximately 20 per cent of all economic activity. The scope of this sector was primarily limited to the utilities (gas, water, electricity) and transport (rail, buses, canals, airlines) with the major addition of the coal industry.[1] This pattern was not that different in its inclusions from other Western European countries, but was notable for its exclusion of both financial institutions (other than the central bank) and manufacturing. This pattern can partly be explained by standard network/natural monopoly arguments, plus notions of 'commanding heights' at a time when public ownership was seen as a crucial underpinning for planning the economy. Nevertheless, the exclusion of both financial institutions and manufacturing suggests that a very particular (and already anachronistic?) notion of what constituted the 'commanding heights' of a modern economy was at play in the debates of the 1940s. Economic historians are rightly still exploring the political and ideological reasons for this peculiar pattern.[2]

This pattern of nationalisation created monopoly suppliers, with whole sectors rather than individual firms being the units of ownership. These sectors were run by public corporations, usually referred to as 'Morrisonian' after the Labour politician Herbert Morrison, who popularised their type with the London Passenger Transport Board in the 1930s. Such corporations attempted to combine public ownership and ultimate ministerial responsibility with freedom of commercial judgement. The controlling boards were made up of experts and professional managers, with interested parties excluded. In particular, after heated and extensive debate in the 1930s, the idea of worker representation on public corporation boards had been rejected by the Labour leadership, and this rejection had been sustained in the nationalised structures of the 1940s. Public corporations were enjoined to break even over a period of years, but other principles of their operation were largely unexplored. Thus, for example, pricing policy was not addressed in detail until *after* public ownership was already in place.[3]

With some exceptions, the major nationalisations of the 1940s were of industries which were in long-run decline before the Second World War, and whose physical assets suffered serious attrition in wartime. While in the short run demand for the output of the two biggest nationalised sectors, coal and rail, was buoyant, neither was in any sense a dynamic source of economic development. A second problem of the new nationalised industries was that their structure could not deliver all the hopes that had been invested in their creation. On the government side, the tension between commercial autonomy for the public corporations and the idea of the industries as the building blocks of national economic planning was soon evident, even before the Attlee government left office.[4] Similarly, the political Left soon registered disappointment with the failure of public ownership to have the radical transformative effects they had hoped. The logic of this disillusion should not be exaggerated; many of the expectations of nationalisation appear Utopian. Equally, the newly nationalised industries did bring about significant improvements in workers' conditions, and though denied board representation, workers' involvement was generally encouraged.[5] Nevertheless, overall by the end of the Attlee government widespread feeling of disillusion with the workings of the new corporations was evident. This was true for the Labour as well as the Conservative Party. The Labour leadership, whilst still defending the principle of nationalisation, and the achievements of the corporations against political opponents, talked the language of 'consolidation' rather than extension of the model. Increasingly the dominant view in the Labour Party was that with a few relatively small additions, the existing set of nationalised sectors (including steel) set the broad limits of this particular experiment. After 1951 and the return of the Conservatives little fundamental in the shape of public ownership changed, beyond the only partially successful attempt to reprivatise steel.[6]

INVENTING DECLINE

Increasingly in the 1950s signs accumulated that British economic performance across a number of criterion was falling short of achievements in other Western European countries. By the end of that decade, public and governmental discussion was coming to accept that Britain was suffering from relative economic decline, and that action needed to be taken to accelerate Britain's growth rate.[7] As was to happen repeatedly over the following decades, perceptions of domestic economic failure led to the search for foreign models of how to achieve success. The first of these models seized upon was that of France and its system of indicative planning. The creation of the NEDC in 1962, followed by the setting-up of a planning ministry (the Department of Economic Affairs) and publication of a National Plan by the 1964 Labour Government attested to this willingness to look elsewhere for how things might be improved. While the extent to which British copying was true to the original in this case (and in others) has been much disputed, the British defied their reputation for insularity, as declinism strongly motivated the search for a panacea for perceived economic ills.[8]

A key text in the perception of the IRI as an attractive foreign model was Shonfield's widely-cited *Modern Capitalism*, published in 1965. This argued a general case for the importance of state intervention in Western Europe's post-war prosperity. It particularly celebrated the explicit or implicit techniques of planning used across Western Europe in underpinning this performance. Alongside this general case it singled out Italy as 'the most extreme example (with Austria) of public sector enterprise and intervention in the whole of Europe'.[9] IRI was the prime example here, its combination of public purpose and entrepreneurial flair being contrasted with the failure of British governments to find and impose a public purpose on Britain's nationalised sector.[10] Shonfield had been a pioneer of declinism in Britain, with the publication of his *British Economic Policy Since the War* in 1958.[11] *Modern Capitalism* suggested that a remedy for this decline should be sought not only in planning, but also in a new type of state-owned enterprise on the Italian model.

THE BRITISH LEFT AND IRI

A striking feature of the discussion of IRI in Britain was the support for such a body found across a large part of the political spectrum. Of course, this did not include the laissez-faire Right, where traditional opposition to state involvement led to the denial of both IRI's importance in Italian development and its usefulness as a model for Britain.[12] But on the Centre Left of the spectrum, support for such a body was very wide. Here it is important to note that the idea of 'competitive public enterprise' had first been put forward by the pioneer Labour Party 'revisionist' Douglas Jay in 1948, even before the completion of the Attlee programme of nationalisations. He saw the extension of public ownership as most fruitfully pursued by public ownership of individual firms in the manufacturing sector, not least because of the belief that this sector lacked dynamism because of the lack of competition between privately-owned firms.[13] Such ideas were taken up by others on the Right of the Labour Party in the 1950s, though at this stage they found little support on the Left, where competition, even between publicly-owned companies was anathema.

The landscape of debate in the Party began to change in the late 1950s as the idea that modernisation could provide a successful rallying-cry progressed. Painful disputes between Party factions about the nature and scope of future nationalisation programmes were slowly displaced by an emphasis on the need to find policies to revivify the economy. After 1961 modernisation and faster economic growth were top of Labour's domestic agenda, and after Wilson's succession to the leadership in 1963 this rhetoric was all-powerful, and seemed to have overcome previous Left–Right divisions.[14] It was in this context of modernisation that the example of IRI was to become widely embraced across the Labour Party.

That different parts of the Left could embrace IRI is nicely illustrated by the contrasting works of Posner and Woolf, and Holland. Posner and Woolf published their study of *Italian Public Enterprise* in 1967. Posner was an adviser to the Wilson government, and might be described as a 'centrist technocrat' (Woolf was an academic expert on Italian history). This book focused on the achievements of IRI as the investor in large-scale high-technology industry, seeing this as central to Italian economic growth. The claims made for IRI were that it escaped the financial constraints imposed on the British public sector, and that it had contributed significantly to the development of the South, but the authors were noticeably less impressed by IRI's entrepreneurialism than Shonfield.[15] Their conclusion was that IRI was an important mechanism for improving Italian economic performance, but one which had not yet been fully deployed because of the absence of clear central government purpose in its use. In particular, IRI seemed to offer alternatives to British shortcomings in respect of the lack of centralised control of the public sector, the absence of an agency for the spawning of new enterprises, the ignoring of possibilities for joint public–private enterprise, and as a means of escaping the Treasury's financial straitjacket. Such a perspective on IRI was broadly compatible with the dominant strands in Labour's economic thinking in the 1960s, which had great faith that a combination of higher levels of investment, especially in new technologies, facilitated by greater state finance and 'indicative' planning could give a major boost to the growth rate of the British economy.

Whilst sharing some of the views of Posner and Woolf, Holland's work gave a much more radical twist to the interpretation of IRI and its relevance to the British economy. In his *The State as Entrepreneur*, published in 1972, an analysis is offered of the problems of the British economy which emphasises the incapacity of Keynesian policies of demand management to address issues of slow growth. He argues that such slow growth is self-reinforcing because of Lamfalussy-style 'defensive investment' by the private sector, and concludes that only state-led investment across wide sectors of British manufacturing can rescue the British economy from decline.[16] Holland is clear that what he proposes represents a stage beyond what has actually been done by IRI, especially with the idea of using multi-sectoral investments to co-ordinate faster growth across the whole of manufacturing industry.[17] The idea that an IRI type of institution is needed because of the breakdown of post-war assumptions about economic policy is more broadly expressed in Holland's contribution to Vernon's volume on *Big Business and the State*.[18] Here, trade and financial liberalisation and the rise in importance of MNCs, coupled with the re-emergence of an important problem of regional unemployment, are seen as undermining the effectiveness of traditional instruments of national economic management, requiring a new expansion of state activity into the major sectors of manufacturing.

The radical analysis underpinning Holland's advocacy of an IRI body reaches its apogee in *The Socialist Challenge* in 1975. In this account, the rise of multinational oligopolies, coupled with trade and financial liberalisation, has undermined the traditional macro/micro-economic distinction. Instead, Western economies are characterised by the 'meso-economic' power exercised by the giant, usually multinational, corporations, against which traditional methods of national economic management are impotent. To restore economic power to government in order to enable them to pursue economic goals of growth and full employment therefore requires a major extension of public ownership across the manufacturing sector, seen as the key sector for overall economic performance. In this schema, a state holding company is part of a semi-revolutionary redistribution of economic power, rather than an instrument of technocratic adjustment in pursuit of specifically economic goals.

BRITISH DREAMS, ITALIAN REALITIES?

All advocates of a state-holding company inescapably drew upon a particular interpretation of the IRI experience, and one which, of course, Italian and other commentators would not necessarily have accepted. The early history of IRI is not a matter of controversy.[19] Initially set up as a temporary rescue body in 1933, it became permanent in 1937. The assets first acquired were holdings in joint stock companies, and this pattern was to be retained. In the late 1930s sectoral holding companies were created to co-ordinate the use of IRI assets, in telephones, shipping, and iron and steel, again a pattern that was to be maintained after the Second World War. Asset disposals as well as further acquisitions were substantial in the 1930s, but were concentrated in areas where private companies saw ready profit opportunities (e.g. electricity) or where no strategic interests seemed involved (e.g. textiles). The war had a devastating effect on IRI assets, especially in shipbuilding and engineering. In the initial post-war period its future was in doubt, both because of its own financial difficulties, but also because of the political debate over the future economic role of the state. On the Right advocates of laissez-faire called for its abolition, while on the Left there were calls for complete state ownership more on the model of the British or Soviet example. In the late 1940s and early 1950s the absence of political agreement seems to have insulated IRI from political pressure, and its activities were uncoordinated by the state until the creation of the Ministry of State Shareholdings in 1956.

Though the status and role of the IRI was still much debated in the 1950s, there was emerging a clear 'philosophy' of its purpose. At the Ministerial level the key emphasis was 'laid upon the notion that public ownership was not an end in itself, but represented an instrument for the furtherance of economic development'.[20] From within IRI itself, Saraceno developed a doctrine of 'market failure', both with respect to monopoly tendencies, and inadequate and poorly distributed investment, which justified a developmental role for state holding companies.[21] This doctrine seems not only to have underpinned the 'official' ethos of IRI, but to have become widely accepted across the range of Italian opinion by the early 1960s. IRI's perceived success in creating an efficient iron and steel industry, in building autostrada throughout much of the country, and aiding the development of the south together seemed to justify its role even amongst Italians who had previously been sceptical. (This range of support for the idea of state-holding companies was undoubtedly also increased by ENI's creation of a successful, autonomous oil and natural gas industry).

This consensus, it should be emphasised, embraced almost all political forces at this time. On the Right, IRI's evident entrepreneurialism and private sector involvement undercut criticism from a laissez-faire perspective, and, of course, the dominant political party of the period, the Christian Democrats, had in any case never been a party of economic liberalism. On the Left, the Communist Party also came round to the view that the IRI was suited to the peculiarities of the Italian political and economic situation.[22] The existence of this (passing) political consensus emphasises that IRI in its heyday, which was when British commentators alighted upon it, did not have the political connotations it had in the British political debate. As Pontarallo stresses 'The heavy and increasing involvement of the Italian state in business is not primarily due to the thrust of ideologies or parties of a socialist type'.[23] This de-politicisation of state holding companies emphasises how different British and Italian circumstances were. In Italy, a poor country by Western European standards in 1945, there eventually emerged widespread support for a 'developmental state' which would allow Italy to take her place as a major economic power in Western Europe. The rapid growth of the Italian economy in the 1950s and early 1960s seemed to suggest that an appropriate formula had been found to achieve that end. There were critics who doubted whether state holding companies really were a key feature of that success, but such views were very much against the grain by the 1960s.[24]

Britain was, by contrast, a rich country in 1945, and for all the rhetoric of decline and modernisation so common from the early 1960s, the idea of a 'developmental state' was much more problematic and controversial. To a large extent political debate about the economy in Britain focussed on the extent of the state's role. On the Conservative side, while their was unwillingness after 1951 to undo the broad settlement of the 1940s, any proposed extensions of the state's role were likely to be anathematised as 'backdoor nationalisation'. On the Left, while some offered a quite narrow, technocratic rationale for an increased state role, many others saw it as part of a wholesale transition to a socialised economy, which was bound to make it much more politically controversial.

Paradoxically, the Italian consensus around the benefits from IRI seems to have started to fade at precisely the time that it was becoming lauded as a model for Britain. Prodi articulates what seems to be a popular Italian view about the phases in the history of IRI: 'It was (in the 1950s) principally the public enterprises that exhibited a capacity for to form a new technostructure and to imbue that structure with a sense of responsibility for industrial growth. But that dynamism was short-lived. The vigour of the public enterprises seemed to diminish in the 1960s, infiltrated and bogged down by the process of bureaucratisation which had long been characteristic of other areas of Italian life'.[25]

A key problem for IRI had always been the extent to which its pursuit of efficiency and growth would be compromised by the political pressures to maintain employment in sectors and companies in decline. Up until the mid-1960s the political pressures had been resisted, partly because of the lack of tight central control over its activities, and partly because IRI itself resisted the politicisation of its activities much more than, most notably, ENI.[26] Such a stance was relatively easy to sustain in an economy that was growing at 8 per cent a year, as the Italian economy was in the 1950s. Sectoral shifts in employment were much easier to accommodate in that buoyant macro environment, and IRI did not have significant holdings in the sharply declining sectors such as textiles. But these factors began to change in the 1960s. The rate of growth of the whole economy slowed. Particular competitive pressure built up in some sectors where IRI was heavily represented. The most notable of these was shipbuilding, which had been originally built up for military reasons in the 1930s. The world trade boom of the 1950s eased the problems of this sector, but in the 1960s the rise of Asian competition made reductions in capacity compelling. But this could only be achieved in a limited and hard-fought manner, given the bitter political resistance, especially concentrated on Trieste and Genoa which led to major upheavals in those cities in the mid-1960s.[27] This was but the most striking example of the difficulties with which IRI was to be faced in sustaining its financial position.

Other factors said to have affected the role of IRI by the mid-1960s were, firstly, the decision made in the late 1950s to leave Confindustria, the Italian employers' federation. This led to a divergence in employment policies from much of the private sector, and arguably a greater willingness to concede claims for continuity of employment.[28] Secondly the issue of the regions. For many Italians and foreign commentators the role of IRI in the Mezzogiorno was a very positive feature of its operations. On the other hand, the obligation laid on it by a law of 1959 to apply a minimum proportion of its resources to investment in the South moved it further from its entrepreneurial role, and opened up more prospects of politicisation.[29]

A clear deterioration in the finances of IRI is evident from the beginning of the 1970s, greatly exacerbated by the effects of OPEC I.[30] In part this was simply a reflection of macro-economic circumstances, and large enterprises in all sectors, privately and publicly owned, were hit hard in this period. However the problems were particularly acute for IRI, partly because of the sectoral distribution of its assets. Iron and steel was, of course, a particularly troubled part of every Western European economy in the 1970s. But beyond this was undoubtedly the continuation of the political pressures to sustain employment. Unemployment was growing, and at the same time the ruling parties, Christian Democrat and Socialist, were anxious to stem the rise of the PCI by using all possible means of gaining political advantage.[31] Increasingly the IRI was becoming a lame duck.[32] To try and escape this role IRI was involved in the early 1970s in the creation of EGIP, intended to be a body for rescuing failing private sector companies, before selling them back to the private sector. Ironically this seems to have been inspired by the example of the British IRC.[33] It is indicative of both the economic and political pressures of the period that this new body failed to sustain this remit, as its lame ducks mainly proved resistant to being 'turned round' into profitability. In parallel fashion, IRI's investments were increasingly loss-making.

IRI struggled through the 1970s, with financial deficits in all years bar one. By the mid 1980s, following a period of radical restructuring, it had once again become financially sound, and ironically was now seen as an example to other countries of how to rescue public sector activities from loss-making. In 1992 it was turned into a joint stock company as a precondition for eventual privatisation.[34]

BRITISH DREAMS AND BRITISH REALITIES I: THE INDUSTRIAL RE-ORGANISATION CORPORATION (IRC)

The example of IRI was used in Britain to support the creation of two agencies, IRC in the 1960s and the National Enterprise Board in the 1970s. Of these, the NEB was both a more radical innovation and owed more to the IRI. But the earlier case of the IRC is not without interest. The IRI did contribute to the decision to set up the IRC in 1966, especially through the role of Thomas Balogh, a senior economic adviser to the Wilson government.[35] The initial case for the IRC was made in terms of the need for greater concentration and rationalisation of British manufacturing industry, in order to combat increased competition from giant foreign, especially American, enterprises. This was very much in line with the 'big is beautiful' beliefs so prevalent in discussion of the British economy at this time. It was recognised that the process of privately-initiated mergers was already extensive, but it was argued in support of state action that some important opportunities were being missed.[36]

However, while the broad developmental thrust of the IRI is apparent in the IRC's remit, in many other ways the differences were substantial. While IRI was a shareholding institution, IRC was, at its inception at least, concerned with short term loans to facilitate mergers with the aim of then withdrawing. While IRI raised most of its money from the private sector, IRC was barred from fund-raising other than by grants from government. On the other hand, similarities can be found in the entrepreneurial approach of both bodies (with personnel drawn from the private sector) and the accompanying distance from supervision by a government department. These characteristics were clearly far removed from the traditional British pattern of public ownership. Also, despite the similarities to a purely banking role in its relations with the companies it became involved with, IRC did place its nominees on the Boards of companies.[37] It seems that while the Labour government resisted the ideas even of centrist advocates of a state holding company (such as advocated in Posner and Pryke's Fabian pamphlet of 1965), once the IRC was established it seemed to move away from its very limited merger-encouraging role towards greater willingness to involve itself in both company personnel and investment decisions. This stemmed in part from the realisation that the encouragement of greater concentration was in itself unlikely to have major regenerative effects. Also, the IRC did successfully establish confidence in itself on the part of industry and the City, which seems to have encouraged a less cautious role.[38]

IRC was an interesting institutional innovation, but its impact on the British economy was probably small. It did support the existence of one 'national champion' against the threat of American takeover, but this seems to be an isolated case. It was involved in only 4 per cent of the mergers in the economy during the period of its existence (1966–70). Some of those with which it was involved were in very important sectors, such as car-manufacturing, electrical engineering and aviation electronics. But it is difficult to know whether IRC's role was vital to these changes or merely helpful. IRC involvement seems to have been used by some companies to evade the likelihood of anti-trust investigations into mergers which they wanted to pursue; it was, in some cases at least, the companies picking IRC, rather than the IRC 'picking winners'.[39]

Overall, the IRC probably owed rather little to the IRI example, or to those who saw a state-holding company as spearheading a fundamental change in relations between the state and industry, and much more to the striking prevalence of the 'big is beautiful' arguments noted above (though these ideas were already waning in influence by the late 1960s). Yet in retrospect this appears one of the most problematic assumptions of economic debate in the 1960s. While in some sectors it could be argued that British companies were too small to gain the economies of scale necessary to compete with the Americans (airframes, for example), it is much less clear that this is true across the board. In any case, even in industries where economies of scale are potentially available, achieving them simply by company merger may not work. In the case of British Leyland the strategy of finding a well-managed company (Leyland) and merging everybody else with it was not a recipe for success, partly because the new management did not pursue the rationalisation of the product range which this merger was supposed to facilitate.[40]

While IRC seems to have been quite successful in gaining the support of industry and the City, and despite its aims being accurately described by one junior Labour Minister as 'not to encourage Socialism to creep but capitalism to gallop',[41] the highly politicised nature of discussion of such issues in Britain led to its abolition by the incoming Conservative government.[42]

BRITISH DREAMS, BRITISH REALITIES II: THE NATIONAL ENTERPRISE BOARD (NEB)

The creation of NEB in 1976 owed much to the arguments of those who promoted IRI as an example to be followed. Holland was a key figure in this, being a crucial insider in the formulation of Labour Party policy on industry in the late 1960s and early 1970s. The impact of his advocacy has to be seen in the extraordinary developments in Labour's policy-making in these years. In the late 1960s disillusionment with the perceived failures of the Wilson government's economic policies, including the apparent failure of IRC to deliver the more dynamic large-scale industry which had been promised, led to a sharp leftward movement in the Party policy-making apparatus. This apparatus was dominated not by MPs or the Parliamentary leadership, but by party members elected from the annual conference to its committees, or co-opted onto these committees at national headquarters. This process led to a widening divergence between the official policy of the Party as drawn up by these committees and the views of the Parliamentary leadership.[43] This divergence was at its sharpest in the case of the role and purpose of the NEB. Holland and his allies got the Party to accept a radical version of the NEB which drew strongly on the analysis later to be given extensive statement in *The Socialist Challenge*. This is starkly evident in a key Party document, *The NEB: Labour's State Holding Company* drawn up in 1973 and endorsed by the conference in that year. Holland was an influential member of that committee, and the IRI figures strongly as the example to be followed. The argument of this paper was that the existing public sector provided an unprofitable infrastructure supporting the profits of the private sector: 'what is now proposed by the Party ... is an extension of the public sector into the areas of manufacturing and profitability.'[44] The aims of this extension were to promote equality by rebuilding the power of government to control investment decisions. Previous government attempts at this control by incentives and encouragement, the paper argued, had failed, and the need now was for a direct role. The NEB had to be in 'the new commanding heights of the modern capitalist economy–manufacturing and services', and here the IRI was cited because of the multi-sectoral spread of its activities.[45]

The NEB was seen as the solution to a very wide range of problems. Its aims would be 'National and regional employment creation, the promotion of major new investment and technology projects, price leadership ..., public purchasing on a new scale, export promotion and import substitution, and counteracting the effects of private MNCs operations ...'[46]

Unsurprisingly perhaps, a Labour government without an overall majority, led by the Centre and Right of the Party, and trying to cope with the economic effects of OPEC 1, was unlikely to regard either the language or substantive proposals of this document as helpful. In the event the proposals were seriously watered down. An NEB was created, but the tone and substance were much altered.[47] Under the 1975 legislation, the main purpose of NEB would be to provide equity investment funds where the private sector had proved unwilling. In addition the NEB was to receive the company shares already held by government in some enterprises notably Rolls Royce (engines) (RR) and British Leyland (BL) which had already been rescued by government. The resounding socialist aims of the original supporters of the NEB found little support. There was none of the rhetoric of the 'transfer of power' and more specific points such as the encouragement of industrial democracy were watered down, and in practice nothing was done about them.[48]

The history of NEB is dominated in large part by the 'lame ducks' of RR and BL which most of their funds were channelled into. NEB's role in relation to these was always unclear. RR bitterly resented that role, and control of its shares was eventually taken away from the Board.[49] The Board had a more constructive relationship with BL, though whether or not it made a major contribution in that case can be argued from many angles. They installed Michael Edwardes as the boss of the company, and he eventually led it onto the path of financial recovery, but ultimately this was only achieved by reducing BL from a major producer to a 'niche' company under foreign ownership. NEB was more successful in 'turning round' the electronics company Ferrantis.[50] In none of these cases could it be said that the idea of focusing on *profitable* enterprises had been realised. Lame-duckery became the abiding problem of NEB.

Alongside this financially most important and best-known activity of NEB was its role as a provider of venture capital. Kramer has argued that this was in fact the most innovative and successful of the Board's functions. In a field where there were very few competitors in Britain, NEB, he argues, provided a useful source of funds for high-tech, high-risk, companies which private institutions were reluctant to take on. In his analysis, the portfolio NEB acquired in this way compared well with that of venture capital companies in the USA, both in respect of failure rates and rates of return on investment.[51] But even if Kramer's case is fully accepted, the venture capitalist role was far removed from that envisaged by the supporters of NEB – a useful but marginal place in the spectrum of company finance institutions.

NEB was the closest Britain had to a body akin to IRI. It was certainly closer than IRC, which had no equity interests and was dominated by the idea of encouraging mergers. On the other hand NEB was hamstrung from the beginning by its 'inheritance' of major loss makers. Its positive, developmental role was limited to a few narrow areas of high technology. It did not play a significant role either in regional policy or in challenging the growth of foreign ownership of manufacturing capacity in Britain. Proponents of the IRI model could reasonably claim that the potential of that body in British circumstances was never tested, because neither IRC or even NEB came close to paralleling the Italian institution; it was not an experiment that failed, but one that was never tried. In assessing such a proposition there are several layers of questions to be addressed.

First, was the role of IRI in Italy a successful one, and therefore a sensible model to consider following? Here the consensus of Italian commentators seems to be that it did play a positive role in the 1950s and early 1960s, though in propitious circumstances. The major transfers of labour from agriculture to industry facilitated a process of export led growth which underpinned almost unheard of growth rates. In this context IRI helped, especially in building up steel capacity. But IRI was probably not the crucial body in this overall dynamism.[52]

Second, granted that IRI played a positive if not overwhelming role in Italian development, was it a model Britain should have followed? Here, it may be argued that in the early post-war period the problems facing Italy were problems of 'underdevelopment', rather than the problems of a mature industrial country like Britain in the 1960s and 1970s. One way of looking at IRI would be as a Gerschenkronian-style substitution of a public–private partnership for the absent private provision of capital/expertise to provide for projects such as steel production. This, of course, emphasises the differences between the needs of the Italian and British economies.

Third, would a British version of the IRI have been able to escape the problems which beset the original from the 1960s? Here the proponents of the British adoption do not seem to have taken on board either the political aspects of this problem or the major economic aspect about dealing with the employment consequences of structural change. In fairness, it should be said that these problems were only just beginning to appear at the time most of the British advocacy of copying IRI was being produced.

Paradoxically, given the widespread sense of failure in discussion of the 'classic' British nationalised industries, they in fact dealt very well in the 1950s and 1960s with the problem of reducing their workforces. British Rail and the National Coal Board both lost hundreds of thousand of workers in these years, with very little struggle. The reasons were partly the humane manner in which this was done, which was certainly encouraged by public ownership, but particularly relied on overall economic buoyancy and full employment. The point of especial relevance here is that *any* publicly-owned enterprise in a Western European country would have come under great pressure in the 1970s as unemployment increased, given the political importance full employment had acquired in these countries. Therefore it is likely that the problems which beset IRI from the late 1960s would have been manifest in any country which established a similar body, even if the extreme form of politicisation which emerged in Italy were avoided in countries where the ruling party changed with greater frequency.

The final point about a British IRI relates to politics. The eventual acceptance of this body in Italy was based on a cross-party consensus made possible because the state–private divide, a cause of such conflict in public policy debate in Britain, was not such a divisive issue in Italian politics. In Britain disagreement about the proper spheres of public and private ownership not only made political consensus on any IRI style body impossible, but it also meant that because of the high level of politicisation of employers organisations, any attempt by a Labour government was bound to run up against the almost insuperable obstacle of private sector opposition. Even the mild version of NEB in the 1970s ran up against virulent opposition; once again (as in the 1940s) a Labour government dominated by mildly reformist elements found that it was impossible to co-operate with those who would not co-operate, and a state holding company, whatever else its conditions of existence, cannot work without such co-operation.

NOTES

* This article began life as a contribution to a joint ASSI/BHU Conference on 'British and Italian Public Sector Performance in Comparative Perspective' at San Miniato, Italy in October 1997.

1. Iron and steel was the last major industry to be nationalised, and the only one where the Conservative opposition contested the principle of public ownership.

2. R. Millward and J. Singleton, *The Political Economy of Nationalisation in Britain, 1920–1950* (Cambridge, 1995); R. Millward 'The 1940s Nationalisations in Britain: Means to an End or the Means of Production?' *Economic History Review* 50 (1997), pp. 209–34. For general accounts of British post-war nationalisation, see W. Ashworth, *The State in Business, 1945 to the mid-1980s* (London, 1991); T. Gourvish, 'The Rise (and Fall?) of State-Owned Enterprise', in T. Gourvish and A. O'Day (eds), *Britain Since 1945* (London, 1991), pp. 111–34; L. Hannah, 'The Economic Consequences of the State Ownership of Industry, 1945–1990', in R. Floud and D. McCloskey, *The Economic History of Britain Since 1700 Vol. 3 1939–1992*, 2nd edn (Cambridge, 1994) pp. 168–94; J. Tomlinson, *Government and the Enterprise* (Oxford, 1994), ch. 8.

3. M. Chick 'Marginal Cost Pricing and the Peak Hour Demand for Electricity', in Chick (ed.), *Governments, Industries and Markets* (Aldershot, 1990), pp. 110–26.

4. J. Tomlinson, *Democratic Socialism and Economic Policy: the Attlee Years* (Cambridge, 1997), pp. 100–102.

5. Ibid., pp. 107–14.
6. K. Burk, *The First Privatisation* (London, 1988).
7. J. Tomlinson 'Inventing Decline: the Falling Behind of the British Economy in the Post-war Years', *Economic History Review* 49 (1996), pp. 731–57.
8. A. Budd, *The Politics of Economic Planning* (London, 1978), chs 5, 6.
9. A. Shonfield, *Modern Capitalism* (Oxford, 1965), p. 177.
10. Ibid., pp. 185–92, 90–1.
11. A. Shonfield, *British Economic Policy Since the War* (Harmondsworth, 1958). This book emphasised Britain's excessive overseas commitments as the prime cause of slow growth.
12. M. Deaglio, *Private Enterprise and Public Emulation. A Study of the Italian Experience with IRI and the Lessons for Britain's IRC*, Institute for Economic Affairs Research Monograph 5 (London, 1966). Aims of Industry, *State Capitalism. Some Reflections on the National Enterprise Board in the Mirror of the IRI* (London, 1975).
13. D. Jay, *Future Nationalisation Policy*, Labour Party Research Department, RD 161 (London, 1948).
14. Tomlinson, 'Inventing Decline', pp. 748–52
15. M. Posner and S. Woolf, *Italian Public Enterprise* (London, 1967), pp. 116–20.
16. S. Holland, *The State as Entrepreneur* (London, 1972).
17. Ibid., p. 21.
18. S. Holland, 'Europe's New Public Enterprises' in R. Vernon (ed.) *Big Business and the State* (Cambridge, Mass., 1974), pp. 25–42.
19. Posner and Woolf, *Italian*, ch. 2; A. Martinelli, 'The Italian Experience: a Historical Perspective' in R. Vernon and Y. Aharoni, *State-Owned Enterprises in the Western Economies* (Beckenham, 1981), pp. 85–98; E. Pontarollo, 'Italy: Effects of Substituting Political Objectives for Business Goals', in B. Hindley (ed.), *State Investment Companies in Western Europe* (London, 1983), pp. 26–9.
20. Posner and Woolf, *Italian*, p. 37.
21. Holland, *The State as Entrepreneur*, pp. 5–8.
22. S. Holland, *The Socialist Challenge* (London, 1975), p. 354.
23. Pontarollo, 'Italy', pp. 23.
24. V. Lutz, *Italy: a Study in Economic Development* (Oxford, 1962).
25. R. Prodi, 'Italy' in Vernon (ed.), *Big Business*, p. 50.
26. Pontarollo, 'Italy', p. 30.
27. S. Steffinizi and S. Tarrow, 'Protest and Regulation: the interaction of state and society in the cycle of 1965–74', in P. Lange and M. Regini (eds), *State, Market and Social Regulation: New Perspectives on Italy* (Cambridge, 1989), pp. 84–6.
28. Pontarollo, 'Italy', p. 32.
29. Ibid., p. 33.
30. Pontarollo, 'Italy', p. 38.
31. P. Bianchi, 'The IRI in Italy: Strategic Role and Political Constraints', *West European Politics* 10 (1987), pp. 269–90; F. Grassini, 'The Italian enter-

prises: the Political Constraints', in R. Vernon and Y. Aharoni, *State-Owned Enterprises in the Western Economies* (Beckenham, 1981), pp. 70–84.

32. Pontarollo, 'Italy', p. 37.

33. Ibid., pp. 50–5.

34. A. Kumar, *State Holding Companies and Public Enterprises in Transition* (Washington, DC, 1993).

35. On Balogh's role, P. Streeten (ed.), *Unfashionable Economics: Essays in Honour of Lord Balogh* (London, 1970).

36. Holland, *The State as Entrepeneur*, pp. 243–4.

37. Ibid., pp. 245–6.

38. M. Posner and R. Pryke, *New Public Enterprise* (London, 1965). D. Hague and G. Williamson, *The IRC: an Experiment in Industrial Intervention* (London, 1983), ch. 14.

39. Holland, *The State as Entrepeneur*, p. 246: B. Hindley and R. Richardson 'UK: an experiment in Picking Winners – the IRC', in Hindley (ed.), *State Investment Companies in Western Europe* (London, 1983), ch. 5.

40. Hague and Wilkinson, '*The IRC*' ch. 7; K. Williams and C. Haslam, *The Breakdown of Austin Rover* (Leamington Spa, 1987).

41. Cited in Hindley and Richardson 'UK', p. 130; Hague and Wilkinson, *The IRC*, pp. 13, 16 emphasise the defeat of the radical view of the IRC held on the Left of the Labour Party, while stressing that its role did move away from just encouraging mergers. These nuances are rather missed by Hindley and Richardson, 'UK', pp. 129–30.

42. Hague and Wilkinson, *The IRC*, p. 3.

43. M. Hatfield, *The House the Left Built: Inside Labour Policy-Making 1970–1975* (London, 1978).

44. Labour Party, *The NEB: Labour's State Holding Company* (Labour Party, 1973), p. 9; Hindley and Richardson, 'United Kingdom: Pulling Dragon's Teeth – the National Enterprise Board', in Hindley (ed.), *State Investment Companies*, pp. 264–9.

45. Labour Party, *The NEB*, pp. 13–14.

46. Ibid., p. 14.

47. Hatfield, *The House*, chs 9, 10.

48. D. Kramer, *State Capital and Private Enterprise: the Case of the UK NEB* (London, 1988).

49. Ibid., ch. 13.

50. Ibid., chs 14, 12; Williams and Haslam, *The Breakdown*.

51. Kramer, *State Capital* chs 2, 3; the financial analysis in Hindley and Richardson, 'United Kingdom' pp. 278–80 is less favourable, but extends only to 1979.

52. V. Zamagni, *The Economic History of Italy 1860–1990* (Oxford, 1993), chs 11, 12; K. Allen and A. Stevenson, *An Introduction to the Italian Economy* (Oxford, 1974), ch. 1.

Steel and the State in Italy and the UK. The public sector of the steel industry in comparative perspective (1945–1996)

Ruggero Ranieri

University of Manchester

This article intends to compare the public sector of the steel industry in Britain and Italy, focusing on the post-1945 period.[1] The comparison has to take into account the different starting points and performances of the two industries. Italy's steel industry emerged from the war as one of the smallest among the industrial countries. In a short time, however, it was able to surge ahead, with the highest rate of output growth in steel production in Western Europe. Britain, on the other hand, emerged from the war with the largest steel industry in Western Europe, only to gradually fall back in the ranking. By 1975 the two industries were of about the same size, but, since then, the UK's position has fallen behind Italy's. Taking the period between the mid-1950s and today the rate of growth of steel output in the UK has been below zero.

The history of the two public sectors is also different. Italy's public steel sector was created in the early 1930s and had a life span of over fifty years. After 1945 it played an important part in raising the industry's output and technological standing. Decline, however, set in as early as the late 1960s, and since then its performance was down hill all the way to a disorderly and piecemeal privatisation process, completed between 1989 and 1996. During the early 1930s a degree of State intervention was imposed on the British steel industry, in a way that was to shape it for at least thirty years thereafter. The issue of nationalisation came to the fore with the election of the 1945 Labour government. The industry, thus, found itself plunged in at the deep end of party political controversy. There were, in fact, two successive nationalisations carried out by Labour governments: the first one, short lived, in 1951, and the second, more enduring, in 1967. Each of these was followed by a return to the private sector, sponsored by Conservative administrations: in the first case denationalisation was carried out gradually between 1953 and 1958; in the second it was accomplished at one stroke in 1988.

Despite these different patterns, there are some broad similarities in the history of the two public sectors. In the first place the rationale for public ownership in both countries was the need to modernise and rationalise the industry, by injecting a measure of technocratic leadership into it. Secondly, once the public sector was set up, one of the crucial dilemmas it faced was how to reconcile its aims of efficiency and competitive strength with being part of the State. Finally, the experience of public ownership in the industry has recently come to an end in both countries, although in somewhat different ways. It seems that, this time, privatisation is here to stay.

I have chosen to look at these problems in three sections. In the first I will give a brief general outline of the history, nature and development of the public sector in the two countries, including an account of the latest privatisation process. Having laid out the main facts, I will go on to examine some of the issues in more depth. In the second section I will look at the period between 1945 and 1967, which, in Italy, was marked by the successful rise of Finsider, the state-owned steel holding company. In Britain, on the other hand, the industry, with a brief interlude, remained in private hands, although with a measure of public supervision. In the third section I will examine events after 1967, the year in which the state-owned British Steel Corporation (BSC) took over all the main private UK companies, comparing the performance of the two public sectors in the 1970s and 1980s. I will conclude with a few remarks drawing attention to the some of the points emerging from this comparative investigation.

STEEL AND THE STATE IN ITALY AND BRITAIN: AN OVERVIEW

In Italy the public sector of industry was created as a result of the Great Depression, when the State stepped in to salvage the large 'mixed' banks, particularly the Banca Commerciale and the Credito Italiano, taking them over together with all their industrial assets. As a result, when the IRI (Istituto per la Ricostruzione Industriale) was created in 1933, it was saddled with a number of important steel companies, accounting for about half of the industry's assets. The old company structure was left intact despite the fact that, a few years later, all the companies taken over by IRI were placed within Finsider, one of IRI's newly formed sub-holdings. In 1938 Finsider accounted for seventy seven per cent of Italy's pig iron production, forty five per cent of crude steel and thirty eight per cent of hot rolled products. At this initial stage, the public sector consisted of four large companies: Ilva, Siac, Terni and Dalmine. Ilva – a vast and shapeless conglomerate – was by far the largest. These four companies owned in the region of twenty steel plants, of which only a few were integrated, while most were either cold-melting shops or simple re-rolling facilities.[2]

Large-scale destruction during the war affected Finsider very badly; particularly the large integrated coastal works of Ilva – Bagnoli, Portoferraio and Piombino – as well as Siac's Cornigliano and Terni, which manufactured steel for armaments production. As a result, the output of the public sector shrank, whereas the private steel companies boosted their share. This, however, was short lived. A massive wave of post war investment meant that Finsider was soon back to its former position and during the 1950s and 1960s it improved upon it considerably. Together with expansion came a degree of rationalisation and concentration of output in the larger, integrated plants. In 1962 the Finsider group accounted for 90 per cent of the country's pig iron, fifty five per cent of crude steel and fifty seven per cent of hot rolled products. In 1980 its share of crude steel was about the same, whereas its share of hot rolled products had moved a couple of points down. This downward shift continued during the 1980s, so that by 1989 Finsider's shares of crude steel and hot rolled products were below fifty per cent. This was essentially due to the competition from privately owned mini-mills, which succeeded in capturing nearly the entire market for long products. In 1989, they held 88 per cent of that market against Finsider's 8.8 per cent.[3]

Finsider did not account for all the steel making facilities directly or indirectly controlled by the State. A number of companies were not originally part of the IRI; among them, for example, was Cogne, a fairly important integrated-cycle producer of special steel products located in the Val d'Aosta. Cogne was nationalised in the 1930s and its ownership was vested in the Ministry of Finance. Another example of a large steel making company lying, for most of its history, outside Finsider, was Breda. Originally a privately-owned, vertically integrated company engaged in steel, heavy engineering and armaments production, after the Second World War, Breda was bailed out by large injections of public money. Later the company, renamed Breda Siderurgica, became part of EFIM, a newly created State Holding Agency. There followed a brief spell within Finsider, after which Breda Siderurgica was moved into the EGAM, yet another state holding company, which during the 1970s also incorporated Cogne, thus bringing about a merger of long product special steel making plant. Soon, however, EGAM went bankrupt, so that in 1981 both Breda Siderurgica and Cogne were brought back into the IRI-Finsider group.[4]

Finsider always had to contend with the presence of an important and often adversarial private sector. Originally the challenge came from established producers. Traditionally the two largest private steel makers were Fiat, an automobile maker that had integrated backwards into steel making during the 1920s, and the family-owned Falck group. In addition there were a number of other small and very small companies, mostly located in the North West of Italy. The dispute between Finsider and the Falcks on the terms of post-Second World War Reconstruction is regarded as a classic of Italy's industrial policy debate. Oscar Sinigaglia, the Chairman of Finsider, insisted on rebuilding large integrated coastal plants based on standardised mass production, whereas the Falcks believed that Italy should eschew the large scale and concentrate on high value-added, small-batch production. In that instance Fiat, however, broke ranks with its private sector partners to support Sinigaglia's plans to install a wide strip mill at Cornigliano.[5]

The contrast between private and public sector was renewed at the time of the second wave of post war investment, in the late 1950s, when private producers tried to stop Finsider from building a large green-field plant at Taranto. Once more, however, they were forced to give way to IRI government-backed expansion plans. While losing market share to Finsider during the 1950s and 1960s, the output of private companies expanded considerably, given the high aggregate rate of growth. Strategically, however, they were no longer in a position to challenge the dominance of Finsider. Fiat, for example, entered into a co-operative deal with Finsider during the 1970s by acquiring a fifty per cent stake in the works of Piombino, only to retreat shortly thereafter, abandoning steel production altogether and selling out to the Finsider. The Falck group increasingly specialised in a narrow range of special steel products; by the early 1990s it had diversified out of steel making.[6]

A new powerful challenge to Finsider was mounted by the mini-mill sector, which emerged as a major player during the 1960s. The mini-mills, also known as 'bresciani' from the Brescia district, where they were clustered, were originally very small electric steel makers and scrap re-rollers involved in the production of concrete reinforcing bar (rebar) and other long products. Faced with very favourable market opportunities during the 1950s and 1960s, such as a strong demand for rebar by the construction industry and comparatively low scrap prices, they became larger and more aggressive. Some of them, such as Riva, Leali, Lucchini grew into large multinational groups, capturing important shares of the European market for long products, and eventually were able to play an important role in Finsider's privatisation.[7]

During the 1970s public sector steel was characterised by crippling financial losses, due to over-investment and poor capacity utilisation as well as poor industrial relations and declining productivity. During the early 1980s retrenchment and cuts under the auspices of the European Commission were designed to meet this crisis. Despite sizeable cuts in capacity and personnel (from over 120,000 in 1980 to 76,000 in 1987), however, Finsider's financial situation remained precarious. At the beginning of 1989 the group's assets were handed over to a new company (with an old name) Ilva, relieved by the government of the burden of Finsider's accumulated debt. This was followed, between 1989 and 1992, by a piecemeal and partial process of privatisation, whereby a number of the group's smaller plants (Marghera, San Giovanni, Sisma, Lovere, and Servola) together with the more important one of Piombino, were sold off. The Lucchini group purchased Piombino. In most cases Ilva retained a minority share.[8]

Again, however, this proved well short of what was needed to turn Ilva around. The final act opened in 1993, against a background of poor performance and heavy losses, Ilva was split into three parts, its most important assets, respectively in the strip mill and special steel departments, handed over to two new companies: ILP (Ilva Laminati Piani) and AST (Acciai Speciali Terni). In 1994 ILP was sold to a consortium, the main shareholders of which were the Rivas, a leading mini-mill dynasty, whereas AST was bought by a group whose stock was shared between the German group Krupp-Thyssen Nirosta and a number of Italian companies. Since then, Riva and Krupp have respectively increased their stake in the two consortia, effectively achieving full ownership of ILP and AST. The remaining bits of Ilva were also privatized between 1994 and 1996; they included both Cogne and Dalmine, a well-known company specialising in tube making, taken over by Techint, a multinational group based in South America.[9]

As a result of privatisation the map of Italian steel has been deeply transformed. Whereas, previously, there was a public sector giant conglomerate, flanked by a number of smaller private companies, currently there are a number of top players, ranging from large to medium sized. Two large private groups, Riva and Lucchini have emerged out of the mini-mill sector and next to them rank two important non-Italian multinational groups, Krupp-Thyssen Nirosta and Techint, which have taken a controlling interest in special steel and tube making. In the rest of the industry, too, there has been a move towards medium-sized, privately owned firms.

The first public body to play a role in the UK steel industry was the IDAC (Imports Duties Advisory Committee) set up in 1932, with the task of enforcing tariff protection and re-organising the industry. It acted in conjunction with the BISF (British Iron and Steel Federation), set up with a mandate to speak for the whole trade. Thereupon, a complex web of trade barriers, price fixing arrangements, cost spreading measures, and domestic and foreign quota allocation was spun around the industry, with the primary objective of fending off foreign competition, particularly competition emanating from Continental European producers. One of the first tasks the IDAC undertook was, in fact, to negotiate a satisfactory agreement with the European Steel Cartel, based on reciprocal market share allocation.[10]

The pattern of an officially sanctioned cartel was further consolidated during the Second World War. The industry was effectively self-governed, but, at the same time, it worked in close co-operation with the Government, either through the machinery of the relevant Ministry or through special public supervisory bodies, acting on the Government's behalf. Thus, during the war, the Iron and Steel Control of the Ministry of Supply absorbed most of the staff of the Federation. After the war a new public body, the Iron and Steel Board, was set up to advise the Government and oversee the industry, with the BISF resuming a key role in setting prices, planning investment and managing foreign trade.[11]

Nationalisation of the steel industry was part of the program of the first post-war Labour government, which came into office in 1945. Because steel was not among the first sectors to be nationalised, the Iron and Steel Board appointed in 1946 was supposed, among other things, to advise the Government over nationalisation and prepare the industry for it. In fact it had very little appetite for this task, given that the BISF was adamantly opposed to public ownership. A dispute broke out between the Federation and the Labour Government: why, the Federation demanded, should the Government want to own an industry that it was able to control and with which such a close and intimate relationship had been struck? The answers of the Labour party leadership to this question were fairly unclear, ranging from an ideological antipathy to steel „barons' to a desire to force the industry to modernise and expand. There was a search for intermediate solutions, much discussion and controversy, but, at the end of the day, the Government imposed its will.[12]

The Nationalisation Bill was first introduced before Parliament in November 1948 and after a prolonged, often fierce debate the Bill became law in November 1949. With Labour retaining a very slim majority in the 1950 election, it came into force, the vesting date taking place on 14 February 1951. The existing company structure was left intact, but a public holding – the Iron and Steel Corporation of Great Britain – was to take all the companies over. Still, the boards of the companies were able to retain most of their powers, while the BISF, formally empowered to represent the smaller firms which had escaped the net of public ownership, also continued to play an important role. Perhaps, things would have eventually changed, but there was too little time for that to happen.

The Conservative Party had undertaken to bring the industry back into the private sector. On 26 October 1951 they won a majority in the General Election. Immediately after the new Government barred the Iron and Steel Corporation from taking any further decision of any consequence. The Bill to privatise the industry received the Royal Assent on 1 May 1953. It set up a new supervisory Iron and Steel Board as well as the Iron and Steel Holding and Realisation Agency, which would temporarily hold the assets and sell them back to private ownership.

Privatisation, or de-nationalisation as it was called, proved a fairly drawn out process. A consortium of leading City houses handled the issue of shares. The public response, especially to the first issues, was good, despite the pledge of the Labour Party to re-nationalise, were they to win again. Some of the companies were sold wholesale to new private buyers; but mostly it was the former shareholders who were able to secure their property back. By January 1955, steel companies accounting for some fifty per cent of steel output had been disposed of. In January 1957 the proportion had risen to 86 per cent, the only major firm awaiting to be sold being Richard Thomas and Baldwins. Its prospects were not very attractive, since it was planning to build a new strip mill in South Wales, amid a certain amount of controversy within the industry and with government subsidy.[13]

A second Iron and Steel Board was set up in 1953 to supervise the industry. It remained in existence for fourteen years until the industry's re-nationalisation. Its powers over investment and prices were not negligible, but they were not enough to make it an effective planning or regulatory body. On many issues if found itself dependent on the BISF, which remained a major force, with its influential leadership and its powerful and pervasive bureaucracy. By 1966 the BISF employed 600 officials, as compared to the Board's 140.[14] The Government, on the other hand, showed that it was prepared to overstep the Board, whenever a major investment decision with electoral implications came up. This proved the case in 1958 when the Cabinet, against the Board's advice, decided to built two new strip mills, rather than one: one went to South Wales and the other to Scotland. Increasingly the Board vented its frustration at being prevented to rationalise the industry.[15]

The Labour Party declared its intention of nationalising steel soon after it was elected, with a tiny majority, in 1964; and set out a White Paper in 1965 outlining its policy. The period between 1964 and 1966 witnessed a new debate over the future of the industry, with counterproposals put forwards by the Industry's Federation for re-organisation under private ownership (the Benson Report) or alternatively for mixed ownership. Some of the arguments already heard in the late 1940s were given a new airing. The outcome was also similar. Having won a second general election in 1966 with a clearer mandate, the Labour Party put forward an Iron and Steel Bill to nationalise the industry, which became law in March 1967.

A few lessons from the past, however, were learnt. Whereas in 1951 all the steel companies, but the very smallest, had been nationalised, in 1967 only the fourteen largest companies were taken over by the State. This left a sizeable private sector in existence, accounting for about ten per cent of crude steel production and 30 per cent of finished steel, ensuring that there would be a measure of competition. Furthermore, one year before nationalisation, in the autumn of 1966, an Organising Committee was set up, composed of government officials, industry leaders and other prominent businessmen and supported by the staff of the Iron and Steel Board. Its mandate was to prepare the details of the take over, including the selection of the top management of the new public holding, and think through some of the measures that needed to be taken. This too was a new departure, since the 1949 nationalisation had not been preceded by any amount of industrial planning.[16]

Thanks to the work of the Organising Committee, the BSC was not simply a grouping of the industry's different sections. It was meant to be a single business organisation, with a centralised management structure, allowing it to pursue a coherent strategy and to achieve its objectives, which were set out as being mainly of a commercial nature. As a consequence, it was agreed that the BISF would be dissolved and that its remaining functions to represent the private sector would be taken over by a new, far less influential body, the BISPA (British Independent Steel Producers' Association).

The life of the BSC extended over a period of 21 years, from 1967 until 1988. It was an eventful life. The BSC's first achievement was to bring together the various companies and subject them to centralised management along technocratic lines. This was accomplished progressively, through a sequence of internal reforms, moving from regional groups, which still reflected the old company structure, to six product divisions. The BSC's main task was to rationalise the industry by concentrating investment in a number of key plants. By the end of the Sixties there was some consensus as to the fact that the main production facilities were to be five integrated plants: Scunthorpe, Teeside, Port Talbot, Llanwern and Ravenscraig. On the other hand, the BSC had inherited twenty two integrated plants in addition to forty seven other units, with a total, much inflated, manpower of over 250,000. Initially it was hoped that rationalisation could be carried out in the context of large-scale expansion and the Corporation's Ten-Year Development Plan approved by the Government in 1973 assumed a huge increase in the demand for steel. However the recession of the mid-1970s hit Britain particularly hard, meaning that any new development had to be offset by radical cuts and massive retrenchment.[17]

The performance of the BSC during the 1970s has been harshly judged. Undoubtedly mistakes were made, and there were compounded by damaging political meddling in the running of the Corporation, on the part of Governments, both Conservative and Labour. While new projects were being launched, the BSC lost significant market share to imports, particularly after UK membership of the European Communities brought to an end the cosy arrangements that had protected the industry. Attention to the needs of final users seems to have slackened and the BSC was found wanting in commercial clout. Local pressures from trade unions and politicians delayed much needed action to close redundant plant. On the other hand, there was an effort to pursue a coherent investment strategy and, by the end of the period, this began to pay dividends.[18]

The private sector of the industry, which during the 1970s was boosted by the entry of foreign-owned mini-mills, succeeded, at first, in exploiting BSC's weaknesses and was able to cut into its market share, particularly for semi-finished goods. Private firms based in Sheffield and Rotherham held on to their profitable business in special steel products. On the whole, however, the private sector never posed the same challenge as in Italy. Private companies were hit by the recession and, particularly in the Sheffield area, were forced to merge defensively and seek joint ventures with the BSC. The division, thus, became blurred. For example, in 1986 the BSC was responsible for 76 per cent of crude steel, with another 15,8 per cent provided by the 'Phoenix' companies, joint ventures in which the BSC was the dominant partner. This left less than 10 per cent of crude steel entirely in private hands.[19]

The turnaround in BSC's performance took place around 1980–81, under the Chairmanship of Ian MacGregor, appointed by the new Conservative Government. The Conservatives had pledged to prepare the industry for privatisation, by cutting back on public subsidies. In the short term, however, this proved impossible and large sums were still needed to bail the Corporation out of its grave financial difficulties. Crucially, however, the Government was prepared to leave the BSC's top management a free hand. The strategy of shutting down all plants except for a few large works was, basically, the same that had been outlined in the 1970s; the difference was that now most, if not all, compromises and delays were ruled out. Between 1980 and 1983, there were about 100,000 redundancies, and BSC's total workforce fell from 166,400 in 1980 to 64,500 in 1985. Labour productivity, on the other hand, more than doubled over the same period. The industry was back to levels of international excellence. It had been helped, although this was seldom admitted by its vociferously free-trade leadership, by the Davignon regime of 'manifest crisis', which, during the early 1980s, when the company was most vulnerable, helped to stem imports from the rest of the Continent, avoiding damaging price wars.[20]

Having concentrated all operations in five most modern plants, pushed up total factor productivity, the BSC, under the chairmanship of Bob Scholey, was privatised for the sum of £2.5 billion. In its last year as a public sector company it achieved profits of £400 million and was able to offer a very attractive dividend. At the time of privatisation, the BSC employed just over 50,000 people.[21]

Since privatisation 'British Steel plc' has built on the strengths acquired during the 1980s. It managed to weather the recession of the early 1990s without too much damage, other than a loss of attractiveness to investors.

In 1995 the BSC was Europe's third largest steel company, and one of the most successful.

THE IMPERATIVE OF RATIONALISATION AND EXPANSION: 1945-67

Despite their very different size and standing, both the Italian and the UK steel industries emerged from the War with a strong need to modernise and expand. Plans for concentration of steel making in a few favoured locations had been laid out during the 1930s by technical reports – the Sofindit-Ilva Plan in Italy and the Sankey Committee report in Britain.[22] Much plant was known to be obsolete, waiting to be re-equipped with new technologies, which had been developed in the US. Both industries, although in different ways, were burdened by the existence of too many small firms and by a pattern of plant location, which was clearly out of date and irrational. Much informed opinion in both steel communities, moreover, broadly supported these aims.

Between the 1930s and the 1960s the 'American model' was widely regarded as the most successful in the steel industry. It consisted of a package of new thin flat rolling technologies, of economies of scale, both at plant and unit level; of standardised production in large batches; and, also, of new organisational methods, designed to maximise management control, work force productivity and company profitability. In this respect, steel makers both in Britain and in Italy found themselves at the deep learning end.

The report on the steel industry of the Anglo-American Council for Productivity was published in 1952. It discussed the reasons for the higher productivity of US steel making and found them, mainly, in the greater size of plant and units of production. Production in the US, moreover, was more standardised than in the UK, and the number of specifications smaller. Some of these features were perhaps unique to American conditions, but others could clearly be adopted. Finsider's top managers were challenged in the same way. Some of the more reform-minded among them embarked upon a steady diet of transatlantic pilgrimages, which was to last for well over a decade.[23]

The British were in a stronger position, retaining areas of considerable competitive advantage, for example in certain special steel productions. This, however, did not necessarily make their task of fundamental restructuring and adaptation to new technologies any easier. It might have made it, in fact, more difficult, by encouraging a misplaced sense of superiority and resistance to change.[24]

In Italy, Finsider's leadership rose to the challenge. Oscar Sinigaglia's first class managerial team, largely drawn from the private sector, was able to provide dynamic leadership.[25] It is worth summarising briefly their main achievements. Foremost among them must stand the construction of the second Cornigliano works (the first had been built and then destroyed during the war) near Genoa. Cornigliano was endowed with a wide strip mill, a cold strip mill and modern coating facilities. It was an 'Americanised' plant: built with American equipment; with the aid of American engineers and consultants; its personnel trained by the American firm, ARMCO; its management structure as well as its organisational design and industrial relations modelled on what was understood as best 'American practice'. Deciding to install a wide strip mill in Italy in the precarious conditions of the late 1940s was a risky gamble: but it paid off; and Cornigliano stood out for many years as the largest, fastest growing and most profitable plant in the industry.[26]

The completion of Cornigliano brought with it a vast rationalisation, with many plants either closing down, or refocusing to process coil made in Cornigliano. Markets for long products, however, were not streamlined in the same way, and much duplication of plant within Finsider and between the private and public sector persisted. Nevertheless, the main ideas of the Sinigaglia Plan were accepted and were developed further when it was decided to build a large new coastal works at Taranto. Also important was the commercial success enjoyed by Dalmine, the tube makers, as well as the launching of Terninoss, a joint venture between Terni and US Steel in the promising field of stainless and electrical cold rolled sheet.[27]

Finally, Finsider were able to secure very favourable terms for Italy within the European Coal and Steel Community. When the Schuman Plan was launched in 1950, there was a danger that Italy, as often in the past, would be at the mercy of a strong Continental combination, forced to accommodate massive steel imports from France, Belgium and Germany. In the event, however, Italy was able to set her own conditions for membership, including a guarantee of being able to complete her investment plans, temporary tariff protection for domestically produced common and special steel, and favourable arrangements for supplies of iron ore, coke and scrap.[28]

What lay behind this record? One noteworthy factor was the mixture of co-operation and competition established by Finsider with the private sector. Fruitful partnerships were struck with final users, such as the contract to supply Fiat with coil produced in Cornigliano – which gave Finsider the cushion of a considerable captive market. In some cases it was a question of bullying and cajoling smaller private producers to buy Finsider's products; while in others – see the Terninoss venture – the aim was to undercut rivals in their hitherto most profitable market niches.

Sinigaglia was very clear on the fact that Finsider should not aim at supplying private companies with semi-finished goods. On the contrary, it should compete with private companies by developing its own finishing units. Sinigaglia believed in mass production not just for the sake of raising output, although this was also a consideration, but because it allowed higher productivity and profits. Therein lay the seed of the dispute with the Falcks, who wanted to restrict the public sector and pursue traditional market sharing practices within the national producers' association.[29]

In the early post war years, moreover, Finsider was able to enjoy the privileges of being a state-owned company, without the burden of having to submit to any substantial external interference. The IRI state-shareholding system, by requiring companies to maintain their market-oriented bias, encouraged the creation of an informal technocracy. It was quite different from wholesale nationalisation. Arguably, moreover, during the Reconstruction the new political ruling elite lacked both experience and a strong power base, and this increased the freedom of the technocrats in charge of the public sector. The creation of the Ministero delle Partecipazioni Statali was the first step by the governing parties to establish some kind of control and direction, but it only happened in 1956.[30]

The strongest resistance to Sinigaglia's rationalisation plans came from inside the public sector itself. Immediately after the war, the IRI was a fairly small organisation, mostly concerned with financial accounting. Nor did Finsider itself, in which most of companies' shares were vested, have much clout, beyond a general say over long-term decisions. To a large extent, the operational companies of the group were independent and, because the system was supposed to operate according to private company law, they could successfully resist outside interference. Thus companies such as Ilva were still firmly embedded in a corporatist, conservative tradition far removed from Sinigaglia's reforming programme. Sinigaglia and his followers had no choice but to carry out their plans at company level. In particular, they entrenched themselves in Cornigliano and eventually sought to reshape Ilva by merging it with Cornigliano into a new company by the name of Italsider.[31]

Italsider brought together all the major steel making plants in the public sector, including Taranto, and was dominated by Cornigliano's executives. It sought to mould itself as a single, centralised corporation. In the intention of its founders it would not only wipe away the outmoded technological and managerial culture prevalent within the Ilva group, but also reduce the influence of the new bureaucracies that had taken hold of Finsider's as well as IRI's headquarters.

Cornigliano-Italsider's technocratic style of management has to be evaluated further in respect to the vital question of financial control. During the late 1960s the IRI model seemed to command general admiration across Europe as a system allowing the best of two worlds: state-control and the market. It was soon proved, however, to contain serious flaws.[32]

The IRI was a shareholding agency integrally owned by the State. The State, thus, conferred to IRI so-called Endowment Funds. IRI held the majority stake of its sub-holding companies and in the case of Finsider it accounted for fifty five per cent of the 1971 capital, the rest being owned by banks and insurance companies (most of which were also part of the public sector). Finsider, in turn, owned controlling stakes in its operating companies, although the more attractive the company, the larger the role of private capital. For example, in 1971 Italsider, which accounted for seventy five per cent of Finsider's assets, was owned for fifty five per cent by Finsider, for sixteen per cent by Sip, a public sector telecommunication company, and for another for twenty one per cent by private investors. Private investors in Dalmine held as much as 48.8 per cent of the company's shares.[33]

These private stakes had been allowed to build up especially through the issue of convertible debentures. Herein seemed to lie a promise for professional managers in the State sector: by running their companies successfully, they might attract enough private capital to dilute, perhaps even to opt out of state-ownership. More broadly, there seemed to be an advantage in being able to tap a wide variety of financial instruments: public endowments and short-term financial credit as well as equity and debenture issues.[34]

The peculiar nature of the IRI formula rested, therefore, in this flexibility and apparently loose financial structure. It is possible that, had Italy possessed a more developed capital market, a piecemeal privatisation might have taken place. In the event, rapid expansion had to be financed by short-term loans, exposing the companies to the vagaries of high interest rates during the 1970s. Their difficulties provided a good excuse for IRI bureaucrats to establish their authority, holding company managers to ransom. Lack of accountability and transparency compounded the problem.[35]

The emergence of a strong IRI was, therefore, the new factor that public steel managers had to contend with. By the early 1960s, IRI had turned into a powerful conglomerate with a commanding voice in the operations of Finsider. This was a far more corrosive and dangerous influence than straightforward government intervention. For example, the decision to build a new strip mill near Taranto, in the Mezzogiorno, was taken by the Christian Democrat-dominated Government, in the same way as the Macmillan Cabinet decided for two strip mills in Scotland, and South Wales. Company executives, however, were able to live with these instructions, since they were granted substantial subsidies to carry them out and were also left free to oversee their details and practical implementation. Much more corrosive were day to day encroachments, backed up by financial blackmail and pressure on appointments, carried out by a powerful technical body such as the IRI, which ruling parties had chosen to use as a vehicle of influence and patronage. This kind of creeping collateral interference eventually undermined good management standards.[36]

In the British case the results of rationalisation and modernisation were more disappointing. Much effort went into laying out Development Plans, but the effort was clearly not enough to maintain the industry in the top league. Particularly marked was the failure to reduce the number of plants and concentrate production. Investment tended to be of the patch-up kind and it peaked at the end of the 1950s, just as major new technological innovations, such as the basic oxygen steel making (BOS) process and continuous casting, beckoned for the industry.[37] Macroeconomic factors did not aid either, with domestic demand subject to considerable fluctuations.[38]

Labour productivity in the UK grew by about twenty five per cent between 1955 and 1965, whereas in Italy and Japan it grew by 150 per cent, and in West Germany, by 58 per cent. This meant that by 1965 the UK ranked below her major international competitors. The industry was slow to take up oxygen steel making and a large proportion of steel was still made in open-hearth furnaces. There was also a failure to develop the special steel sector, particularly stainless. During the early 1960s while some parts of the industry were well managed and healthy, the larger works were incurring losses, and total profitability of the 14 major companies consistently declined.[39]

One of the main features was the persistence of the corporatist mode of industrial self-government. It had the effect of stifling the emergence of an effective technocratic culture. The first post war nationalisation offers a good case study. It was initially conceived at least by some in the Labour Party as a means to rationalise and expand the industry. Soon, however, it turned out to be something different: an ideological exercise, undertaken perfunctorily by a Government, whose real inclination lay in collaborating with the industry's association along traditional lines. Thus, while the politicians and civil servants were wrestling with nationalisation the much more vital question of carrying out the first post war plan was left in the hands of the BISF. Equally the Iron and Steel Board, appointed after 1953 was little more than a hostage to the industry did, and could do very little.[40]

The corporatist pattern consisted in a tightly cartelised market and a carefully organised pricing system, supported by a system of levies and compensations, designed to minimise inter-firm competition and maximise stability. The BISF established itself as a semi-official industry regulator, undertaking a number of functions, such as price-fixing, collecting of levies, payment of subsidies and regulation of foreign trade. It also purported to act as a planning body, reviewing companies' investment schemes.

More often than not, however, it failed to be effective, given that it could only act where there was agreement among the largest companies, on which its authority ultimately rested. The most dynamic companies were, thus, unable to pursue competitive, cost cutting strategies and the strongest regional groupings, such as the sheet producers in South Wales, were held back by the declining, but powerful and well established, heavy product trades of Scotland and the North East.[41]

The BISF regime was particularly damaging in foreign policy. The choice of joining the European Coal and Steel Community was clearly barred by the Government's decision of 1950 to turn down the Schuman Plan. However, it was within the industry's possibilities to reach a genuine agreement with the Six, submitting to certain common rules over pricing and dismantling reciprocal tariff barriers. This would have had the positive effect of maximising reciprocal trade.

After a fractious internal debate the industry turned its back to such a solution: the UK market remained practically cut off from the Continental one, protected by quotas and tariffs and screened by its baroque cross-subsidies and artificial pricing rules. While preferential access to Commonwealth markets could be raised as a justification for this state of affairs in the short term; in the long term, given that those markets were becoming less dependable, this meant postponing inevitable choices.[42]

The more positive notes during these years, therefore, are to be found at the company level, wherever a professional management with a technocratic approach to the problems of investment rationalisation and technological innovation emerged. The industry's main areas of strength were the United Steel Company, and the two companies running the large wide strip mills in South Wales: the Steel Company of Wales and Richard Thomas and Baldwins. These three companies were to provide the BSC with most of its management expertise.

The emergence of a technocratic management culture in South Wales can be traced back to Sir William Firth, who, during the 1930s, strove to introduce the first wide strip mill into the UK, eventually succeeding at Ebbw Vale. Firth was an abrasive moderniser and a believer in mass production and Americanisation. Ultimately he suffered rejection on the part of the leading figures in the Federation; but his message, that company structures and old traditions had to be overhauled, lived on.[43]

The construction of the new Port Talbot works, one of the most impressive feats of post war investment, was made possible by company amalgamations abetted by government regional subsidies. The Steel Company of Wales was, thus, the result of an ambitious pooling of capital and management teams and it brought to the fore a new generation of professional managers, including administrators ready to entertain a close relationship with Whitehall such as Sir Ernest Lever. In addition experienced technical

Directors such as John Cartwright, mastered first American, and later Japanese technologies and managerial systems.[44]

The new development of Llanwern undertaken by Richard Thomas and Baldwins in the early 1960s, although much criticised at the time for its heavy reliance on public capital, was carried out using the latest BOS technology and adopted a very modern lay-out. Finally the large-scale facilities for long products at Appleby-Frodingham, the so-called 'Anchor' project, initiated by United Steel in 1966, were also based on oxygen converters, as well as on the alternative route of EAF (Electric arc furnace) together with continuous casting. They were the result of the company's plan to rationalise common grade and special steel operations. The Anchor project, in an upgraded version, was to form the centrepiece of BSC investment during the 1970s.[45]

LOSERS AND WINNERS IN THE QUEST FOR PROFITABILITY: 1967–96

The cyclical swings in the steel market affected the two countries in a similar way. At first, during the late 1960s and early 1970s, there was a period of bold optimism, marked by ambitious expansion plans – in Britain the BSC's Ten Year Development Plan and in Italy the decision to double Taranto's capacity, to over 10 million tonnes. British and Italian public sector steel makers were mesmerised by the Japanese model, consisting of huge water front green field plants. Emphasis fell decidedly on quantity, rather than quality. The upward trend in the market came to an end in the mid-1970s, although at first this was understood to be temporary. When the signs of a prolonged crisis appeared, sooner in the UK, rather later in Italy, painful retrenchment became necessary.

From 1978 up to 1986 steel policy was managed mainly at the European level, by national governments, in conjunction with national trade associations and the European Commission. The energetic Belgian Commissioner, Davignon, by officially introducing the 'manifest crisis' regime restricted output, prevented price cutting and set in motion a process of nationally negotiated cuts. This might not have been ideal from the point of view of efficiency, but it certainly suited the higher cost countries, such as both the UK and Italy were at the time. It was only by the mid-1980s that the BSC, having improved its productivity quite dramatically, began to voice its unease, calling for more competition.[46]

Sheltered by the Davignon regime, the public sector tended to act as a lifeboat for the rest of the industry. Thus, a number of private-public partnerships were agreed upon: in Britain there were the 'Phoenix' schemes, mainly involving the BSC with Sheffield producers; while in Italy, Finsider offered Fiat-Teksid and other producers very generous terms for surrendering their assets and leaving the trade.[47]

Enduring wide-scale losses prompted a rethink in steel making culture. The emphasis shifted towards recapturing profitability, by enhancing product quality and by better marketing.

Here, however, the similarities end. Unlike the BSC, Finsider was never able to rediscover the magic of profitability, which had blessed its earlier post war performance. This stark contrast is made more poignant by the fact that, if anything, it was the Italian group that enjoyed an advantage. The mid-1970s recession in Italy was by far less severe than in the UK. Apparent crude steel consumption in Italy had reached the all time high of 23.2 million tonnes in 1973. It fell back to 17.5 million in 1975, but by 1979 it was back to the 1973 level, peaking at over 25 million in 1980. Once more, during the early 1980s, demand was curbed by deflationary policies, but in no year did domestic consumption fall much below the 20 million tonne mark. In step with this trend, Finsider's steel output grew steadily until 1974 and did not significantly fall thereafter, at least until the late 1980s. In the UK, on the other hand, both domestic demand and the output of the BSC fell quite dramatically after 1974; and then fell even further in the early 1980s. This difference can be traced back to a different level of structural maturity in the two economies, as well as to a more robust performance on the part of Italy's manufacturing, particularly engineering, sector.[48]

A second advantage for Finsider was that, by the early 1970s, it had already carried out major technological modernisation. Taranto, in particular, was a very modern plant and there were other important centres of technological excellence. Despite this, however, low capacity utilisation, spiralling costs and high debt increasingly bogged down Finsider. If, therefore, as has been claimed, the turnaround in the BSC at the beginning of the 1980s was 'one of the most remarkable in business history', the sinking of Italy's public sector must stand out, at the other end, as a quite unique business debacle.[49]

The weaknesses of the public sector in Italy were, at least partly, rooted in the preceding affluent years of expansion. During the 1960s the balance of production between Finsider's main works was lost. The creation of Italsider was supposed, among other things, to bring about a balance between Taranto on one side and a renewed and expanded Piombino works, on the other. Soon, however, all the effort was put into Taranto. This reflected the infatuation with the Japanese huge-plant model, but did not pay the same attention to other features of that model, such as efficient unit management, flexible human resource management, dedication of the workforce, enhanced by teamwork and high levels of training. Furthermore concentrating so heavily on one plant created construction bottlenecks, hampering orderly production schedules.[50]

Taranto would have probably been able to sustain a capacity of a few million tonnes. Pushing it above that figure, exposed its handicaps, such as the distance from the steel users, most of which were in the North of Italy. This was partly overcome by carrying out finishing and coating of Taranto's coils at Novi Ligure, between Genoa and Turin. Nevertheless it encouraged a supply, output-oriented culture and a loss of feel for the market. Italsider, in particular, often fell back on supplying semi-finished goods to rival private steel companies, a practice that Sinigaglia had sought to discontinue.

Marketing was weak. The fragmented nature of steel demand in Italy required producers either to cater directly for small batch orders, thus exposing their mills to frequent and uneconomic changes of roll size and gauge, or to vertically integrate with well-equipped merchants, who could carry out appropriate customising operations. Italsider never chose the latter option, tinkered with the first, while in fact conceding more and more ground to independent steel traders. Traders, however, ran producers against each other and it was mainly through them that cheaper imports from the ECSC made inroads into Italsider's market share for coil and sheet. At the same time, domestic mini-mills were capturing the long product market.[51]

Further problems were wrought by persistent labour unrest during the 1970s. This was not peculiar to the steel industry, but part of a larger national pattern of trade union unrest. Frequent unannounced stoppages in the fixed, continuous-cycle installations of the steel plants, particularly the large blast furnaces at Taranto, caused immense financial damage. Industrial relations gradually improved during the early 1980s, the trade unions becoming more responsible and opting for negotiation rather than confrontation. By that stage, however, radical restructuring measures were required, which could hardly be accommodated within a negotiated framework. There was no appetite for outright confrontation with the unions.[52]

The actions of government ministers and other politicians were part of the problem, rather than the solution. At all levels Finsider's managers were subjected to uneconomic pressures to create jobs. The group became rife with political patronage. It has been claimed that such pressures were increased by weak coalition governments, facing frequent electoral tests, inducing them to surrender long term goals to short term political expediency.[53] In any case, the seeds of this problem had been sown at the time when IRI-Finsider had encroached on the organisational autonomy of Italsider, undermining its former leadership. Seasoned bureaucrats contaminated by the increasingly corrupt ethos of Italy's political class replaced the younger generation of executives, who had followed on the steps of Sinigaglia A few facts stand out to illustrate the scale of the disaster. Finsider's labour productivity, for example, failed to show any progress between 1968 and 1980, despite massive new investment. The number of employees, in fact, continued to grow, reaching a record number in 1976. The first cut back had to wait until 1981. In no year, between 1975 and 1988 did the group make a profit, and huge sums of public money were poured into it.[54]

Steps to redress the situation during the 1980s were too little and too late. By 1987 Finsider was unique within the EEC for still being unable to stand on its own feet. The creation of Ilva in 1989 brought only temporary respite. What was still lacking was the capacity to face some of the key problems of restructuring, restoring profitability to the group's main works at Taranto and Terni. Closing down or privatising marginal plants was largely irrelevant. Furthermore, there was no indication from the Government that a failure to redress the situation would lead to privatisation. Up to 1992, in fact, the message was that the public sector would be allowed to prosper, even to expand.

Only at the end of 1992, under the threat of bankruptcy, was there a national economic and political change of direction. It became unthinkable for the Government, struggling to regain its own financial credibility, to dish out more money to a public sector industry with such a poor record. The Commission, for its part, was setting more stringent requirements for bailing out Ilva; these included a prescription to sell off its main plants at a short notice. A few hurried measures were taken in order to make Ilva's assets more palatable to prospective buyers, but it was little more than a facelift. Ultimately, some potentially first class steel works were sold off for very little money.[55]

The first two chairmen of the BSC, Lord Melchett and Monty Finniston, inherited the recommendations included in 'Benson Report', the so called 'heritage strategy', of upgrading and enlarging the five largest integrated existing sites. Furthermore there would be enlarged port facilities at Teeside and Port Talbot. To this they added a sixth new plant on Teeside, to be built on Japanese lines. At the same time one hundred thousand jobs would have to go. Forecasts were optimistic, to say the least. Home steel consumption was expected to rise by 50 per cent between 1970 and 1980, although it had risen by only 16.5 per cent in the previous decade. Exports, too, were expected to make a quantum leap.[56]

Ambitious planning and radical, expensive modernising did not help to meet customer requirements in the short term. The BSC soon found itself unable to produce enough good quality steel. Average delivery times went up and there were problems with major customers, such as Ford, British Leyland, GKN, who began to 'second source' extensively. Figures for labour productivity remained well below those of Germany and other continental competitors.[57]

Nor was the legacy of the corporatist regime easy to overcome. UK membership of the ECSC in 1973 meant that tariff protection against Continental imports was scrapped; the ECSC rules were adopted, ending the long standing, artificial separation between the UK and the Continental markets. Among other things, this meant that domestic price fixing was replaced by the Community basing-point system, requiring each company to publish its own price schedule. Prices in the UK consequently rose, and there was a surge of imports from the Continent, particularly from Germany. In 1970 the share of imports in total steel consumption had been as low as five percent, but in 1977, for example, it had risen to twenty per cent and in 1981 to twenty eight per cent.[58]

Such shares were by no means extraordinary; they simply brought the UK in line with the rest of Europe. Nevertheless in the short-term import penetration hurt, and it was the BSC, not the independent producers, to suffer more. Moreover the BSC found it difficult to re-adjust exports towards the European market, where it lacked established links with major customers.

To all this was added a fair amount of damaging political interference. The Heath Government, in office between 1970 and 1974, started a time-consuming debate as to whether parts of the BSC should be sold back to the private sector, and whether the rest should be split into two separate companies. This came to nothing; in fact, the Government endorsed the Corporation's long term plans.[59] On the other hand, the following Labour government was not very pleased with the programme of manpower cuts the BSC had in mind, and it was also reluctant to face up to the huge costs of its ambitious capital programme.

In 1975, as a result of the Beswick Review, closures, amounting to three quarters of the manpower cuts the BSC was asking for, were deferred, without any steps taken to compensate the BSC for the additional financial burden. From 1975 onwards, the financial position of the Corporation deteriorated and expansionist talk gradually went out of fashion. By 1977 the Ten Year plan had been virtually abandoned and a new incremental step by step approach, with a focus on rationalisation was adopted, under the Chairmanship of Sir Charles Villiers. The new approach consisted of 'soft' closures, carried out in consultation with the unions, and smoothed by generous severance allowances. The BSC also undertook to encourage job creation schemes through its subsidiary BSC (Industry). Some reductions in workforce and in capacity were achieved, but the severity of the downturn called for more radical measures.[60]

Poor industrial relations were another handicap. The workforce was represented by a multiplicity of trade unions. In the late 1970s there were twenty three of them in the industry. This encouraged the existence of a variety of wage payments systems, each with different time rates and bonuses. Demarcation disputes and union rivalry made the management of technological change and falling employment extremely laborious.[61]

Matters came to a head in late 1979, when the BSC made decentralisation of pay bargaining a key issue, introducing a local lump sum scheme, to be negotiated at a plant level, on a multi-union basis. The union's response was a national steel strike lasting for over three months during early 1980. The strike, however, was ill timed, since the industry was in a recession; it played into the management's hand, offering it the opportunity to raise the stakes. After the collapse of industrial action, a number of plants were closed, over sixty thousand workers were dismissed within little over a year and labour productivity rose by forty per cent.[62]

Despite the setbacks, the 1970s also brought some achievements, the importance of which became clear in the following decade. A BSC leadership emerged with a strong sense of purpose and an equally strong esprit de corps. Whereas Ministers retained considerable statutory powers over the Corporation, in actual fact, inside knowledge and technical expertise gave BSC's executives an edge. In their negotiations with the Government, occasionally they had to give ground, but they never reverted to short-termism. Gradually, therefore, most of the original plans drawn up upon nationalisation were carried out. Concentration of operations in five major coastal centres, flanked by number of more specialised works was achieved. By 1980 all major works were based on large-scale oxygen steel making plant, and a massive switch had taken place away from low-grade expensive domestic ores to high quality foreign ones.[63]

Financial constraints were never serious enough to undermine the BSC's strategy. Very soon after nationalisation the Government had turned the BSC's fixed rate debt towards the Treasury into more flexible Public Dividend Capital, which was remunerated by dividends, raised in the light of the Corporation's yearly performance. Further borrowing followed, but again the Government proved fairly generous, in so far as much debt was subsequently written off. Financial targets were repeatedly imposed and then lifted.[64]

Coming to power in 1979, the new Thatcher government's declared aim was to privatise the BSC. There would be no more public money – it was said – to cover the Corporation's losses. The message, however, was premature: already in 1980 BSC's borrowing limits were increased. Other, less conspicuous, signals proved more effective. For example, BSC's statutory duty to promote the supply of iron and steel and further the public interest was scrapped. The Corporation was told to concentrate on restoring profitability, and it would also have to publish performance ratios, to show progress on labour productivity and capital efficiency.[65]

The Government appointed a new Chairman, Ian MacGregor, with a reputation for toughness, and gave him full confidence, telling him to get on with the job. Thereupon, each sector of the BSC was considered a Profit Centre and a number of collateral activities were de-merged from the Corporation to be set up as separate companies, whose performance could be monitored. After the 1980 strike, a new plant level bargaining pattern was enforced and previously taboo topics such as craft demarcation, and the use of subcontract labour were back on the agenda.[66]

The strategy now was to cut total manned capacity by nearly 50per cent, bringing it down to around 15 million tonnes a year. This required closing down all the non-core facilities, with the additional slimming down of the two major strip mill plants in South Wales. The Scottish strip mill at Ravenscraig, on the other hand, was given a reprieve, despite the fact that its market prospects had become fairly poor after the closure of the Linwood car factory. This was a political decision, just as the one in 1958 to build it. Nevertheless the cuts were substantial, and between the financial years of 1980/1 and 1986/7 the number of employees was halved, while labour productivity more than doubled.

Perhaps even more important was the shift of emphasis towards quality production and customer satisfaction. Efficiency in the use of existing plant became the benchmark for the top management; and quality improvements were pursued in key market segments, such as coated sheet for automobile and 'white goods' producers, and long products for the construction industry. Some important customers began to show satisfaction with these changes.[67]

There was also an effort towards acquiring a larger presence among stockholders and traders, both on the domestic and on the European market. Exports to the EEC were still hampered by declining steel demand, as well as by the Commission's market regulation measures. Imports from Germany and the Netherlands continued to make big inroads in the UK. Nevertheless the improvements were dramatic enough to bring the BSC back from the red. The first profitable year was 1985/6 and two years later the trend was fairly clear enough to make the BSC a good prospect for private investors. Steel output was rising, and optimum capacity utilisation rates were being achieved.[68]

The privatisation of the BSC has become somewhat of a landmark for the steel industry, since it opened the way to a string of other steel company privatisations across Europe and overseas. It was not unproblematic, however. The Corporation still had a considerable debt burden, and the Government had to engage in some nimble financial restructuring to make its shares more attractive. A golden share was held by the Government in order to restrict the size of individual shareholding. The BSC's Chairman, Bob Scholey, one of the Corporations old hands, who had been in leading positions for over a decade, and was to remain in charge for another few years, played an important role in pushing the process through. He insisted that the company should be privatised as a single entity, rather than broken up. The Trade Unions did not offer any resistance. The Royal Assent having been given in July 1988, the new company became British Steel plc.[69]

Since privatisation British Steel has been free to pursue the successful course that had led to its earlier recovery. Capacity was further reduced, with the closure of the Ravenscraig strip mill. Further efforts were made to link up with steel users, particularly the Japanese-owned car factory transplants in the UK. Export penetration in Europe has been improved, while important initiatives were launched in the US as well. Decentralisation of pay and conditions bargaining has been taken a step further.

The steel industry has long since ceased to be a leading, strategic sector. But neither has it become one of the most profitable businesses. Setbacks in the market, such as the one in 1990–2 that brought European prices down by an average thirty per cent, meant that British Steel's share value slumped and dividend payments were interrupted. In recent years there has been a comeback, but not a remarkable one.[70]

CONCLUDING REMARKS

A brief comparative survey, such as this one, offers only limited opportunity for wide-ranging generalisations. Some tentative conclusion, however, may be drawn in regards to both the structure and the performance of the two public sectors.

Some of the most far sighted reformers and modernisers in the two steel industries, men like Sir William Firth and Oscar Sinigaglia, fought their battles against the steel establishment, the national steel association's body. They say the national cartel, as stifling innovation and rationalisation. By all accounts, Sinigaglia was the more fortunate of the two, since after the war he was put in charge of Finsider and thus had a chance to carry out his plans. The steel establishment in the UK was more powerful, and not easily overcome by ambitious outsiders. The BISF remained at the forefront of the industry up to 1967, by which time evidence of under-performance was striking.

Even within Finsider, however, the path towards reform was not a smooth one. Sinigaglia and his successors had to carry their battle at the company level, by taking charge of Cornigliano. The fact that Finsider proved to be an effective agent for modernisation in the early post war years was not, contrary to what many thought at the time, due to any fundamental merit of the IRI formula, based on the State being a majority shareholder rather than the outright owner. Rather it was due to particular circumstances, empowering an enlightened group of steel executives.

That the IRI formula contained important flaws was revealed during the crisis years of the 1970s and 80s. The companies of the IRI-Finsider group proved not to be sufficiently alike private companies to be subject to the disciplines of the market; nor, however, were they sufficiently demarcated as part of the State to fully commit the politicians to restoring their viability. They lived in a limbo, exposed to the worst of both worlds. The top management drifted along without a sense of direction.

A better balance was probably achieved with the creation of the BSC, which was a nationalised, one hundred per cent state-owned company, but at the same time enjoyed a certain amount of freedom to conduct its operations on a long term basis, and with commercial success as its purpose. This had not been the case at the time of the 1949 nationalisation. Many lessons had since been learnt. In other words, the long and tortuous debate held in Britain since the early 1930s on how the steel industry should be run in a mixed economy had not been entirely in vain. The first step was to establish the need for long term planning for the whole industry, not just its single companies. Once that was achieved, the steel managers should be left to do the job, with as little interference as possible from the Government or the politicians.

The lessons in regard to the public sector's performance are possibly easier to draw. First of all there was a need for rationalisation. Alongside this, there was the imperative and the attraction of expansion. The great boom of the 1950s and 1960s shifted the attention to raising output and nurtured a dangerous supply-side culture, which reached its peak in the early part of the 1970s. The market for steel seemed assured; it was just a question of how to organise production. The politicians also enjoyed a stake: they could trumpet millions of tonnes and thousands of jobs for under-developed or under-achieving regions, and shore up their electorates. Steel making, however, suffered from becoming a symbol. The lessons of the market were forgotten and this, more than anything else, brought the Italian public sector to its knees. Cutting jobs and closing plants was only part of the painful answer; without an improvement in quality performance the dramatic recovery of the BSC in the 1980s would not have happened. A lesson that Sinigaglia would have had no difficulty with.

NOTES

1. The first draft of this paper was presented at the Anglo Italian Business History Conference, *British and Italian State Owned Companies in comparative perspective*, (San Miniato, Pisa, 31 October–1 November 1997). I have since expanded upon it, drawing on both my own published research and on a selection of the secondary literature. I have greatly benefited from conversations with Jonathan Aylen.

2. On the origins of Finsider see F. Bonelli (ed.), *Acciaio per l'industrializzazione – Contributi allo studio del problema siderurgico italiano* (Turin, 1982); V. Castronovo, 'L'industria siderurgica e il piano di coordinamento dell'IRI (1936–1939)', *Ricerche storiche*, VIII (1978), no. 1, pp. 163–88.

3. Figures are drawn from M. Balconi, *La siderugia italiana (1945–1990) – Tra controllo pubblico e incentivi del mercato* (Bologna, 1991), p. 258, p. 481 and p. 517.

4. On Breda see AAVV, *La Breda. Dalla Societa' italiana Ernesto Breda alla Finanziaria Ernesto Breda, 1886–1996* (Milan, 1996). More broadly, on Italy's public sector in the post-war period M. Maraffi, *Politica ed Economia in Italia – La vicenda dell'impresa pubblica dagli anni Trenta agli anni Cinquanta* (Bologna, 1991); M. Baldassarri (ed.), *Industrial Policy in Italy 1945–1990* (London, 1991).

5. O. Sinigaglia, 'The Future of the Italian Iron and Steel Industry', *Banca Nazionale del Lavoro Quarterly Review,* IV (1948), pp. 240–45; G. L. Osti (ed.), *L'industria di Stato dall'ascesa al degrado – Trent'anni nel gruppo Finsider, conversazioni con Ruggero Ranieri* (Bologna, 1993); R. Ranieri, 'Assessing the implications of mass production and European integration: the debate inside the Italian steel industry (1945–1960)', in M. Dumoulin, R. Girault and G. Trausch (eds.), *L'Europe du patronat de la guerre froide aux années '60* (Berne, 1993), pp. 77–100.

6. On the construction of Taranto see R. Ranieri, 'La grande siderurgia in Italia: dalla scommessa sul mercato all' industria dei partiti', in G. L. Osti, *L'industria di stato dal successo al degrado,* cit, pp. 70–81. On Fiat see D. Velo, *La strategia Fiat nel settore siderurgico 1917–1982* (Turin, 1983); on the Falck group see M. Balconi, *La siderurgia italiana,* pp. 536–9.

7. On the mini-mill sector M. Balconi, 'The Notion of Industry and Knowledge Bases: The Evidence of Steel and Mini-Mills', *Industrial and Corporate Change,* II (1993), pp. 471–507; R. Castellani, 'The Ultimate Role of the Italian Mini-mill Sector', *Steel Times,* (January 1996), pp. 12–14; *Riva 1954– 1994* (Milan, 1995).

8. On developments in Finsider-Ilva during the 1980s, see F. Venturino, *La politica industriale in Italia. Il caso della siderurgia pubblica 1951–1990* (Genoa, 1991); A. Pichierri, 'Crisis and Restructuring in the Steel Industry', in R. Y. Nanetti and R. Catanzaro (eds.), *Italian Politics: A Review,* IV (1992) pp. 58–70; M. Balconi, 'La gestione comunitaria della crisi siderurgica (1975–1987)', in R. Malaman and P. Ranci (eds.), *Le politiche industriali della CEE* (Bologna,1988), pp. 15–55.

9. On the privatisation process see M. Balconi, 'The Privatisation of the Italian State-Owned Steel Industry: Causes and Results', in R. Ranieri and E. Gibellieri (eds.), *The Steel Industry in the New Millennium: vol. 2, Institutions, Privatisation and Social Dimensions* (London, 1998), pp. 51–64.

10. On the steel industry in the 1930s see, J. C. Carr and W. Taplin, *A History of the British Steel Industry,* (Oxford, 1962); S. Tolliday, *Business, Banking and Politics – The Case of British Steel 1918–1939* (Cambridge Mass., 1987). On negotiations with the European steel cartel see C. Wurm, *Business, Politics and International Relations. Steel, cotton and International Cartels in British Politics, 1924–1939* (Cambridge, 1993).

11. See D. L. Burn, *The Steel Industry 1939–1959 – A Study in Competition and Planning* (London, 1961), pp. 3–128; B. S. Keeling and A. E. G. Wright, *The Development of the Modern British Steel Industry* (London, 1964), pp. 24–84.

12. On the 1949 nationalisation see G. Ross, *The Nationalisation of Steel – One Step Forward, Two Steps Back?* (London, 1965); M. Chick, *Industrial Policy*

in Britain 1945–1951, Economic Planning, Nationalisation and the Labour Governments (Cambridge, 1988); R. Ranieri, 'Partners and enemies: the decision to nationalise steel, 1945–1948', in R. Millward and J. Singleton (eds), *Industrial Organisation and the Road to Nationalisation in Britain 1920–1950* (Cambridge, 1995), pp. 275–305.

13. On de-nationalisation see K. Burk, *The First Privatisation: the Politicians, the City and the Denationalisation of Steel* (London, 1988); On the steel industry during the 1950s, D. L. Burn, 'Steel' in ID (ed.), *The Structure of British Industry*, Vol.1 (London, 1958), pp. 260–308; J. Vaizey , *A History of British Steel*, (London, 1974), pp. 150 ff.

14. On the staff of the BISF and the ISB see K. Ovenden, *The Politics of Steel* (London, 1978), p. 18 and p. 214.

15. J. Vaizey, *A History of British Steel*, p. 169–77; D. L. Burn, *The Steel Industy 1939–1959*, pp. 639 ff; K. Warren, *The British Iron and Steel Sheet Industry since 1840* (London, 1970), pp. 254–81.

16. On the 1967 nationalisation the fullest account in K. Ovenden, *The Politics of Steel*, pp. 102 ff.; also H. Abromeit, *British Steel. An Industry Between the State and the Private Sector* (Leamington Spa, 1986), p. 118 ff.

17. Details on the BSC investment plans in D. W. Heal, *The Steel Industry in Post War Britain* (London, 1974), pp. 174–81.

18. R. Pryke, 'British Steel' in ID, *The Nationalised Industries. Policies and Performance since 1968* (Oxford, 1981), pp. 183–209; G. F. Dudley and J. J. Richardson, *Politics and Steel in Britain 1967–1988 – The Life and Times of the British Steel Corporation* (Dartmouth, 1990); A. J. Cockerill, 'Steel', in P. S. Johnson (ed.), *The Structure of British Industry* (London, 1980), pp. 131–53.

19. On the development of the private sector A.J. Cockerill, 'Steel' in P. S. Johnson (ed.), *The Structure of British Industry*, p. 141 ff; T. T. Jones and A. J. Cockerill, 'The Steel Industry', in ID, *Structure and Performance of Industries* (Oxford, 1984), p. 171 ff.; on market shares in 1986 see G. F. Dudley and J. J. Richardson, *Politics and Steel in Britain 1967–1988*, p. 241.

20. On the BSC in the 1980s see J. Aylen, 'Prospects for Steel', *Lloyds Bank Review*, no. 151, (1984), pp. 13–31.

21. J. Aylen, 'Privatisation of the British Steel Corporation', *Fiscal Studies*, IX, no.3 (1988), pp. 1–25 and C. Beauman, 'The British Steel Case – How History Determines Strategy', in R. Ranieri and E. Gibellieri (eds.), *The Steel Industry in the New Millennium: vol. 2, Institutions, Privatisation and Social Dimensions*, (London, 1998), pp. 39–49.

22. On the Sofindit – a holding agency set up under the auspices of the Government to oversee the assets taken over from the Banca Commerciale – and its plans for restructuring Ilva see L. Scalpelli, 'L'Ilva alla vigilia del Piano Autarchico per la Siderurgia (1930–1936)', *Ricerche storiche* , VIII, no.1 (1978), pp. 241–9. On the Sankey Committee report of 1930s see S. Tolliday, *Banking and Politics*, pp. 294–5 and D. L. Burn, *The Economic History of Steelmaking 1867–1939 – A Study in Competition* (London, 1940), p. 436 ff.

23. Anglo-American Council on Productivity, *Iron and Steel Productivity Team Report* (1952); Nick Tiratsoo and Jim Tomlinson, 'Exporting the "Gospel of

Productivity": United States Technical Assistance and British Industry, 1945–1960', *Business History Review*, LXXI (1997), pp. 41–81; see R. Ranieri, 'Learning from America. The Remodelling of Italy's public sector steel industry in the 1950s and 1960s', in M. Kipping and O. Bjarnar (eds.), *The Americanisation of European Business. The Marshall Plan and the transfer of US management models* (London,1988), pp. 208–28.

24. On the strength of the UK special steel sector see G. Tweedale, *Sheffield Steel and America: A Century of Commercial and Technological Interdependence 1830–1930* (Cambridge, 1987). The UK steel community was resistant to change at the time of the wide strip mill, although finally, thanks to the more far-sighted industrialists, that innovation was adopted. See R. Ranieri 'Between America and Europe: The Introduction of Wide Strip Mills in Britain and Italy', in E. Bussière and Michele Dumoulin (eds.), *Milieux Economiques et Integration Européenne en Europe Occidentale au XXe Siècle* (Arras, 1998), pp. 215–34. Further indications of reluctance to face up to innovation came in the 1950s, when the discussion in the UK on the introduction of the oxygen converter revealed marked scepticism and attachment to existing technologies see D. W. Heal, *The Steel Industry in Post War Britain*, p. 91.

25. Oscar Sinigaglia's original team consisted of Ernesto Manuelli, Guido Vignuzzi, and Mario Marchesi. After Sinigaglia's death in 1953, a new generation emerged with people like Gian Lupo Osti, Alberto Capanna, and Enrico Redaelli. See P. Rugafiori, 'I gruppi dirigenti della siderurgia 'pubblica' tra gli anni Trenta e gli anni Sessanta', in F. Bonelli (ed.), *Acciaio per l'industrializzazione* (Turin, 1982), pp. 335–68.

26. On Cornigliano see F. Amatori, 'Cicli produttivi, tecnologie, organizzazione del lavoro. La siderurgia a ciclo continuo integrale dal piano autarchico alla Italsider (1937–1961)', *Ricerche Storiche*, X, no.3, (1980), 557–611; R. Ranieri, 'Il Piano Marshall e la Ricostruzione della Siderurgia a ciclo integrale', *Studi Storici*, XXXVII, no. 1, (1996), pp. 145–90; G. L. Osti, *L'industria di stato*, pp. 42–72 and 167–90.

27. On Terninoss see V. Borgami, 'L'evoluzione produttiva e l'espansione industriale della Terninoss', *Rassegna Economica (Terni)*, XIV, no. 1, (1978), pp. 15–21; on the market for stainless steel in Italy see R. Ranieri and M. Marmottini, 'La Terni durante la gestione Osti (1965–1975): I mercati, gli impianti e le strategie aziendali', in R. Covino, A. Grohmann, L. Tosi (eds.), *Uomini economia cultura: saggi in onore di Giampaolo Gallo* (Naples, 1997), p. 296 ff.

28. R. Ranieri, 'La siderurgia italiana e gli inizi dell'integrazione europea', *Passato e Presente*, III, no. 7, (1985), pp. 65–85; R. Ranieri, 'The Italian Steel Industry and the Schuman Plan negotiations', in K. Schwabe (ed.), *Die Anfänge des Schuman Planes 1950. The Beginnings of the Schuman Plan* (Baden Baden, 1988), pp. 345–56.

29. G. L. Osti, *L'industria di stato*, pp. 104–12

30. B. Bottiglieri, 'Le partecipazioni statali negli anni Cinquanta: alcune premesse al dibattito odierno', *Economia e Lavoro* , XV, no.2, (1981), pp. 79–101.

31. On planning within Finsider and the creation of Italsider see G. L. Osti, *L'industria di Stato*, pp. 191–218.

32. The following is a selection of literature extolling the virtues of the IRI model: M. V. Posner and S. J. Woolf, *Italian Public Enterprise* (Cambridge, Mass., 1967); S. Holland (ed.), *The State as Entrepreneur New Dimensions for Public Entreprises: the IRI State Shareholding Formula* (London, 1972); Giuseppe Petrilli, *Lo stato imprenditore. Validità e attualità' di una formula* (Rome, 1968).

33. Figures for cross-holdings in 'Diagram of IRI's major shareholdings as of May 1952', in S. Holland (ed.), *The State as Entrepreneur*, pp. 314–15.

34. M. V. Posner andi S. J. Woolf, *Italian Public Enterprise*, pp. 116–20, contains an interesting discussion, comparing financial arrangements in the Italian and in the UK public sectors. Also see S. Holland, 'The Finance Formula' in *The State as Entrepreneur*, pp. 184–201. On the views of top IRI-Finsider managers on the dilution of State control see G. L. Osti, unpublished paper for the conference, 'Perche' l'impresa pubblica?' Ciriec, Club Turati, May 1970, now at Ciriec, Milan; also G. L. Osti 'Iniziativa pubblica e sviluppo economico', in *Mondo Economico*, XVIII, no.27, (1963), p. 28.

35. On the financial difficulties of Finsider see M. Balconi, *La siderurgia italiana*, pp. 310–23.

36. A good analysis of the involution of the IRI model is in F. Amatori, 'Growth via Politics: Business Groups Italian-Style', in T. Shiba and M. Shimotami (eds.), *Beyond the Firm. Business Groups in International and Historical Perspective* (Oxford, 1997), pp 121–33. An important testimony is A. Fantoli, *Ricordi di un imprenditore pubblico* (Torino, 1995), p. 46 ff.

37. For a basic illustrations of the key technological developments in the industry see J. Aylen, 'Innovation in the British Steel Industry', in K. Pavitt (ed.), *Technical Innovation and British Economic Performance* (London, 1980), pp. 200–234.

38. Fluctuations in demand in the UK steel industry are illustrated in B. S. Keeling and A. E. G.Wright, *The Development of the Modern British Steel Industry*, pp. 89–95.

39. Performance figures for the UK steel industry are in R. Pryke, 'British Steel', p. 184; and K. Ovenden, *The Politics of Steel*, pp. 20–21.

40. On the steps leading to the 1949 nationalisation see R. Ranieri 'Partners and Enemies', pp. 285–97. On the powers of the Iron and Steel Board, see D. L. Burn, *The Steel Industry*, p. 671 ff.

41. Within the Government there was also unease with the BISF regime, see. R. Ranieri, 'Attempting an Unlikely Union: The British Steel Industry and the European Coal and Steel Community, 1950–1954', in P. M. Stirk and D. Willis (eds.), *Shaping post war Europe: European Unity and Disunity 1945–1957* (London, 1991), pp. 112–23.

42. On the attitude of the UK on the Schuman Plan see Roger Bullen, 'The British Government and the Schuman Plan: May 1950–March 1951', in K. Schwabe (ed.), *Die Anfnge des Schuman Plans 1950/51 – The Beginnings of the Schuman Plan,* pp. 199– 210. A less apologetic view is in E. Dell, *The Schuman Plan and the British abdication of leadership of Europe* (Oxford, 1995); on the British steel industry and the ECSC see R. Ranieri, 'Inside or outside the magic circle: the Italian and British Steel industries face to face

with the Schuman Plan and the European Coal and Steel Community', in A.
S. Milward, F. Lynch, R. Ranieri, F. Romero, V. Sorensen, *The Frontier of
National Sovereignty – History and Theory* (London, 1994), p. 129 ff.
British steel exports to the Commonwealth accounted for between fifty and
sixty per cent of total exports in the early 1950s, whereas exports going to
the countries of the ECSC were very modest.

43. S. Tolliday, *Banking and Politics*, p. 136 ff.; W. E. Minchinton, *The British
Tinplate Industry – A History* (Oxford , 1957), pp. 193–204.

44. On the development of the Steel Company of Wales see K. Warren, *The
British Iron and Steel Sheet Industry since 1840* (London, 1970), p. 205 ff.
and p. 293 ff.; W. F. Cartwright, 'The Steel Company of Wales Limited – Its
Development to Date', *Iron and Steel Engineer*, XL, (1963), pp. 69–97.

45. On Llanwern and on the Anchor Project see D. W. Heal, *The Steel Industry
in Post War Britain*, p. 93 ff.

46. Y. Meny and V. Wright (eds.), *The Politics of Steel: Western Europe and the
Steel Industry in the Crisis Years (1974–1984)* (Berlin, 1987). Also E.
Davignon, 'The Future of the European Steel Industry', *Annals of Public and
Cooperative Economy*, LI, no. 4, (1980), pp. 507–19. On the UK's attitude
towards the Davignon Regime see G. F. Dudley and J. J. Richardson, *Politics
and Steel in Britain 1967–1988*, pp. 7–9. On the Italian attitude see F.
Venturino, *La politica industriale in Italia*, p. 119 ff.

47. For Finsider and the private companies see D. Moro, *Crisi e ristrutturazione
dell'industria siderurgica italiana* (Milano, 1984), p. 104 ff.; on the Phoenix
schemes see H. Abromeit, *British Steel*, p. 235 ff.

48. Comparative trends for steel intensity, i.e. the relationship of steel and GDP
are shown in F. Audino, 'The Steel Market in Italy. The Trend of Steel
Consumption: Macro-economic Aspects', in R. Ranieri and J. A. Aylen, *The
Steel Industry in the New Millennium. Vol. 1, Technology and the Market*
(London, 1998), pp. 237–52; on the performance of Italy's manufacturing
sector see R. Ranieri, 'Italy: After the Rewards of Growth, the Penalty of
Debt', in B. Foley (ed.), *European Economies Since the Second World War*
(London, 1998), p. 84 ff.

49. J. Aylen, 'Privatisation of the British Steel Corporation', p. 1 ; at the other
end stands the following quote from Professor Balconi, '...the Italian taxpayer contributed about Lire 38000 billion at 1994 prices to the misadven-
ture of the public steel sector' in M. Balconi, 'Introduction to Section I,
Privatisation and New Business Strategies', in R. Ranieri and E. Gibellieri,
The Steel industry in the new Millennium, vol. 1, p. 14.

50. On the investment plans of Italsider see G. L. Osti, *L'industria di Stato*, cit p.
191 ff.

51. M. Balconi, *La siderurgia italiana*, pp. 276–90.

52. On industrial relations in the steel industry M.Balconi, *La siderurgia italiana*,
p. 291 ff. For a broader summary see E. Reyneri, 'La politica del lavoro', in
B.Dente (ed.), *a cura di, Le politiche pubbliche in Italia* (Bologna, 1990), pp.
237–55; for a further testimony from the steel employers' point of view see
A. Ciglia, 'Restructuring and Industrial Relations in Italy's Big Steel: The

Experience of Dalmine', in R. Ranieri and E. Gibellieri, *Steel in the New Millennium, vol.1*, pp. 219–34.

53. M. Balconi, *La siderurgia italiana*, pp. 223–8.

54. Figures are taken from M. Balconi, *La siderurgia italiana*, pp. 258–9.

55. On the final crisis of the Ilva group and the role of the EC see A. C. Masi, 'Steel', in H. Kassim and A. Menon (eds.), *The European Union and National Industrial Policy* (London, 1996), pp. 70–78; the best overall account is M. Balconi, 'The Privatisation of Italian State-Owned Steel Industry'. Also Fim, Fiom-Uilm, *La siderurgia in Italia 1992–1996*, mimeo, (March 1997).

56. J. Aylen, 'Prospects for Steel', p. 23, highlights the optimistic, expansion-led culture of the BSC's management. On the unrealistic forecasts of the Ten-Year Development plan, R. Pryke, 'British Steel', p. 189.

57. R. Pryke, 'British Steel', p. 195; G. F. Dudley and J. J. Richardson, *Politics and Steel in Britain 1967–1988*, p. 238.

58. A. J. Cockerill, 'Steel', p. 135 and T. T. Jones and A. J. Cockerill, 'The Steel Industry', p. 182.

59. K. Ovenden, *The Politics of Steel*, p. 173 ff.

60. A. J. Cockerill, 'Steel', pp. 139–40; G. F. Dudley and J. J. Richardson, *Politics and Steel in Britain 1967–1988*, pp. 79–108; C. Beauman, 'The British Steel Case', p. 41.

61. J. Aylen, 'Plant size and efficiency in the steel industry: an international comparison', *National Institute Economic Review*, no. 100, (1982), pp. 74–5; A. J. Johnston, 'Industrial Relations and Workforce Management at British Steel', in R. Ranieri and E. Gibellieri (eds.), *The Steel Industry in the New Millennium: vol. 2*, pp. 219–27.

62. A. J. Johnston, 'Industrial Relations and Workforce Management at British Steel', p. 221; J. Aylen, 'Prospects for Steel', pp. 19–20.

63. J. Aylen, 'Innovation in the British Steel Industry', pp. 222–8; G. F. Dudley and J. J. Richardson, *Politics and Steel in Britain 1967–1988*, p. 263 ff.

64. K. Ovenden, *The Politics of Steel*, p. 188 ff.

65. Jonathan Aylen, 'Privatisation of the British Steel Corporation', p. 10.

66. G. F. Dudley and J. J. Richardson, *Politics and Steel in Britain 1967–1988*, p. 143 ff.

67. G. F. Dudley and J. J. Richardson, *Politics and Steel in Britain 1967–1988*, p. 261–3; C. Beauman, 'The British Steel Case', p. 42.

68. G. F. Dudley and J. J. Richardson, *Politics and Steel in Britain 1967–1988*, pp. 238–9.

69. G. F. Dudley and J. J. Richardson, *Politics and Steel in Britain 1967–1988*, pp. 225–30; C. Beauman, 'The British Steel Case', p. 43–4; A. M. Blair, 'The British Iron and Steel Industry Since 1945', *Journal of European Economic History*, XXVI (1997), pp. 580–82.

70. C. Beauman, 'The British Steel Case', p. 45 ff.; Patrick Heenan, 'British Steel PLC', in *International Directory of Company Histories*, IV, (London, 1991), pp. 42–3.

Business Scandals in the Weimar Republic

Martin Fiedler

University of Bielefeld

With the 1997 Schneider affair, large banks once again found themselves in the crossfire of criticism: their careless awarding of credits was faulted for having practically provoked fraudulent behaviour. Dazzled by 'fool's gold', banks were basically allowing credit in order to enter into business with allegedly successful companies.[1] Some observers even see a structural failure of the 'network-capitalism' established in Germany for decades in the increasing appearances of spectacular company collapses in the 1990s (Metallgesellschaft, Bremer Vulkan, Balsam). The privileged position of banks in the controlling organs of companies; the accumulation of supervisory board seats; the network of personal relationships; and cross-over capital participation is suspected of creating a climate of careless trust, just ripe for abuse.[2]

The scolding that banks received in the aftermath of one of the biggest business scandals in the recent years of the Federal Republic harks back to the public debate about sensational finance scandals in the final years of the Weimar Republic. Highlights of this chronicle of scandal included the crash in August 1929 of the Frankfurter Allgemeine Versicherungs-A.G. (hereafter Favag); followed by the collapse in July 1931 of the Norddeutsche Wollkämmerei (Nordwolle), which heightened the banking crisis and pushed one of the D-Banks to the brink of disaster; and finally the scandal surrounding the Schultheiss-Patzenhofer brewing company in October of the same year. While a critical public made accusations of guilt and was no longer content to blame the recurrent appearance of such crises solely on economic depression, the serious trade press, with no vested interest in attacking the capitalist system, remarked on the moral crisis of industry leadership: 'Be it Favag, Nordwolle, Schultheiss, Karstadt, Wicking, Miag, Blumenstein, Linoleum-Trust, Zeche-Ewald or other cases,' commented the editor of the *Deutscher Volkswirt* after the Schultheiss affair, 'everywhere there is something amiss. There is at least a degree of foolhardiness at play that lets the general crisis become an individual catastrophe, that in turn because of its magnitude further affects the general crisis.' Stolper responded clearly to the question of guilt in these circumstances: 'The principal fault is carried without a doubt by the banks. None of the finance scandals of these years would have been possible if the banks had not made them possible...'[3]

Stolper's conclusions on the question of guilt were not unique. But his comments rang resoundingly true during the turbulent events of the summer of 1931, when the big banks sank into their most serious crisis so far, therefore creating anything but a good impression. Was such a verdict against 'the banks' truly justified, when no banker in the ensuing criminal proceedings was indicted with legal responsibility? Was the system of supervision and control really so inefficient, that it would lay the blame decisively on the banks, who after all divided the large part of supervisory board memberships among themselves?

In his portrait of Jakob Goldschmidt, Gerald Feldmann pointed out that the problem of the business scandals in the Weimar Republic received far less attention from historians that the it deserved.[4] Goldschmidt, the rapidly risen director of Danatbank, expressed the strong wish that – after a speedy resolution of the Favag case – 'the curtain could be allowed to fall on this affair which has agitated the public'.[5] Two years later he himself was, in the Nordwolle as well as in the Schultheiss affair, the object of criticism. Focusing on this example, Feldman pleaded for fair judgement: The Weimar economy was ill and therefore possibly more susceptible to risky manoeuvres and business practices than in any previous or succeeding period. Additionally, it should be borne in mind that the borders between 'healthy and unhealthy speculation,' between 'entrepreneurship' and 'bad business practice' are constantly shifting. No one embroiled in the business scandal conceded an awareness of any wrongdoing. Whereas the personality of the actors is normally accorded a major role, Feldman's portrait opens up the question of whether what Stolpler diagnosed as a 'degree of foolhardiness' manifested a widespread attitude that tended towards quick profit, speculation and risk. Just a few years earlier, during the inflation, such behaviour had in fact been rewarded.

Business scandals should not just provoke a discussion of guilt, which inevitability becomes the centre of public debates. A satisfactory examination of the problem should extend beyond an enumeration of management mistakes, which as a rule precede 'moral hazard,' account balance falsification, disloyalty, and other illegal activities. Severe business crises should also initiate a learning process and lead to improvements within institutions. The degree of public criticism functions here as a catalyst.[6] What did these cases cause, besides a bad balance sheet; destruction of capital and jobs; trust gambled away; the end of a few careers; and the already economically and politically fragile constitution of the Weimar Republic being exposed to a further ordeal?

If in this article the collapse of the second largest German insurance company, the largest textile and largest brewing combine (Konzern) are treated as the most prominent of the business scandals of the Weimar Republic, then it is because they clearly had the most damaging impact on the economy. Moreover, they differ from other business group crises of the time in one important way, which is often referred to in the same breath as these scandals:[7] Favag, Nordwolle and Schultheiss resulted in courts cases. The criminal proceedings in turn meant that public attention prolonged. The necessity of a legal reappraisal lent the then as now often too quickly expressed accusation of a 'scandal' a certain justification.

THE SCANDAL COMPANIES: SOLIDITY AND MEGALOMANIA

I

The origin of Favag was a glass insurance society founded in 1865, which Paul Dumcke, member since 1892 and chairman of the board since 1897, wanted to turn into the largest German insurance company. Dumcke was the 'business motor of expansion,'[8] and he created from a multiple branched society, which in 1911 took on the name Frankfurter Allgemeine Versicherungs-AG, the second largest German insurance business until the outbreak of the war. In 1914 Favag, with a capital of 20.5 million mark, stood in first place of the German property insurers. Measured on the premium acquisitions – the more significant indicator for the size of the insurance business – Favag was half as large as Allianz.

During the period of inflation, Favag proceeded with its expansion course. The foreign shares and the increasing activities in the transport insurance business provided financial backing for further activities. Companies in south-eastern Europe and in Switzerland were added, and Favag took over the Karlsruher Lebensversicherungsbank, die Vereinigte Berlinische und Preußische Leben and the 'Hammonia' Allgemeine Versicherungs AG in Hamburg. Among the larger companies that belonged to the Favag were also the Helios Rückversicherung, the Nürnberger Leben and the Aachen-Leipziger. The gross premium incomes of Favag were in 1928 at 80.7 million Reichsmark, of Allianz at 178 million – the life insurance portion achieved with 1,656 million almost the size of the branch star Allianz, which after its merger with the Stuttgarter Verein weighed in at 2055 million.[9]

When the chairman Paul Dumcke died on 14 February 1929 at the age of seventy years, the future of Favag seemed to be quite in order. One of the obituaries claimed: 'The future historian of the development of the German private insurance industry of the last fifty years will list Dumcke's name among the first, and will have to name him as one of the men who prepared the way for the modern economic reorganization and the introduction of big companies in the insurance trade.'[10]

Six months before the collapse of the business group, apparently nobody outside of the closed board knew that the gold mark opening account balance of 1924 was based on falsified figures.[11] The end of inflation also meant a break for insurance companies, in which the business policy had to be directed towards more careful strategies. Dumcke and his financial director Becker, who followed Dumcke as chairman and in the branch was praised as 'one of the best bank directors of Germany,' could not be won over to a policy of small steps. They wanted to continue the path of quick growth and fast profits, the price of which was of course increased risk. The board of directors roped in Favag with newly founded subsidiaries in numerous financial non-insurance practices, including especially the installment plan – already established in the United States for the prefinancing of goods – which brought in ever larger losses. As an expert accurately concluded in a later trial, Favag had become a 'financial house of cards' in which the management, bypassing the supervisory board, reigned high-handedly in a 'mess of businesses' in consortia and non-transparent limited companies, which did not publish account balances. Of the complex building of sixty four companies of Favag and a further nineteen companies which were only controlled by the executive board were among other things three instalment plan businesses, several Frankfurt private banking companies such as the Südwestdeutsche Bank A.G., which – most unusual for a financial company – entered the money market as credit seekers.[12]

The circumstances for the disclosure of the financial disaster of Favag were curious and does not speak well of the members of the supervisory board or of the supervising authority of the governmental Reichsaufsichtsamt für Versicherungswesen. Even if Favag was officially regarded as a solid business right up until its demise, whose shares on 15 August, one day before the losses became generally known, were quoted at 221 per cent (885 mark), thus a good tenth above the average rate, information had been circulating at least since the new year 1929 which seriously called the standing of the business' administration into question. Artur Lauinger, member of the economic editorial office of the *Frankfurter Zeitung*, played a key role in the disclosure. He described in his memoirs how even before Dumcke's death, the businesses practices which were atypical for an insurance company were being discusses on the stock market. Based on this, he decided to 'get to the bottom of these things.' He was strengthened in this resolution even more when one day the director of the Frankfurt branch of a major German bank walked in and, showing him a bond issued by Dumcke, asked 'if such a bond could be discounted.'[13] Lauinger reported having responded,

...he should know that better than I, particularly since his bank sat on and could vote in the supervisory board of the 'Frankfurter Allgemeine Versicherungs-A.G.,' so that he should be better informed than I about the company. My opinion was at any rate that an insurance company that after all is or at least should be an exceptional reservoir of capital never should attract money from outside the company, be it through the acquisition of bank debts or through the issue of bonds. I further explained that banks should in no way support such a business policy through discounting of bonds, and that I planned to take Mr. Paul Dumcke, the chairman, to task for this and ask for an explanation. Interestingly, the response was: 'You are in for a surprise.'[14]

Dumcke disputed any irregularities and in response to Lauinger's demand 'for complete transparency about the amount of acquired funds, their purpose, and the amount of guaranties and securities issued,' suggested a discussion with Dumcke's financial director Becker. Lauinger wrote further that he had no other choice but to wait for the meeting with Becker, 'because I was afraid to take a public stance in the newspaper before having attempted every possibility of receiving an explanation from the company's administration.'[15]

Certainly in the months before the collapse there was no lack of warning signs clear enough for those interested to see them. The *Magazin der Wirtschaft* of 22 March 1928 noted of the Südwestdeutche Bank that it would have to show in the future if the existence of a bank under the roof of the company didn't lead 'to an excessive emphasis of banking business, and with this a distraction from its actual obligations.'[16] Even clearer was the *Frankfurter Zeitung* of 2 June 1929, when Lauinger complained of the company report for Favag that its banking and credit businesses were not transparent. Thus he stated that the company report – in contradiction to every reality, as it soon turned out – which claimed net profits of 3.1 million 'did not satisfy the need for sufficient information.'[17] On June 18 the administration declared at its regular general meeting the intention to distribute a dividend of twelve and a half per cent of the net profit.[18] At this time, the internal audit commission of the supervisory board, which in the spring after Dumcke's death had been called in to investigate the rumours of irregularities in business procedures, did not yet have results in hand and possibly had not even begun its investigation yet. The events then occurred rapid-fire in August when the special commission found indications of the actual losses.[19] Lauinger received a telegram from the company at his vacation spot in the Black Forest, inviting him to a special session of the supervisory board in Frankfurt:

The time had come. I was asked to a supervisory board session of the 'Frankfurter Allgemeine Versicherungs-A.G.' – quite an unusual occurrence – and found the management in heavy consternation, the supervisory board in dissolution. The representatives of the big banks and other large banking houses in the commission of the supervisory board asked for my counsel. I demanded the presentation of an accurate balance sheet and the ascertainment of the responsibility for the obvious catastrophe of the company...[20]

On 16 August the *Frankfurter Zeitung* reported considerable losses, although the survival of the Favag was not yet called into question. Three days later, in light of the first figures for the amount of the problematic liabilities, which were estimated to be at least 160 million Reichsmark, of which 40 million was apportioned to foreign creditors, the newspaper judged that the continued independent survival of the Favag could no longer be considered feasible. In the meanwhile, the head office of Allianz had announced a guaranty for all liabilities which had resulted directly from the insurance business of Favag. The supervisory board of Favag had no other choice but to agree to the offer of Allianz on 20 August, who thereby took over the entire insurance holdings of its competitor, while the other affected banks had to create a guaranty consortium for the financial debts of the business group. The mountain of debts was taxed a few months later at 241 million.[21]

The fact that the insured came away without serious consequences after the collapse of Favag was thanks to the quick intervention of Allianz, which, however, had already been considering a co-operation or a takeover for a long time.[22] The 'Black Friday' of the German insurance business was not only the first in the round of major financial scandals of the Weimar Republic, it was one of the biggest losses for banks in regular credit business, 'the first forecast of the big crisis,' the 'prelude for the decline in trust of foreign creditors.'[23] These judgements do not appear to be exaggerated: the scandal surrounding Favag marked 'almost precisely the link between the phase of stabilisation and the descent into the financial crisis.'[24]

II

When it became known in July 1931 that Nordwolle was no longer tenable, the public's memory of Favag's ruin was immediately reawakened. The 'Nordwolle Case' appeared to contemporary observers to be a new production of the Frankfurt drama, from comparable scale and economic implications as well as having a similar cast of lead characters. On the other hand, the supervisory board had tolerated an absolutist management whose good name was certainly beyond all reproach. Even more than the head of Favag, the Bremen patrician family Lahusen enjoyed limitless prestige. The Lahusens and the Norddeutsche Wollkämmerei and Kammgarnspinnerei A.G. stood for wealth, industrial competence, solidity and credit worthiness.[25]

The Bremen business family Lahusen had been an important figure in Bremen's oversees trade since the 1840s, although they specialised themselves in South American business as of 1853, and after the acquisition of Argentine properties they concentrated on wool importation. In 1873 they ventured the leap into the processing of wool with the purchase of a wool cleaning and carding shop in Bohemian Neudek. Thereafter the business interests of the family shifted from trade to industry. In 1884, Nordwolle was successfully founded as a joint-stock company in Delmenhorst. A year later it merged with Neudek. With a policy of rapid acquisition, in a decade Nordwolle became one of the largest wool processing combines in Europe. In 1913 Nordwolle counted 8,000 employees, and its share capital amounted to 22.5 million mark.[26]

Since 1920, with Gustav Carl, Lahusen the third generation determined Nordwolle's business policy. He relentlessly continued his father's expansion policy, but serious mistakes occurred under his leadership, so that here, too – as with Favag – the course towards an economic collapse of the business group had already been set some years earlier. The largest expansion followed in the years 1927 and 1928, during the good years of the Weimar economy, when the Nordwolle management changed from a previously horizontal expansion to a vertical one, taking over end-production factories, and with them defaulting clients, introducing them into the newly formed subsidiaries Toga Vereinigte Webereien A.G. and Alrowa Deutsche Strickerei A.G. The share capital of Nordwolle was raised to 75 million Reichsmark. Thus Nordwolle was by far the largest combine in the German textile industry. Including open reserves, the balance sheet of 1928 showed company capital of 101.3 million,[27] although liabilities at the end of 1928 had actually grown to 124 million Reichsmark.

Retrospective analyses of the business management up to the collapse have assigned the management of Nordwolle a mixture of megalomania, incorrigible optimism, stubbornness, and a failure to face reality.[28] The business economist Wilhelm Kalveram, who served as an evaluator for the bankruptcy proceedings that began in July 1931, saw the vertical expansion as one of the crucial administrative mistakes. Kalveram remarked that 'increase in turnover at any price' was enforced by taking over dependent, economically weak customers 'without the advisable practice of taking into consideration the customers on the open market and the existing market conditions'. In so doing one did not consider that price discounts and subsidies which had to be continually granted to the annexed processing factories affected a 'dangerous dumping' towards the other solid customers.[29]

This was not the only area into which the Nordwolle management had sunk millions of marks. The speculation conducted by Lahusen on the price of wool was fatal, which he counted on increasing in price in spite of its continuous fall since 1927. In the business reports of 1928 and 1929, the Lahusen announced the approaching end of the price descent, and in light of this assumption, the stock of raw materials was continually enlarged in order to be able to profit from the expected price increases. The announced upward trend in price never manifested itself, though. Instead the wool quotations continued to fall, without the management of Nordwolle rectifying its balance sheets. Additionally, the Lahusens, who never failed to remark in every business report that the general wage-tariff was a misfortune for the German economy, instigated a costly labour dispute in their factories, which resulted in a loss of production for several months. At the same time the company erected a new administrative headquarter in Bremen, which surpassed the initial cost estimate of 3 million three-fold. During the ensuing trial, G. Carl Lahusen was asked if this project didn't represent an obsession with grandeur. His justification for the size of the selected construction site was almost naive, stating that it had resulted 'from fencing off the four streets.'[30]

What made the 'Nordwolle Case' a scandal was the proof that the balance sheets had been falsified, thus year after year concealed the increasing losses. Dividends and percentages were paid out in the years 1926–28 on the share capital in the sum of 25 million along with the payment of a corporation tax of approximately 4 million based on fictitious profits. Not until 1929, a 'catastrophic year for the wool world,' did the accounts balance for the first time note a loss of 2 million. In this balance sheet, the value of the wool supply was estimated far too high, and a sum of 92 million Reichsmark was recorded under debtors, which contained claims of wares owed by a Dutch company.[31]

The bank director Max Doerner discovered the role that this company played in the consistent balance falsification of Lahusens on 7 May 1931. Doerner was entrusted with the assignment of auditing by Danatbank, the company's bank and the consortium director in the summer of 1930, but was strung along for almost a year until Lahusen finally provided him with the first honest figures.[32] The N.V. Handels-Maatschappij Ultra Mare was founded by Nordwolle in the period of inflation in order to relieve the foreign exchange circulation. It functioned at first only as a clearing-house of the business group companies, but as of 1926 was systematically used to improve the German accounts balance of Nordwolle. Furthermore, it served as a concealed collecting point for the tax relief of the company's own stocks and speculations on them – as well as for concealed withdrawals and credits.[33] The excessive debts of Nordwolle were noticed so late primarily because Nordwolle had always worked very much with foreign capital in order to prefinance the annual production of stock. The actual dimensions slowly turned into a problematic overall situation of foreign credit, finally making its way to the public. On 18 June the business announced a loss of 24.05 million, followed daily by increasingly higher estimates. On 24 June the trade press named the existence of the 'Ultra-

Mare,' and on 7 July, a few days before the eruption of the banking crisis, the total losses of Nordwolle were listed publicly at 240 million, a sum which had been fixed in a financial statement at the end of June.[34]

As the trigger for the credit crisis in July 1931, the 'Nordwolle Case' was from the beginning a political issue of the first degree. This was first of all true for the mistrust that spread like wildfire among foreign creditors, who upon learning of the difficulties of the large German textile business group withdrew their credit on a large scale, thus contributing to the dynamic of the events in July, during which time Danatabank had to close its counters forever.[35] Many commentators at this time thought ahead, though, concerned about the future of the capitalist system. It called its own existence into question with such practices that made their way to the public and forced voters into the arms of the right and left edges of the party landscape. With the question 'Will capitalists wake up?' the *Frankfurter Zeitung* (10 June) predicted possible consequences of the Nordwolle scandal, finding these bitterly confirmed a year later in the Reichstag elections:

> ...it is today the case that the leaders and rulers of our capitalist machine have a unique chance – some believe their last one – to preserve and strengthen the system by a renewal of the capitalist mindset and its methods. In September 1930, a little less than half of all those persons entitled to vote slated their vote against the capitalist system and for some version of socialism. If elections were today, the number of radical opponents would probably now be much higher.[36]

The claim of a direct connection between the effects of the business scandals among the public and their later voting behaviour must of course remain speculative. However, the next in the rounds of major financial scandals clearly added fuel to the flames of extremist propaganda. This was even more the case since the excitement about the dramatic events in the summer months had just died down. Furthermore, the emergency decree to reform the share laws and account audits that had been passed in late September promised a fundamental improvement of the situation. Now, Jewish board members, too, as main persons in a financial affair became targets for right-wing propaganda.

III

As the prime culprit in the 'Schultheiss Scandal,' which came out into the open during late October 1931, Ludwig Katzenellenbogen was considered to be the 'financial acrobat who, with his sly transactions, captivated and stole the breath from directors of the German big banks, the stock exchange, and the public for a decade,' one of 'the few profiteers of the inflation who have thus far been able to maintain their standard.'[37]

Katzenellenbogen came from Krotoschin in the province of Posen, son of a
respected and branched-out Jewish family. Having taken over the direction
of his father's Breslau alcohol refinery in 1903, with a series of clever
moves he turned it in to a promising conglomerate. In April 1921 the
parent company Breslauer Spritfabrik was turned into a holding company,
hereafter called Ostwerke A.G. and whose home office was transferred to
Berlin. Within a few years, Ostwerke controlled the equity holdings of
Katzenellenbogen in the Silesian brewing, mill and cement industries, in
machine construction and in glass and bottle production. In the same
month, Ostwerke entered with Schultheiss-Patzenhofer brewery of Berlin
into an alliance of mutual interests. The Schultheiss Brauerei A.G. had
already acquired brewery property in Silesia before the war and in July
1920, under the direction of the chairman Walter Sobernheim, advanced
to the largest brewery in Berlin after the merger with the Patzenhofer
Brauerei. The connection to Katzenellenbogen, who shortly before had
entered the Berlin beverage industry through an alliance with Kahlbaum,
came about by the initiative of Sobernheim's stepfather Eugen Landau.
Landau, who came from Breslau, worked as a financial and industrial
expert, and was active in the clubs and numerous supervisory boards as a
'business mediator of grand style.'[38] Landau and Walter Sobernheim, whose
brother Curt belonged to the board of the Commerz- and Privatbank,
belonged to the capital's respected Jewish business elite.[39]

The essential element of the strategic alliance that was renewed in July
1926 consisted of pooling the annual profits of Ostwerke and Schultheiss-
Patzenhofer Brauerei and dividing them up according to a ratio of two-
thirds of the total amount for Schultheiss and one-third for Ostwerke. The
increasingly close co-operation between both companies, manifested by
such elements as Schultheiss-Patzenhofer taking over the brewery shares of
Ostwerke, led in September 1930 to the decision of a complete merger.
The account balance of Ostwerke on 31 August 1930, which Schultheiss
enclosed with its annual report of 1929/30, closed with an account balance of 78,429,692 Reichsmark. The legal reserves were given as 15.2
million, the bank debts and the bank credits each as 12 million, the
outstanding accounts as 14.7 and the securities as 49.5 million
Reichsmark.[40] The majority of these figures were pure fiction, feigning a
liquidity that was non-existent. The missing true value of the Ostwerke
account balance was later excused with the explanation that because of
the retroactive decision to merge dated from 30 September 1929, the
balance was no longer approved by Ostwerke's official boards and therefore 'only had informational character.'[41] No one seemed to be bothered
by the fact that this account balance was included in the stock-exchange
prospectus which as a result of the capital increase of Schultheiss by
offering new stocks was legally required. In the March 1931 published

prospect, which was more importantly signed by the banks represented in the supervisory board, some of the joint ventures were listed whose only purpose was to administer the company's own stocks.[42] However, nothing indicated the extent and losses of the speculative activities of Katzenellenbogen in Schultheiss stocks, although when the prospectus was published, Walter Sobernheim and the other members of the board were completely aware of them, and the representatives of Danatbank and Commerzbank sitting on the supervisory board of Schultheiss were at least partially informed of the situation. Katzenellenbogen's costly stock-exchange manoeuvres, whose goal was ultimately to gain the stock majority for Schultheiss but resulted in ever larger losses due to the falling exchange rate, caused the scandal, whose circumstances and details were more embarrassing than the now notorious mistakes and negligence of Favag and Nordwolle. The public was just as surprised at the 'Schultheiss case' as at its predecessors in the chronicle of scandal, because the popular Berlin brewing group was 'always believed to be a wonderfully sound big business that nothing could happen to.'[43]

As the leading bank of Schultheiss-Patzenhofer, including Danatbank and Commerzbank in the case of Ostwerke, the Deutsche Bank as early as 1928 had inspired a consortium in order to buy stocks of both companies with the goal of price support. Intervention purchases in a company's own stocks was neither an offence nor unusual. The stock-exchange quotations continued to turn downwards, providing again and again reason to make selected purchases in order to stabilise the market value of a company. This was increasingly the case as of late summer in 1929, when the scandal surrounding Favag resulted in a sharpened reflux of German stocks in foreign possession and the Berlin Stempelvereinigung publicly considered creating a general consortium to buy German stocks.[44] Given this situation, Katzenellenbogen obviously easily made the decision to move further creditors to his accounts for the purchase of Ostwerke and Schultheiss stocks, and then also – unbeknownst to the management – to move them to the account of Schultheiss. Although the official consortium ended its official activities in 1929, the board director of Ostwerke, whose financial assets were overestimated, instructed Danatbank as well as a consortium founded in Amsterdam – made up of one of the Eidgenössische Bank in Zürich, the Hugo Kaumann & Co's Bank in Amsterdam and the Trust- en Administratiekantoor 'Aquila' – to purchase further stocks. Behind the Dutch-Swiss consortium were the Commerz- and Privatbank, since they had the majority of stocks for the Hugo Kaumann bank, while these in turn controlled several business shares of 'Aquila.' The securities purchases on the Berlin stock-exchange were 'concluded preferably by mediation of Commerzbank.'[45] Through Danatbank, up until the beginning of 1931 Katzenellenbogen had acquired nominally a total of 10.3 million

Reichsmark Schultheiss stocks for the price of 31 million, and through Commerzbank nominally 4.7 million at the cost price of 13.8 million Reichsmark. Although these figures already resulted in a loss of almost 30 million, the debts continued to climb from month to month, especially since the exchange rate of Schultheiss stocks fell from 265 per cent at the end of 1929 to 162 per cent at the end of 1930 and after a brief interlude of increases in March, plummeted further until being below par in early September.[46] Goldschmidt and Reinhart, the representatives of Danatbank and Commerzbank on the supervisory board of Schultheiss, claimed after the disclosure of the speculations not to have known or noticed anything about the stock purchases of each other. The Schultheiss board received actually one year before the unveiling of the scandal information about Katzenellenbogen's stock activities, when Danatbank announced in a communication of September 9, 1928 that the company's books presently showed a charge of 25 million. Walter Sobernheim, who after the merger shared the chairmanship with Katzenellenbogen, stated during the trail that he felt as if he had been 'struck by lightening.'[47] He then gave in to the 'siren song' of Katzenellenbogen, who continued to count on a successful end to his stock speculations, had placed his entire personal estate at risk and convinced the entire board not to inform the supervisory board yet. At the crisis meeting of the supervisory board on 23 October 1931, a week after Katzenellenbogen and Sobernheim had finally given up their reserve towards the chairman of the supervisory board von Stauß, Sobernheim justified his decision to remain silent:

> I would like to expressly note that I am not of the opinion that Mr. Ludwig Katzenellenbogen was attempting to draw personal gains from this, but rather it was just that his attitude was very optimistic. We took the view that – otherwise we would have gone to the supervisory board earlier – this very wealthy gentleman with all of his connections would be capable of relieving us of the stocks with limited damaged for us, for the company, I mean.[48]

The material damage for Schultheiss was considerable, but it was not as high as had been the case for Favag or Nordwolle. The continued independent existence of the company could be assured, although Katzenellenbogen's fortunes were destroyed and his career ended. In the cleaned-up account balance for Schultheiss for the business year 1930/31, 23 million Reichsmark had to be paid off from the stock purchases and 63 million was written off as shares and outstanding debts. The stock capital of the still largest German brewery had fallen in July 1932 to 41.4 million.

IV

Contemporary investigations by the economic press of the reasons for the crises consistently blamed the 'business group mania' the attempts of chairmen – trained under the conditions of inflation – to keep companies on a course of unconditional expansion and to ensure the reign over companies through the ownership or purchase of the stock majority at any price. This usually meant the absence of a healthy, harmonious structure of the combines, as the cases clearly showed. Instead, a non-transparent jumble of encapsulations and shares was erected, as characterised by so many of the 'Inflationskonzerne', that for the most part failed miserably by the end of the decade.

The Nordwolle was a mature company and not a product of the period of inflation, but the vertical expansion in end-production in the years of 'dastardly optimism' after the stock upturn of 1926[49] contributed decidedly to the financial collapse. Nordwolle had simply grown too big, and its largely independently operating affiliated companies, which were forced to react quickly to the ever-changing trends, were forced into the corset of a central arrangement of buying, selling and scrutiny, which did not allow for the extremely necessary manoeuvrability.

Katzenellenbogen's multi-branched holding included numerous non-characteristic shares, a 'mixed ware shop,' for which the shares in the glass and bottles manufacturer Siemens-Glas and in the Norddeutsche Hefeindustrie (yeast production) made sense from the point of view of a beverage combine. Others areas were harder to justify, such as the bought-up shares in machine and construction engineering, the purchased shares in the Silesian cement industry – bought with the help of the private banker Alfred Jarislowsky – or the stock portfolio of the Mitteldeutsche Creditbank that was maintained until it was taken over by the Commerzbank.

The contemporary trade press had for years before Favag's collapse been very critical of its working in non-insurance areas. A clear indication of financial activities that had nothing to do with insurance *per se* came about from the shares in the Südwestdeutsche Bank and other financial companies through which the board conducted its dubious transactions. According to Arps, the cautious and critical observers should have come to the conclusion,

> ...that no clear insurance policy concept stood behind the extension of Favag. The only goal to be seen was pure enlargement, ruling for the sake of ruling. ... Before those companies brought together in the group of businesses up until the end of Inflation set about to harmonize the insurance concept, the purchase of shares continued, although the question was still in last place of whether and how the purchased companies fit into the business group, whose business policy was still unorganized.[50]

On the other hand, the self-confident chairmen of the boards of those scandal businesses – Dumcke and Becker, Lahusens and Katzenellenbogen – bubbled over with optimism at the business situation and the future economic developments. Their positions in the financial landscape and their apparently successful courses of growth lent them credibility, which also prevented an open criticism on the business management up until the end. As late as 3 January 1931, Katzenellenbogen used the general meeting of Schultheiss for the declaration that he and his colleagues on the board were not seized by a 'pessimism psychosis.' As long as the other shareholders and creditors believed this picture of a solid brewing company that year after year put forth profits and dividends, critical concerns about questionable holdings or unprofessional business practices were kept at bay.[51]

Even the director of Nordwolle was characterized as a 'born bull' and 'incorrigible optimist,'[52] with whom reality caught up at the height of his career. On 1 January 1931, G. Carl Lahusen had taken over the presidency of the Bremen Handelskammer, and Jakob Goldschmidt, whose bank had become the largest creditor of Nordwolle, noted for the protocol of the subsequent trial that Lahusen 'always so self-confidently' defended his position, and 'that it took quite a bit of forcing oneself to be critical with Lahusen' to talk with him about the business.[53] In response to the question if he had ever considered the possibility that Lahusen had not been honest with him, Goldschmidt was quoted with the statement that he considered it impossible, '... that a man from this tradition, from this familial pride and familial self-containment could do something of that nature. Do not forget that I am not good enough to just be able to associate as an equal with the society of this gentlemen.'[54]

Obviously, such statements served towards personal defence and a weakening of personal responsibility, of which the economic press and the public were unwilling to overlook its insufficient, if not negligent practice. The formula, which Curt Sobernheim, the representative of Commerzbank in the supervisory board of Favag, used to comment on the scandal cases contained a grain of truth, but it was too simple: '[I]t has become obvious that in all the big collapses of the last years, there has been a personality in each of the affected firms who had everyone in his pocket, including the supervisory board and the board of directors.'[55]

What the critical observers of these incidents missed was a statement that did not focus on helplessness and impotence and would explain the lack of resistance on the part of inspectors and creditors to be put in somebody's pocket. By at least the impression of events in the Schultheiss affair, the business scandals of the Weimar Republic had been declared a 'Case of Big Bank Directors'[56], whose passivity in the supervisory boards was considered to be just as reprehensible as the now public activities of individual offenders on the boards. However, at no time were the supervisory boards exposed to such criticism as their insufficient ability to act being an educational or cultural problem which made the German financial elite look shabby compared with their Anglo-Saxon counterparts. It was claimed that in London or New York, no leading banker or industrialist could 'afford disrespectful ignorance of all things political ... which is practically good form in the leadership of the German economy.'[57] Whether or not the sharp criticism of the 'impossibly clueless' bank directors[58] on the supervisory boards is justified will be considered in the last section.

THE GUILT OF THE BANKS

According to an inquiry about the bank credit of the committee for the investigation of manufacturing and sales conditions of the German economy, the loans of Berlin big banks with their branch network at the end of 1928 were as follows: five point seven per cent of the total amount of granted loans went to the mining industry, four point two per cent to the chemical industry, two point two percent to the businesses of machine engineering and vehicle manufacture, only 1.1 per cent to the electronic, optical and precision engineering industries, but twelve point eight per cent to the food, and 13.6 per cent to the textile industry.[59] The literature on this subject even characterises the attitude readable from these figures of the big banks to loans as 'something grandmother-like.' The directors of big banks tended towards safety, never towards risk. Business in the brewing industry and textile trades was considered as particularly 'safe', whose stocks even the grandmothers used to buy on the stock-exchange.[60]

Since insurance companies *per se* radiated quite a high degree of solidity and liquidity, the careless awarding of credit and the exceedingly negligent supervision of management at Favag, Nordwolle and Schultheiss in no way indicated a tendency towards risk on the part of the banks. On the contrary, it was a manifestation of an entirely absent or at best very weakly developed awareness of risks. The large amount of faith in the individual branches does not however adequately establish reasons for the absolute inactivity of the supervisory boards of the scandal companies in the face of the newspapers' reports, rumours at the stock exchange or discussions in their social circles.

One determining factor must be seen in the limited scope of action possessed by the representatives of the big banks, brought about through intense rivalry among themselves and the temporary competition with foreign creditors. The collapse of Favag had already exposed an essential problem of the German banks. With a solid reputation and with bank guaranties, big business could access foreign creditors without great difficulties up until 1929, and these in turn did not particularly bother 'to bring in German banks as intermediaries or even to consult them for advice and information.'[61] The problem of insufficient information was accompanied by the pressure of competition among the German big banks.

There is every reason to believe that up until the salutary shock of the summer of 1931, the everywhere visible and never-ending rivalries among the big banks in these scandal cases prevented not only a concerted action by creditors but also an early intervention and limiting of the damages.

The bank rivalries at Favag even interfered with the authority of the supervisory board, since the Berlin big banks could not agree on a chairman from their ranks – not even on a private banker of a Frankfurt oder Berlin house. The final compromise candidate – at the request of the board of directors – was the Frankfurter businessman Adolf Hoff, who was entirely out of his league among all the complicated legal, financial and insurance questions. Furthermore, he did not possess the least amount of authority to put critical questions to the practically self-ruling management. His 'meagre cognitive faculty,' as was determined in the trial, even protected Hoff from criminal prosecution, although he had always signed everything put before him, including quite a few blank powers of authority.[62] The supervisory board representatives of the big banks did not take second place to Hoff in the question of responsibility, though, since they had been too willing to believe whatever the board of directors presented with figures, especially if these showed profits. After Dumcke's death, Kurt Schmitt of Allianz called on Hoff's acting representative Sigmund Bodeheimer of Danatbank in order to talk with him about the arrangement for a successor. When he took this opportunity to express his critical attitude to Becker, Bodeheimer let him know, '...he knew the circumstances perfectly, and the financial businesses of the Frankfurt branch also were running profitably. If the banks weren't in agreement with all the business transactions, there was still no doubt that Frankfurt was a first-class company that earned well and was making progress.'[63]

The scandal cases also delivered several lessons about self-confident heads of business being about to turn the rivalries among the big banks to their own advantages. Contemporary observers generally pointed to the inactivity and naiveté of creditors, but they also showed sympathy for being in a weak position. In the journal *Die Bank*, an author concluded that, in the case of Lahusen, one should not incorrectly judge the prevailing power relationships between the board 'of a global company' like Nordwolle and the supervisory board. According to the law, he went on, the supervisory board did have far-reaching powers of authority, but de facto 'companies with such international prestige quickly replace a difficult, inspection-mad supervisory board member with another, and if he represents a bank, the company quickly changes banks.'[64] How realistic such a threat was at Nordwolle is not known. However, the example of the Dresdner Bank demonstrates that it was extremely desirous of entering into business with Nordwolle. Until the summer of 1930, the Dresdner Bank had made available a credit of 12 million to Nordwolle. The raising of the credit limit by another 16 million ensued with the entry of the Dresdner Bank board member Paul Schmidt-Branden to the supervisory board of Nordwolle. In the competition for the good addresses in the industry, a competitor of Danatbank paid dearly for this view towards closer business relationships.[65]

Wherever competition reigned, it was standard procedure to withhold information. This occurred in the Schultheiss scandal, where neither the Commerzbank nor the Danatbank deemed it necessary to inform the Deutsche Bank and Disconto-Gesellschaft in their capacity as bank of the business group that, under instructions from one of the two board directors, they participated in stock purchases on a large scale that went to the liabilities of the company. The competition mindset was omnipresent in the Schultheiss case, even before Katzenellenbogen had granted his problem-filled purchase orders to both consortia. In a protocol about the possibility of a merger between Ostwerke and Schultheiss, von Stauss noted a sentence in October 1927 that specified the worry about faster competitors:

> Katzenellenbogen will most likely return with his old plan to (since he now needs money for the payment of the young stocks) sell his approx. nom. 4 million Mitteldeutsche Creditbank stocks to Ostwerke, which I have of course thus far refused. But someone will probably help him to accept these of the Ostwerke stock as collateral. *If we don't do it, Jacob Goldschmidt will.*[66]

Even the DD-Bank had its part in the Schultheiss affair, because it could not and didn't want to stand on the sidelines as Katzenellenbogen's creditor. For one thing, one of the subordinate companies, the Katzenellenbogen Familien GmbH, which controlled the shares of the of the Ostwerke empire, was extremely indebted to the bank. Additionally, the trade press reported a 10 million credit to the subsidiary Norddeutsche Hefeindustrie, which von Stauß had pushed through.[67] Katzenellenbogen's defense insisted that the leading bank for Schultheiss, which went behind the backs of the other banks, had no reason to behave as a judge, working from the motto 'Dishonesty is when the other does it.' Furthermore, the defense continued, in spite of the self-interested and concealed credit activities of the competition, all the big banks acted similarly. After all, the DD-Bank didn't let the profit from the first consortium business escape either. Any anyway, the company bank should be criticizing itself, since its supervision had failed: 'If Mr. von Stauß had paid more attention, he would have learned what kind of consortia the so-called secret consortia were. The DD-Bank has 150 representatives in supervisory boards.'[68]

The directors of the Danatbank also preferred to assign the leading bank the role of scapegoat. During a session break of the supervisory board on the first day of crisis after the disclosure of the losses to the secret consortia, Goldschmidt supposedly said that while in the official explanation the bank was hypocritical, it had been 'seen as going without saying' that the chair of Schultheiss had informed the DD-Bank of the stock transactions:[69] this was nothing more than as with the planned Salzdetfurth stock purchases by Solmssen 'without the knowledge of other board members.' He had 'accepted this without even a protest,' even though he functioned as the acting representative of the supervisory board chairman in that company.[70]

Even if accurate reconstructions of the state of knowledge and the conscious withholding of information in these scandal cases were hardly possible, the public reaction did not find the justification strategies and the mutual accusations of guilt among the big banks credible. The ruling opinion was that those bank directors in question could 'impossibly have been clueless' because they were omnipresent in the supervisory boards. The reports and comments of the economic press were most outraged over the 'interrelatedness and amalgamation of business and private friendships.'[71] It was seen as less significant that the way in which bankers executed the supervision of their creditors revealed less their power than their impotence. The reciprocal intertwining between representatives of the Bremer Wirtschaft and Danatbank had already been conspicuous at Nordwolle. This stemmed from the Bremen source of the Berlin big bank, which in 1920 had resulted from the merger of the Deutsche Nationalbank in Bremen with the Nationalbank in Berlin and – two years later – with the Darmstädter Bank. Even more conspiratorial seemed the relationship entanglement of Katzenellenbogen, whose connections to Commerzbank were so close and numerous that they appeared to be almost predestined towards the culmination of secret purchase orders. Until 1929, Ludwig Katzenellenbogen's nephew Albert belonged to the board of directors of the Mitteldeutsche Commerzbank alongside with Friedrich Reinhart, in which Ostwerke temporarily was active as principal shareholder. After the merger of their bank with Commerzbank, both changed over to its board. Reinhart represented the interests of Commerzbank in the supervisory board of Schultheiss. Walter and Curt Sobernheim, the one on the board of directors of Schultheiss, the other on the board of directors of Commerzbank, were brothers. Their stepfather Eugen Landau, who had prepared the 'marriage' between Ludwig Katzenellenbogen and Walter Sobernheim, handed over to von Stauß the supervisory board chairmanship after Ostwerke had merged with Schultheiss, but maintained his function as acting chairman on the supervisory board of Commerzbank. Against the background of this network of familial and business interests, Reinhart, as responsible representative of Commerzbank, almost had no choice but to become the object of public criticism, which his bank with extremely weak arguments tried to refute.[72]

In conclusion, a more lenient judgment of the 'banks' guilt' seems appropriate than was usually expressed in the majority of contemporary reactions. Certainly, the affected banks and some of their lead actors gave themselves the bad image of having acted out of clumsiness, negligence and elbow-room mentality. But their behaviour resulted more from a position of weakness in a competition which encouraged rather than prevented such abuses. Not until the influence of the deep financial and confidence crises of the summer of 1931, to which the collapses of Favag and the ruin of Nordwolle contributed with their dangerous signal for the safety of foreign credit, did the intense competition mentality among the big banks make room for a more cautious harmonising of interests. After free market conditions, regulated competition followed, which influenced the relationships among the big banks in the following years and decades. Even if the business scandals can be categorised as spectacular individual cases that were only possible because respected and highly trusted business accumulated enormous losses because of bad decisions which were then usually covered up, the opinion has gained acceptance that not only the blame of the individual but also 'mistakes in the system' were at fault. Especially in the 'question of the supervisory boards' and the elimination of the long-discussed deficiencies in stock regulations, the business scandals have brought about movement. When the German bank president Luther described the situation of Nordwolle at the German government ministerial meeting of 1 July 1931, the government decided to try and prevent the repeat of such an incident by pushing through a reform of share law, which had been sitting in the drawers of ministerial bureaucracy for months. Surprisingly fast, on 19 September, the 'Reform of Share Law within the Framework of Emergency Regulation about Share Law, Bank Supervision and Tax Amnesty' went into effect, whose regulations aimed at the elimination of those abuses which had been practiced by Favag, Nordwolle and shortly thereafter Schultheiss.[73]

NOTES

1. Frankfurter Allgemeine Zeitung, 31 October 1997.
2. Martin Rhodes and Bastiaan van Apedoorn, 'Capitalism versus capitalism in Western Europe,' in Martin Rhodes et al. (eds.), *Developments in West European Politics* (London, 1997), pp. 171–89, here p. 178.
3. Gustav Stolper, 'Finanzskandale,' in *Der deutsche Volkswirt* (6/1, 1931/32), pp. 179–81, here p. 179.
4. Gerald D. Feldmann, 'Jakob Goldschmidt: The History of the Banking Crisis of 1931 and the Problem of Freedom of Manoeuvre in the Weimar Republic,' in Christoph Buchheim et al. (eds.), *Zerissene Zwischenkriegszeit – Wirtschaftshistorische Beiträge. Festschrift für Knut Borchardt zum 65. Geburtstag* (Baden-Baden, 1994), pp. 307–27, here p. 327. This statement

corresponds to the conclusion made almost twenty years earlier by Borchardt that in general 'the crises of companies that occurred further back have been more concretely examined than those of the twentieth century, for which general economic explanations often stand in for the actual histories of the companies.' Knut Borchardt, 'Wirtschaftliche Krisen als Gegenstand der Unternehmensgeschichte,' in *Zeitschrift für Unternehmensgeschichte* (22, 1977), pp. 81–91, p. 85.

5. Gerald Feldman, 'Die Deutsche Bank vom Ersten Weltkrieg bis zur Weltwirtschaftskrise 1914–1933,' in *Die Deutsche Bank 1870–1995* (Munich, 1995), pp. 271–314, here p. 276.

6. Cf. Borchardt, 'Wirtschaftliche Krisen,' p. 88, where the 'learning from earlier crises' is identified as the first reason for insisting on taking more notice of crises in business history. 'Institutions' is here used according to Douglass C. North's definition, as guidelines or rules of the game that serve to guarantee a stable or more stable order. The law for shareholdings followed the scandals of the first years of industrial expansion, the reserve funds for banks followed the Herstatt scandal, and a new organisation of the mortgage business of the Deutsche Bank and a reorganisation of loan allocation followed the Schneider collapse.

7. Erich W. Abraham offers a contemporary panorama of the business crises in *Konzernkrach. Hintergründe, Entwicklung und Folgen der deutschen Konzernkrisen* (Berlin, 1933). A more political scandal was the now well-known 1929 corruption affair surrounding the textile wholesaler brothers Sklarek, who forced the Berlin mayor Gustav Böß to resign. For a discussion of the Sklarek case, see Harold James, *Deutschland in der Weltwirtschaftskrise 1924–1936* (Stuttgart, 1988), p.100 f.; Stephan Malinowski, 'Politische Skandale als Zerrspiegel der Demokratie. Die Fälle Barmat und Sklarek im Kalkül der Weimarer Rechten', in *Jahrbuch für Antisemitismusforschung ,5* (1996), pp. 46–61.

8. Ludwig Arps, *Durch unruhige Zeiten. Deutsche Versicherungswirtschaft seit 1914, I. Teil: Erster Weltkrieg und Inflation* (Karlsruhe, 1970), p. 424.

9. Numbers and figures taken from: Georg Kantona, 'Der Frankfurter Versicherungs-Krach', in *Der deutsche Volkswirt*, 3, Jg., No. 47 (1929), pp. 1591–5; Frankfurter Zeitung (hereafter FZ) (No. 618, August 20, 1929); Arps, p. 424 ff.

10. Cited in Arps, p. 426.

11. According to Borscheid this was done only for reasons of prestige, 'in order to outdo Allianz.' Cf. Peter Borscheid, *100 Jahre Allianz 1890–1990, Bd. 1,* (Munich, 1990), p. 69.

12. Cf. Abraham, p. 20 ff; Borscheid, p. 68; Peter Drucker, 'Nach dem Favag-Prozeß', in *Der deutsche Volkswirt,* 6, Jg., No. 23 (4 March 1932), pp. 742–5.

13. Artur Launiger, *Das öffentliche Gewissen. Erfahrungen und Erlebnisse eines Redakteurs der Frankfurter Zeitung.* (Frankfurt, 1958), p. 19. Unfortunately the name of the banker is not known.

14. Launiger, *Das öffentliche Gewissen.* After the Favag scandal, Lauinger (1879–1961) became a member of the advisory council of the Reichsaufsichtsamt

für Versicherungswesen. Being Jewish and prohibited from practicing his profession after 1933, Lauinger was incarcerated in the Buchenwald concentration camp, but in 1939 was able to emigrate to England. He returned to Frankfurt in 1946. Cf. Wolfgang Klötzer (ed.), *Frankfurter Biographie. Personengeschichtliches Lexikon* (Frankfurt, 1994), p. 445.

15. *Das öffentliche Gewissen*, p. 20. The discussion with Becker, 'who smoothly tried to evade every question that seemed incriminating', must have taken place at the end of July or the beginning of August; that is, at least half a year after the discussion with Dumcke. Lauinger reported that he threatened to publish the unanswered questions in the *FZ* if he did not receive detailed information from the administration, and a week after this discussion the scandal surrounding Favag began to heat up.

16. Cited in Borscheid, p. 69.

17. *FZ*, no. 404, 2 June, 1929.

18. Selmar Spier, 'Der Zusammenbruch der Frankfurter Allgemeinen Versicherungs A.G. und das Aktienrecht', *Zentralblatt für Handelsrecht*, 4, Jg., No. 10 (October 1929), p.289.

19. According to Borscheid, p. 70, the internal special commission struck gold on July 29. According to Abraham, *Konzernkrach*, p. 35, the commission of the supervisory board – to which Ludwig Hahn (Deutsche Effekten- und Wechselbank), Eduard Rothschild (Deutsche Bank Frankfurt) and Sigmund Bodenheimer (Danat) belonged – did not meet until August 21, five days after the losses were made known. The date may be considered incorrect, however, since the meeting of the supervisory board described by Lauinger must have taken place before 16 August.

20. Lauinger, p. 20.

21. *FZ*, no. 613, 18 August 1929; no. 614, 19 August 1929; no. 619, 21 August 1929; Abraham, p. 36 ff.

22. Cf. the informative reflections of the board members Hilgard and Schmitt, who prepared these specifically to counter the accusation raised during the Favag trail that Allianz had forced the company to its knees in order to acquire it cheaply: BA Berlin, R 8119/ P 5785 (Deutsche Bank, Allianz). The lack of foundation for this accusation was also discussed in the summary of the *FZ* on the day after the judgement was pronounced: *FZ*, no. 156, 27 February, 1932.

23. *FZ*, no. 732/33, 2 October, 1931; Abraham, p. 39.

24. Feldman, 'Deutsche Bank', p. 74.

25. Journalistically, the Nordwolle case caused a greater sensation than did the downfall of Favag. Research about the 'Nordwolle catastrophe' has also been more thorough, not least because of the direct connection with the banking crisis of July 1931 and the state and financial crisis in Bremen. Cf. inter alia Georg Kantona, 'Die Nordwolle-Katastrophe', *Der deutsche Volkswirt*, 8, Jg., No. 41 (1931), pp. 1386–8; Abraham, pp. 41–60; Eberhard Voelcklin, 'Der Zusammenbruch der Nordwolle', in Alfred Lansburgh, *Die Bank* (1931), pp. 966–72; Wilhelm Kalveram, 'Lehren aus Irrtümern der Vergangenheit. Der Zusammenbruch der Nordwolle', *Zeitschrift für Betriebswirtschaft* (1950), pp. 95–104; Herbert Schwarzwälder, *Geschichte*

der Freien Hansestadt Bremen, Bd. 3 (Bremen, 1983), p. 526 ff.; Otmar Escher, *Die Wirtschafts- und Finanzkrise in Bremen 1931 und der Fall Schröderbank* (Frankfurt, 1988), p. 79 ff.; Dietmar von Reeken, *Lahusen – eine Bremer Unternehmer Dynastie: 1816–1933* (Bremen, 1996), p. 82 ff.

26. For the history of the firm, see von Reeken, p. 71 ff.

27. Cf. 'Der Konzern NWK', *Die Wirtschaftskurve* (1929), pp. 290–95.

28. Cf. von Reeken, p. 82, who sees the key to the downfall of Nordwolle in the sharp contrast 'between the complicated – some judge too complicated – business group structure that demanded a modern business management and the personal rule of G. Carl Lahusen.' The joint-stock company was run like a family business, Carl Lahusen was chairman, his brother Heinz became a director in 1922, and his youngest brother joined the board in 1929.

29. Kalveram, p. 97. A similar scepticism had already been expressed in the discussion of the economic performance of the Nordwolle combine in *Die Wirtschaftskurve* (footnote 27 above).

30. *FZ*, no. 645/46, 31 August, 1933.

31. Kantona, 'Die Nordwolle-Katastrophe', p. 1387.

32. A thorough report by Doerner on his investigation activities, written in November 1956 to the former board member of the DD-Bank Georg Solmssen, is printed in Manfred Pohl, 'Zwei Dokumente zur Bankenkrise des Jahres 1931', *Bankhistorisches Archiv* 7 (1981), pp. 52–61, here p.55 ff. Doerner described the desperate back and forth manoeuverings of G. Carl Lahusen to cover up the situation as long as possible, even including an attempted bribing.

33. Cf. Kalveram, p. 98 ff.

34. Cf. *FZ*, no. 446, 18 June 1931; no. 458, 20 June 1931; no. 463, 24 June, 1931; no. 496, 7 July 1931. According to the trust evaluation of 28 June 1931, the liabilities amounted to 238,161,700 Reichsmark, of which 41 million was apportioned to foreign creditors. The credit of German banks to the sum of 100 million was categorised as unsecured. Of these, 40,370,000 Reichsmark were apportioned to the Danatbank, 24,450,300 Reichsmark to the Bremen Hansa-Bank, 10,397,000 Reichsmark to the Commerzbank, 9,085,500 Reichsmark to the Deutsche Bank and 6,264,000 Reichsmark to the Schröderbank. Cf. BA Berlin, 31 January/ 17887, Bl. 32 f.

35. A very thorough literature exists depicting these dramatic events, beginning with the classic study from Karl Erich Born, *Die deutsche Bankenkrise 1931. Finanzen und Politik* (Munich, 1967), p. 64 ff.

36. *FZ*, no. 506, 10 July 1931.

37. Cited in Abraham, p. 85; *FZ*, 23 October 1931.

38. Felix Pinner, *Deutsche Wirtschaftsführer* (Charlottenburg, 1924), p. 251.

39. For biographies of the main figures, see for instance the entries *in Biographisches Handbuch der deutschsprachigen Emigration nach 1933*, vol. 1 (1980); Walter E. Mosse, *The German-Jewish Economic Elite 1820–1935*, (Oxford, 1989), p. 76 ff., p. 170. For the history of the companies: *Handbuch der deutschen Aktiengesellschaften*, vol. 1 (1927), p. 1372 ff; Erich Borkenhagen, *125 Jahre Schultheiss-Brauerei* (Berlin, 1967), p. 128 ff.

40. Borkenhagen, p. 131.

41. BA Berlin, R 43 I/ 1205, Bl. 114, 'Schreiben der Danatbank an die Reichskanzlei' (28 October, 1931).
42. FZ, no. 176, 6 March 1931.
43. Abraham, p. 86.
44. Cf. FZ, no. 713, 9 September, 1929.
45. BA Berlin, R 43 I / 1205, Bl. 125, 'Bericht des Reichskommissars für das Bankgewerbe Ernst' (3 November, 1931). Also Bl. 129 ff. for the text of the agreements between Katzenellenbogen and the Commerzbank-consortium of October 1929, which presented Katzenellenbogen with rather unfavourable conditions and also demanded, in addition to the credit interest, another 60 per cent of the remaining profit, which was not however achieved. In contrast, Danatbank enjoyed a profit share of 10 per cent, then later with a 25 per cent share exceeding the sum of 1.5 million Reichsmark. Cf. ibid, Bl. 110.
46. BA Berlin, R 8119 / P 4634 (Deutsche Bank, von Stauß), Bl. 64, 72 ff.
47. Abraham, p. 93.
48. BA Berlin, R 8119 / P 4641, Stenogr. Niederschrift der AR-Sitzung, 23 October, 1931.
49. Stolper, 'Finanzskandale', p. 180.
50. Arps, p. 425.
51. The reporting about several affiliates of the Katzenellenbogen empire in the run-up to the Schultheiss scandal showed that there was plenty of reason for critical concerns, such as those involving the Industriebau Held & Franke A.G., cf. FZ, 27 August, 1930.
52. Voelcklin, p. 967.
53. FZ, no. 791, 4 November, 1933.
54. Cited in von Reeken, p. 103. Cf. also the explanations of Doerner (Pohl, p. 57), whose request to take a look at various bank statements of Nordwolle were brusquely refused by Lahusen with the explanation that 'he was president of the chamber of commerce and couldn't tolerate his statements not being fully trusted.'
55. Cited in Stolper, 'Finanzskandale', p. 179.
56. Cf. inter alia: Georg Kantona, 'Das Schultheiss-Urteil', Der deutsche Volkswirt (25 March, 1932), pp. 843–5.
57. Stolper, 'Finanzskandale', p. 181.
58. Basler Nationalzeitung, no. 540, 20 November, 1931.
59. Ausschuß zur Untersuchung der Erzeugungs- u. Absatzbedingungen der deutschen Wirtschaft: Der Bankkredit, (Berlin, 1930), p. 168. Figures rounded off. Cf. also Martin Gehr, Das Verhältnis zwischen Banken und Industrie in Deutschland seit der Mitte des 19. Jh. bis zur Bankenkrise von 1931 unter bes. Berücksichtigung des industriellen Großkredits (Tübingen, 1959), p. 104.
60. Harold James, Deutschland in der Weltwirtschaftskrise, p. 148.
61. Feldman, Deutsche Bank, p. 274.
62. Drucker, p. 743; FZ, 24 October 1931. Experts in questions of insurance were not members of the Favag supervisory board: the only member from

the insurance branch, the chairman of the Karlsruhe Lebensversicherungsbank
Rudolf Kimmig, directed a subsidiary of Favag and thus more or less super-
vised himself.

63. BA Berlin, R8119/P5785 (Deutsche Bank / Allianz). The former board member of Allianz Hilgard wrote in his memoirs that, among others, the director
of the Frankfurt filial of the Disconto-Gesellschaft had made the accusation
'that we at Allianz were true amateurs in the area of financial administration
in comparison with the generous gentlemen in the Frankfurter Allgemeine.'
Hilgard, 'Mein Leben in der Allianz', (Ms.), cited in Borscheid, p. 70.

64. Voelcklin, p. 970.

65. Abraham, p. 57.

66. BA Berlin, R 8119 / P 4640, 'Aktennotiz from 12 October, 1927'. Emphasis
is mine.

67. FZ, 30 March, 1932.

68. BA Berlin, R 8119 / P 11479, 'Plädoyer Dr. Alsberg am 16. Verhandlungstag'.

69. Cf. R 43 I / 1205, Bl. 113, 'Schreiben des Vorstands der Danatbank an die
Reichskanzlei', (28 October 1931) and Bl. 127 about the same attitude of
Commerzbank.

70. R 8119 / P 4634, Bl. 136.

71. Stolper, 'Finanzskandale', p. 179.

72. Cf. FZ, no. 804, 28 October 1931 and no. 805, 29 October 1931. The
argument was embarrassing because Reinhart had not been a member of the
supervisory board and therefore had no knowledge about the incorrect
figures in the stock-exchange prospectus. The evaluation of the
Reichskommissar für das Bankgewerbe in his investigation of Reinhart (R 43
I / 1205, Bl. 124 ff), was against his discharge, since 'blame of the banker in
question' could not be proven. The accusation of being an accessory of
Goldschmidt and Reinhard for the prospectus falsification, which the silence
of their banks would have made likely, was not considered in the Schultheiss
trial because the already expired statute of limitations of six months protected both from being tried for this crime.

73. Cf. RGBl I, 1931, p. 916 ff.

Catching-up?
The Evolution of Management Consultancies in Portugal and Spain

Celeste Maria Dias Amorim

University of Reading[1]

INTRODUCTION

Over the last two decades, great attention has been given to aspects of work organisation, firm strategies and organisational practices. There has been an increasing interest in the role of managerial know-how and on its transferability across national boundaries. Likewise, access to 'soft' aspects, such as organisation and management knowledge, are recognised as playing a paramount role in the innovation processes of firms.[2] Research in comparative management concluded that organisations are quite diverse in the way they solve similar problems and in the way they are organised. Much of modern organisational theory seeks to explain such variations.[3] The common argument is that companies' behaviour and organisation reflect country-level specificities. Without questioning the significance of national characteristics, there is a certain level of convergence among companies as far as management practices and work organisation are concerned.[4] Although the evidence is scarce,[5] some authors argue that there are a number of widely diffused management techniques and models.[6] These phenomena may reflect managers' searches for 'best practices', but they may also have harmful effects on organisations operating in contexts different from those where management ideas were created.

In this respect, consultants, and international consultancies in particular, are characterised as important 'outsiders'[7] contributing to the process of diffusing management knowledge. Moreover, there seems to be an increasing awareness of how they may advance and accelerate a country's technological level and a firm's competitiveness.[8] Even those academics and practitioners who are critical regarding the consultant's job have recognised the role of international consultancies in the dissemination of management innovations and 'best practices' across time and space. In this respect it can be argued that consultants are homogenisation agents.[9] Not only do consultancies tend to apply the same practices to different companies, but they are also becoming more homogeneous among themselves.

However, there are considerable differences between countries concerning the evolution of consultancy businesses and the role of consultants as diffusers of new ideas and techniques over time.[10] In this respect, some authors argue that the evolution and role of management consultancies as conduits of management principles may be limited by a country's 'systemic context'. Besides macroeconomic factors, the characteristics of the provision of consultancy (from private and public sector), the type of institutions offering consultancy services, domestic companies' organisational structures, and management education appear to be among the most influential factors determining the evolution of consulting businesses: Kipping,[11] for example, has shown the relevance of these factors for the cases of Britain, France and Germany.

This view is particularly pertinent when dealing with issues of managerial change in countries like Portugal and Spain. Until the 1970s and even 1980s, these two countries were relatively insulated from mainstream management methods, such as scientific management, human resources management techniques, just-in-time and total quality management.[12] Portuguese and Spanish firms have, nevertheless, with variable time lags, adopted, management techniques, products and/or processes developed by other organisations. Moreover, the economic, social and political events that occurred in the last decade may have stimulated competition and created a new awareness of the importance of the efficiency of business operations, and thus the introduction of management innovations.[13] At the same time, by the end of 1980s, there was evidence of an upswing in the consultancy business in Portugal and Spain. In the 1990s, this process intensified and the market structure changed significantly.[14] Furthermore, there are signs that the lack of an appropriate network of business and technical services has been one of the weaknesses of the Portuguese and Spanish business system and a barrier to their further development.[15]

The two countries selected are therefore highly suitable locations for attempts to analyse the role of consultants as important agents of management modernisation. Thus, the aim of this article is to explore the role of consultants as conduits of management innovations. By adopting a comparative and evolutionary approach, the article attempts to demonstrate how the systemic context influenced the evolution of consultants' activities in the two selected countries over time. This paper is subdivided into two main sections for each country. The first explains the development of the consultancy business, which appears to have reflected deep changes in each country's business system. The second part focuses on current market structure. The paper draws upon forty interviews conducted in the period July to October 1998 with management consultants in both countries, as well as documentary materials from those organisations, and other relevant literature available.[16]

THE EVOLUTION OF THE PORTUGUESE CONSULTANCY MARKET

Three major phases can be distinguished in the evolution of the consultancy business in Portugal. In the first stage, from the 1940s up to the revolution of 1974, Portugal underwent deep changes. However, it lagged behind in terms of industrialisation processes.[17] The second phase started with the end of the dictatorship in 1974 and lasted until the early 1980s. The revolution of 1974 and the subsequent nationalisation of the larger Portuguese firms had a powerful impact on the Portuguese business system. Until the early 1980s, socio-political instability and government intervention, combined with increasing economic liberalisation, undermined Portuguese economic development. The third phase began with European Community (EC) accession in 1986 which stimulated the Portuguese economy, and since then Portugal has undergone profound structural changes, at both economic and social levels.[18] Thus, this article aims to investigate whether these changes had an important impact on the role of consultants and the evolution of the consultancy market.

It is worth noting that the Portuguese national statistics are scarce and do not allow a clear identification of the management consultancy business. Only in 1974 was the statistic categorisation for such activities created, and as late as 1993 management consultancies (MC) were included in the large category of business services. Since then the national statistical system has improved, but the group of management consultants still encompasses too large a number of activities. Furthermore, the national professional body for consultants, Associação Portuguesa de Projectistas e Consultores (APPC), founded in 1975, has low representation both in terms of its number of members and in the size of its members' businesses. Moreover, only 19 per cent of APPC members in 1995–96 were providing management consultancy services.[19]

FROM 1940 TO 1974 – THE ORIGINS

The information on professional business services[20] suggests that management consultancy activity developed later in Portugal than in many other European countries and, indeed, appears to be a relatively recent activity. The consultancy and engineering businesses developed together as an independent sector only from the 1940s to 1950s, and empirical studies in 1993 found that about 90 per cent of the existing engineering and consulting firms had been created after 1974.[21]

The origins of the consulting business in Portugal can be traced to two types of consultants. First, to consulting centres founded by university professors some of which have developed strong connections with industry and public administration, and have evolved into medium-sized and large professional firms. Second, to the consulting departments of large economics groups which had been servicing group and non-group companies. In both cases, large structural investment in the public administration and industrial projects of the large industrial groups played an important role during the initial stages of their expansion.[22]

Before 1974, the potential clients for management consulting firms were mainly in public administration and a few large diversified groups. Public administration demanded mainly engineering consultancy in large-scale and infrastructural projects. Moreover, public institutions have used consultants to monitor the massive infrastructural investments in the former colonies, thus furthering and hastening the demand for engineering consultancy in the 1960s. Later on, those institutions demanded complementary consulting, such as in management, processes organisation, and planning.[23]

From the 1950s up to the early 1970s, Portuguese private industry was characterised by government intervention and a dualist structure. There were a few large, diversified, private groups[24] that were oriented mainly to the internal market and to the Portuguese colonies. In addition, there were a large number of small firms involved in labour-intensive, export-oriented industry. Apparently, few companies were concerned with professional management and 'state-of-the-art' management practices. Medium and small firms, in particular, lacked the capacity to develop their technological and managerial knowledge and their success was mainly based on low-quality products and cheap labour.[25] Within this context, the necessary conditions for stimulating the development of support business services, such as financial services and management consultancy, did not yet exist.

However, the large groups, most of them of family origin, showed a certain fascination for foreign management models, such as strategic planning techniques and human resources management.[26] Moreover, during the 1960s, steady economic growth, industrialisation plans and plant modernisation stimulated interest among large and medium-companies in scientific management and industrial engineering. Some of these companies contracted the services of consultancies specialised in the efficiency of shopfloor work processes. Because of the lesser development of the domestic supply, domestic firms looked to foreign consultancies. The interviews carried out in Portugal revealed that in the 1960s there was a particular interest in French techniques and, in fact, the French firms CORTE and Paul Plaunus (PP) were among the consultancies benefiting from this development. As stated by a former CORTE consultant, during the 1960s CORTE had assignments with multinational subsidiaries (e.g. IBM) and with the large Portuguese groups, namely with Champallimaud where PP had also a strong penetration.

In the 1960s, the larger groups became attracted by qualitative innovations in management, those with implications for business strategy and corporate organisation, work relations and human resources development.[27] It was within this context that those international consultancies specialised in strategy and organisation entered the Spanish market. The first was, perhaps, McKinsey (through the London office) and then the Hay Consulting Group (1979). At that time CUF, the largest Portuguese group before 1974, was known as the most innovative at the level of management techniques. The CUF Group professionalised management earlier than any other Portuguese firm and invested strongly in training. Some of its managers, who were sent abroad to attend conferences, seminars and postgraduate degrees in foreign schools (e.g. Harvard and London Business School), were important conduits for transferring popular management techniques to Portugal. The literature and information gathered during the interviews suggest that CUF had an important role in the development of the domestic consulting business. The first assignment of McKinsey in Portugal was with CUF in 1969–70. This American consultancy firm was engaged in elaborating and implementing one strategic plan for CUF.[28] In order to take advantage of the lessons learned from McKinsey consultants, CUF created a new consulting firm, Norma, with CUF staff. This proved to have been a good investment once Norma became one of the largest consulting firms in Portugal, serving its own group as well as non-group firms. Furthermore, spin-offs from CUF became larger users of management consultancy services after 1974 (such as Quimigal, involved in the chemical industry).

However these cases were exceptions. The bulk of the Portuguese economy was made up of small and medium family-owned and family-controlled firms. Most were undercapitalised and run by owner-managers who lacked professional qualifications. Managers were more akin to short-term supervisors, neither exposed to, nor concerned with, the implementation of new technology. Further, by restricting competition, the industrialisation plans and government intervention reduced the pressures on domestic firms to increase efficiency. There were few professional managers in managerial positions, and the most talented tended to enter the public sector, one of the few leading economic groups or multinationals.[29] Small and large professional offices supplying mainly legal consulting, accounting and auditing did, however, develop. And, although the evidence is scarce, the interviewees affirmed that most of these accountancies, both foreign and domestic (for example Price Waterhouse and CETEL) also carried out some consultancy-type work.

FROM 1974 TO THE MID-1980s

After the 1974 April revolution the whole financial sector was national-ised, as were the larger industrial firms. Some companies were expropri-ated and many of the well-known entrepreneurs, managers and some skilled workers emigrated. Often, political appointees with no formal managerial skills then replaced the owners of the companies. Consequently, problems of small size and lack of managerial capabilities were aggra-vated,[30] further impoverishing the Portuguese business system. The coun-try became dominated by the large public firms (nationalised financial and industrial firms) and by small and medium-sized family-owned and family-managed companies. In addition, Portuguese firms had to contend with the 1970s oil shocks. By the early 1980s, the largest industrial and finan-cial firms were state-owned and characterised by reduced productivity.[31] Moreover, empirical studies have found that even in the late 1980s popu-lar management and work methods (e.g. team-work, quality circles and job rotation) were scarcely known or implemented by Portuguese indus-try.[32] These studies highlight the scarcity of professional managers. Ac-cording to Tordoir,[33] this feature may had been a barrier to the development of the management consultancy business.

The political, economic and social changes that occurred during the 1970s and early 1980s created a disequilibrium between supply and de-mand in the consultancy market. On the one hand, consulting firms ori-ented to the former colonies were forced to change their strategies, and some others declined as Portugal lost control over those markets. On the other hand, the domestic consultancy firms were not equipped to satisfy the consultancy needs of the large public firms and the service sector.[34] Furthermore, the economic recovery and the technology imports of the late 1970s hastened the demand for consultancy. New domestic and/or international consulting firms were established, offering new products and services, and diffusing new methodologies and management techniques. Some of them combined management consultancy with consultancy in industrial engineering or accounting services (for example Partex, Cachudo Nunes & Associados).

After 1974, labour conflicts demanded that increased attention be paid to industrial relations and social issues. As a result, in medium-sized and large companies, personnel or human resource management gained higher status within managerial concerns and increased numerically.[35] Personnel management evolved into human resources management and new services (for example, related to selection, training, labour relations and work performance) were created. Hay was perhaps the most significant diffuser of modern human resources management techniques (including organisa-tion, job definition and development) in Portugal. Indeed, several interviewees mentioned Hay interventions, such as those in the Portuguese public chemical company, Quimigal, at the level of job definition, training and recruitment. In addition, as the market expanded, some industrial engineering or accountancy-based firms diversified into management consulting. This development was accompanied by a boom in individual consultants and consultancies, with lean structures and charging very low fees, that led to a supply surplus in certain areas.[36]

FROM THE MID-1980s

The Portuguese business system was profoundly affected when Portugal joined the EC in 1986. In the last decade several companies have been privatised; others have become larger and have diversified their activities,[37] while others, private and public firms, have been restructuring. The growth in FDI inflows, increasing market and capital liberalisation, and privatisation stimulated the process of change. Consequently, Portuguese companies were forced to look for solutions to cope with their growing organisational complexity and to make themselves more competitive. A new generation, graduating either from Portuguese or foreign universities, has brought modern management concepts to Portuguese companies as well as a greater awareness of contemporary ideas. As a result, there has been a growing demand for new management techniques, expertise, and management consultancy.[38]

These demand conditions considerably affected the market, and since the late 1980s consultancy business has undergone significant changes. Management advisory service departments of the large Anglo-American accountancies (i.e. the 'big five') were well positioned to enjoy this growth in demand: most of them had established offices in Portugal after the late 1950s (see table in Appendix 1). However, until the mid-1980s their activities mainly involved accounting and auditing. It was not until the late 1980s to the early 1990s that they began to invest massively in consulting, namely via information technology. This international trend was referred to by partners of some of the 'big five'. The consulting fees of one of these consultancies grew from less than 5 per cent of the total turnover in 1990 to 25 per cent in 1997. Yet, at the same time, Portugal has witnessed the emergence of a large number of domestic small and medium-sized consulting firms. Very small consulting firms were created, while larger firms, such as Norma, GSI, CETEL, SISMET, were forced to adapt to new market conditions. Some of the larger consultancies either reduced the number of permanent professionals, or established alliances with other firms and/or focused on services that were in higher demand (for example training and human resources management (HRM); the implementation of quality systems aiming at the International Standards Organisation (ISO) certification; information technology (IT) consulting). Moreover, human resources management was recognised as paramount to achieving enhanced competitiveness. As revealed by a partner of one of the largest consultancies in the field of human resources, as wages and labour costs increased some companies displayed greater concern about labour aspects, and even conducted their own salary surveys with which they could compare themselves to their counterparts.[39] Simultaneously, companies were becoming concerned with reducing their own headcount. This had two main effects. First, personnel departments were reduced in staff and, second, human resources activities were externalised. These demand conditions may explain the flourishing of several consultancies in the area of human resources in the last decade.[40] There was also an upsurge in public and semi-public institutions, such as university centres, competing directly with the consulting firms, particularly in the context of applying for funds and in economic viability studies. As a result, there has been an increase in consultancy work involving small and medium enterprises (SMEs), even in traditional and less technically advanced sectors.[41] In the late 1980s, until the early 1990s, a wave of international service providers entered the Portuguese consultancy market (see table in Appendix 1), and many of them focused on corporate-level consulting and organisational strategy and structure. One group of entrants was already providing services in Portugal either from its foreign offices or in association with other consultancies already established in the market. For example, McKinsey, whose first assignment in Portugal was in 1969, opened an office in this country only in 1989, and The Boston Consulting Group (BCG) opened an office in 1995, although both of them were supplying the market through their London or Madrid branches. The interviewees explained that the small scale and the later development of the Portuguese market justified such cautious entry strategies. When John Clarkeson, president of BCG,[42] was asked why his company had not opened an office in Portugal before 1995, he explained that 'we do not want to grow explosively. We are slower than the market'. However late their entry, the interviews revealed that the majority of these large foreign consultancies managed to obtain a number of high-profile assignments with the large and well-known Portuguese companies (such as with Caixa Geral de Depositos (CGD), Portucel, Telecom, Jerónimo Martins, Grupo Sonae). Moreover some consultancies gained large market shares in certain industries (for example McKinsey in financial services).

CURRENT MARKET STRUCTURE

Since the early 1990s consultancy activities have expanded and the market structure of the industry has changed drastically. Recent statistics indicate that consulting fees in Portugal grew by about 20 per cent from 1996 to 1997, reaching about 80–85 billion Portuguese Escudos (PTE) in 1997.[43] Information collected during the interviews, and the ranking of the ten leading consulting firms (see Table 1), suggests that international consulting firms achieved a major market share and came to dominate the management consultancy market.

The ranking of the fifty largest consulting firms[44] must be analysed with caution as it only ranks those firms answering a questionnaire and it is suspected that many of the larger consulting firms did not respond. As an example, Ernst Young's (EY) 1997 turnover was certainly above 3000 million PTE but EY was not ranked. Likewise, companies such as McKinsey, A.T. Kerney, Hay Consulting Group, and even other domestic consultancies such as GSI or CESO CI, do not appear. In spite of these deficiencies, the study sheds some light on the market growth and on the most important businesses. It indicates that the consulting market grew by about 20 per cent from 1996 to 1997 and that IT-related consulting is the fastest growing service.[45] Nearly twenty of the fifty largest firms are specialised in IT consulting, and the market leader Edinfor, part of the Portuguese electricity group EDP, provides IT services to its own group as well as to its clients. Andersen Consulting is one of the leading firms with a turnover of 4500 million PTE in 1997 but it has declined in the period 1995–97. However, McKinsey is one of the largest as far as strategy consulting is concerned, perhaps because it was the first firm to enter the Portuguese corporate market and it did not have significant competitors for years. The German firm Roland Berger and the Franco-American firm MacGroup/

Table 1: The Ten Leading Consulting Firms in Portugal 1997

	Consultancy	Turnover (Mn /PTE)			Employers		
		1995	1996	1997	1995	1996	1997
1.	Edinfor	8020	9849	10311	314	350	378
2.	Andersen Consulting	5518	4725	4500	276	n/a	n/a
3.	Arthur Andersen	3000	3421	4200	224	317	373
4.	E.S. Data Informática	1230	2940	3965	56	85	118
5.	Price Waterhouse	2700	3200	3500	300	280	320
6.	Partex	n/a	2373	3500	n/a	161	150
7.	Grupo Reditus	n/a	1407	2606	n/a	70	98
8.	Cap Gemini	n/a	n/a	2544	n/a	n/a	239
9.	CPC-IS	n/a	1870	2207	n/a	160	200
10.	Deloitte Touche	1381	1478	1727	170	169	160

Source: DN: 1998, pp. 22–3

Gemini Consulting are two other leaders within the business strategy.[46] The interviewees revealed that, as in many other markets, the success of foreign consultancy firms appears to arise from their first-move advantage, from their reputation and knowledge as well as from 'the connectors'[47] they have used to gain access to potential clients. According to information gathered during the interviews and from the business press, in Portugal a number of former top managers of large companies are partners or consultants of those leading consultancies that can afford to pay their high wages. These former managers facilitate access to new clients through the good relations they have established within the Portuguese business system. In addition, a large number of former consultants (such as from Arthur Andersen) and managers who had close contact with international consultancies during consulting assignments (such as with McKinsey and Hay) occupy leading positions in Portugal's leading groups. Moreover, consulting firms have had an important role as a kind of business school. It is clear from the interviews conducted, and confirmed by the business press, that working for large consultancies, or with their consultants, during the assignments has been a passport to entering larger companies. This has been especially true for international consultancies since the 1970s.[48]

Together with these large international groups, there are some Portuguese consulting firms, but a few of them are focused mostly upon strategy consulting. One of the largest Portuguese consulting companies is Iberconsult, which was created in 1989, and which, by 1992, was already fourth in the market for strategic consulting. Its revenue grew from 300 million PTE in 1992 to 467 million PTE in 1997.[49] The liaison with MacGroup enabled Iberconsult to access new management practices and new methods for conducting business.[50]

Side by side with the large consulting firms, there is a group of small and medium consultancies (SMCs) with an important role, especially in the market of SMEs. Many of these SMCs (such as Tecninvest, IBER, Fórun Atlántico) are spin-offs either from engineering groups or from other large companies, while others were founded by individual consultants, former academics, managers and politicians. Information from a variety of sources,[51] including the interviews, suggests that EC membership furthered the development of these SMCs. A large majority focused on giving advice on EC-related issues (such as investment projects, applications for EC funding), recovery projects for firms in bankruptcy (so-called Plano Mateus), and ISO quality certification projects and training (both funded by EC structural funds). Most of these SMCs remained competitive due to their flexible structure. With few permanent professionals, they work on a project-by-project basis with external consultants.[52] As mentioned by a few interviewees, this structure allows them to act in a large range of industries and to provide a large range of services. Some firms have a large network or database of potential individual consultants which are subcontracted to work in different projects according to their functional and industry expertise. With this system, small and medium consulting firms are able to face periods of recession as well as sudden increases in demand in any management practice. Yet another group comprises the legal consultancies, very active at the level of mergers and acquisitions, spin-offs etc.

Some banks (including Banco Portugues de Investimento, Banco Portugues Negocios and Banco Nacional Ultramarino) and several professional, industrial and semi-public organisations (for example Instituto de Apoio a Pequena e Media Empresa or IAPMEI, and Associacao Industrial Portuguesa or AIP), also play an important role in the consultancy market.[53] The professional and technical institutions in particular became more active from the mid-1980s to the early 1990s, not only by creating management consulting offices but also by organising seminars, conferences and management courses.[54]

Globally, the market developed considerably during the 1990s. The management advisory service departments of the big accounting firms have been the biggest players in the consultancy market, although their power should not be overestimated. As referred to above, recent studies have shown that some Portuguese IT-specialist firms and other consultancies profited from the growth in demand. In 1997 not only was the largest consultancy in Portugal Portuguese (specialising in IT), but five of the ten largest were also Portuguese. Moreover, the 20 per cent growth in 1996 and 1997 is partly based on the rapid growth of some Portuguese firms.[55]

Based on consultants' statements and consulting firms' client portfolios, clients come from all sectors. However, in terms of value, finance and telecommunications seem to have been by far the major users of management consulting. Since the late 1980s both of these sectors have undergone a massive reorganisation, mainly due to privatisation and capital liberalisation.[56] Elsewhere, in heavy industry, public firms in the process of privatisation (for example Portucel, Cimpor, Soporcel) have been important users of management consulting services. In the private sector, the larger groups that had begun diversifying in 1986 and 1987 with the boom in the financial market, were forced to rationalise and reorganise their businesses. In some companies this goal was met with help from management consultants.[57]

This analysis reveals that applications for EC funds and economic-viability studies have been important activities, especially for small consultancies. Otherwise, training, implementation of quality systems and, more recently, business re-engineering and IT consulting have been growing practices. Recent studies highlight the size and significance of IT consulting based firms. IT consulting has been growing fast, and in 1997 systems (implementation and development) accounted for 35 per cent of consultancy turnover, with the IT specialised firms dominating the market. Larger consulting firms can afford to develop customised products; however, many firms have decided to represent foreign firms such as SAP, Oracle and JBAS, and implement well-known computing packages, such as SAP and BAAN.

From all that has been stated, it appears that the evolution of management consultancies in Portugal has been largely determined by the country's 'systemic context'. On the supply side, the growth of consulting businesses appear to have been mitigated by the penetration of large international consultancies, the reduced significance of domestic consultancies and the role of other institutions (for example AIP) as conduits of managerial knowledge. The penetration of a large number of international consultancies and the foundation of a large number of public or semi-public institutions, targeting mainly the SMEs, propelled the usage of external support. There are signs of change, but the lack of an appropriate network of business and technical services is still one of the weaknesses of the Portuguese business system.[58] On the demand side, clients' organisational structure and the level of professionalisation at management level have been determinant factors. There is still a relatively low usage of consultants and business services in general, with MC accounting for only 0.4 per cent of GDP while the European average is nearly 0.8 per cent.[59] Late industrialisation, the dualist economy, resistance to using external support, and the small size of companies and markets, partly explain the scarce use of the national network of technical and management support services, and the delayed development of the consultancy business in Portugal. Moreover, Portuguese entrepreneurs seem to show insufficient concern with the management of 'soft' technology issues, such as information, quality and marketing. A recent survey showed a sharp contrast between Portuguese and Spanish firms, with the Spanish firms placing far greater emphasis upon these three factors.[60] By contrast, periods of economic expansion, restructuring, increasing bureaucratisation and higher numbers of salaried managers have propelled the use of consultants.

THE EVOLUTION OF THE SPANISH CONSULTANCY MARKET

Four major phases can be identified in the evolution of the Spanish consultancy market. In the first stage, from the end of the Civil War in 1939 until the early 1950s, the Spanish economy underwent a long period of stagnation. In the second period, between the 1950s and 1974, with the economic liberalisation, and her readmittance into Western economies, Spain achieved the highest rates of growth of the entire OECD. The third period, which can be defined as a transition phase, started in 1974 and lasted until the mid-1980s, when Spain entered the EC. In this period there was an increasing awareness of Spain's backwardness regarding technological development.[61] The last stage of the process of assuming EC membership inaugurated a new period during which the economic cycle, the restructuring of companies – due to increasing competition, deregulation and privatisation – brought important changes for the Spanish business system. The evolution of the consultancy business must be understood within this context as these changes had an important impact on the role of consultants and the evolution of the consultancy market.

There is more data and information on consultancy activities in Spain than in Portugal. However, there are problems in analysing consultancy activities until the 1970s. As in Portugal, statistical categorisation for such activities was only created in 1974. However, in the case of Spain, publications and more detailed information gathered by the national professional body for consultants are available. Nowadays, the members of the Associacion de Empresas de Consultoria,[62] in which the larger consulting, accountancy-based firms are included, account for about 55 per cent of the consultancy turnover in Spain.[63] Thus, the AEC statistics and reports on members' activities are good sources from which to analyse trends in the Spanish consultancy market.

FROM 1940 TO THE 1950s: THE ORIGINS

Many of the earlier consultancies in Spain had grown out of the associations of individual engineers, or other academics, and the governmental national institutes set up during the 1940s. There were also foreign consultancies, most of which were French and American.[64] As a result, foreigners have dominated the Spanish consultancy business almost from the outset. In the 1970s, the larger consulting firms were either international consultancies (such as TEA-Cegos, Bedaux and Mercer) or firms and consortiums involved in foreign equity (see table in Appendix 2).

The scientific-management movement played an important role during the initial stages of the expansion of market consultancy. From the end of the Civil War in 1939 until the early 1950s, Spain remained excluded from the Marshall Plan and went through a long period of stagnation. During the 1940s and 1950s, the state took the lead in the economy, by administering import-substitution industrialisation policies. In order to favour the spread of scientific management, the state holding company Instituto Nacional de Industria (INI) and the National Institute for Work Organisation (INOT) were created in the 1940s. INOT was founded in collaboration with industrial engineers and top managers and became an active and influential organisation for the diffusion of scientific management. Moreover, bureaucratisation and firms' complexity were growing rapidly in most industrial sectors[65] creating new management challenges. At the same time, shortages in terms of supplies, technology and capital propelled employers and engineers to implement scientific-management techniques in order to reduce waste and raise productivity. This allowed the successful introduction of modern mass-production techniques in a variety of industrial sectors. During that period, the companies that implemented scientific-management most comprehensively were the new firms created with foreign capital and technology (such as Marconi Española, Hispano-Olivetti, SEAT) or the state-owned companies (such as ENASA and RENFE).[66]

FROM THE MID-1950S TO 1974/5 – THE FIRST UPSURGE

A new period opened in the mid-1950s. Economic liberalisation created the conditions for accelerated economic growth, and with growth came an increasing demand for consulting activities. The undeveloped domestic supply prompted Spanish companies and public administrations to use foreign consulting firms in specialised fields.[67] The continuous increase in demand was hastened by the indicative development plans of the 1960s and propelled the establishment of an increasing number of consulting and engineering firms. Some consultancies resulted from associations between individual professionals and professors. But, the older foreign consultancies with international activities also profited. Probably the first consultancy to benefit fully from this development was Bedaux,[68] created in Spain in 1940 (restructured in 1953). The system created by Bedaux, a set of practices based on scientific-management principles, enjoyed good receptivity in Europe, and there is evidence of its implementation in Spain (for example in Duro-Felguera, a metal industry company, in 1953).[69] Moreover, Bedaux appears on the list of the largest consultancies in Spain in the 1970s (see Table 2). This firm was subsequently bought by Roland Berger, and was finally closed down in the 1980s.

American human resources approaches and psychological techniques also found their way into Spain. Several organisations created by the state to improve organisational methods were soon dominated by experts favouring the human relations paradigm. In this context, the state created the National Commission for Industrial Productivity in the 1950s and two technical missions of Spanish managers travelled to the US to acquire on-site knowledge of human relations techniques. Moreover, a relatively large group of leading intellectuals (including José Ortega and Gasset) facilitated the reception of American human relations ideas and diffused them through their teaching and consulting work. For instance, the Association for the Advancement of Management (AAM), created by some leading management intellectuals, had assignments for the most important firms.[70]

Table 2: The Largest Consulting Firms in Work Organisation in Spain- 1975/77

Consultancy	Year Est.	Foreign Partner	Spanish Partner	FFTS*	Employees 1975	1977
TEA	1952	Grupo Cegos (Fr)	Abengoa	Cegos (Fr)	101	15
A.C. Nielsen	n.a.	A.C. Nielsen (USA)	–	A.C. Nielsen (USA)	139	143
ICSA	n.a.	Diebold (USA)	Banco Banesto; B. Viscaya	Diebold (USA); Gallup Int (USA)	162	47
Arthur Andersen	1965	Arthur Andersen (USA)	–	Arthur Andersen (USA)	142	215
SOFEMASA	1962	Grupo Metra (Fr)	Banco Bilbao	Sema-Metra (Fr)	70	82
Fraser	1968	–	Individual partner	Weir & Associates	105	53
Price Waterhouse	1956	PW (UK)	–		202	195
COC	n.a.	Group COC-CCE (Fr)	–		155	–
Bedaux	1953		E. Maso	Institute Bedaux (Fr)	68	66
Metra Seis	1964	–	Grupo Banco Atlantico		74	66
Seresco	1962	–	Banco Ind. Cataluna		289	279

Source: Molero (1979, 66); Dun Brudstreet (1996); Egurbide (1976)
Información Comercial Española.
** FFTS: Foreign firms from whom they have received technical support.

Furthermore, this sudden interest in human relations attracted other foreign consultancies. TEA-Cegos, a venture between the Spanish firm TEA and the French group Cegos, was created in Spain in 1952, and became the most active consultancy at the level of organisation, training and selection. During the 1970s TEA-Cegos was one of the leading MC firms (see Table 2).

Abundant FDI and accelerated economic growth resulted in the consolidation of modern mass-production industries. Furthermore, manufacturing firms became more bureaucratised, the size of top management teams increased substantially, and professional executives became more numerous.[71] However, the bureaucratisation levels in Spain were half of those in Germany or Britain.

Other international firms were established, as can be seen in the table in Appendix 3. These firms had moved away from shopfloor organisation towards a focus upon corporate organisation, strategy and even IT. However, apart from Sofemasa (Sema Group), it seems that they were not very active, and they do not appear among the largest consultancy suppliers of the mid-1970s (see Table 2).

FROM 1974/5 TO THE MID-1980s

In the 1970s the Spanish consultancy market was characterised by the significant capacity of the larger economic consortia to determine the structure of the consulting industry. These groups had been either acquiring or merging with small consulting firms, or creating independent consulting units from their previous consulting departments. For example Auxiesa and Inctesa, two of the largest firms in consultant engineering, were owned by INI and Dragados y Construcción, respectively. The data provided by the table in Appendix 2 indicates that in the 1960s and 1970s the market was rather concentrated and dominated by a few large consortia involving the larger banks and companies, the INI and foreign companies. However, as in Portugal, interviewees revealed that the largest international accountancies that had set up offices in late 1950s and early 1960s also carried out some consultancy-type work. It should be noted that the most important consultancies and engineering firms in 1976 were also receiving some type of technical support from foreign firms (see Table 2). This level of internationalisation among Spanish consulting and engineering firms is one of the arguments used by Eguirbide (1976) and Molero (1979) to highlight the role of these companies as conduits for new technologies during the 1970s.

It appears that scientific-management was considered highly attractive. By contrast, empirical studies in the 1980s found that human relations and decentralised or matrix structures were only operating in a very few indus-

trial firms, most of which were very large, highly bureaucratised and frequently foreign-owned.[72] Moreover, few attempts at structural reorganisation have been detected. Thus, it is unclear whether influential consulting
firms such as TEA and Hay Consulting Group, or the seminars promoted by
NCIP, were actually successful in diffusing American human relations philosophy and organisational principles. This research suggests that the main
impediments to the implementation of human relations techniques were the
low level of bureaucratisation of Spanish firms, and a consequent lack of
resources. Indeed, the largest companies in Spain remained small and nationally oriented. The service sector also remained comparatively small.[73]
There was, in addition, an absence of support for structural ideas (such as
line and staff organisation, divisionalisation) from both the management
theorists and the state and labour unions. Leading international consulting
companies (such as McKinsey, established in Spain in 1977, and A.D. Little)
were either absent or not very influential (see table in Appendix 2). Empirical studies have found that in 1977 the majority of the consulting and
engineering activities were clustered around five major sectors, almost all
engineering related.[74] This feature suggests the greater relevance of engineering-related firms within the group of consultancies active at that time.
Against this background, an important restructuring process was initiated
within the Spanish consultancy market in the early 1980s. While the demand for engineering-related consulting has declined, it has increased demand for consulting in organisation, market and economic viability studies.
Moreover, there were concerns about the use of foreign firms by local and
central administration, as well as about the lack of a controlling body to
ensure the qualifications of those operating in the industry.[75]

FROM THE MID-1980s ONWARDS

The political changes of the early 1980s seem to have had a healthy impact
upon the consultancy business. Increasing awareness and information on
how consultancies could help business led to a growth in demand, and
consultancy exports also increased.[76] The expansion of consultancy business activities has continued more or less unabated in the subsequent
decade, during which a second generation of service providers has emerged
(see table in Appendix 2). Unlike in many other European countries,
German and French consultancies penetrated the Spanish market quite
early. For instance, Spain was one of the two countries in which Bossard, a
long established French consultancy, had affiliates before 1989[77] and Roland
Berger, founded in 1967, and today the largest German consultancy provider, opened an office in Spain in 1985.

Different sources indicate that the 'take-off' of the consultancy business
began in the second half of the 1980s. Based on annual surveys carried out

by AEC, the market volume of management consultancy services in Spain declined slightly from 1991 to 1993, after an increase from 1989 to 1991. The graph in Appendix 4 shows that from 1993 onwards Spain has experienced a strong growth in the demand for consulting, reaching 163 billion pesetas (ESP) in 1997. In terms of total fee income, Spain is already the fourth-largest market for consultancy within Europe, after Germany, the UK and France.[78] The boom in consultancy demand is related to some specific features of the Spanish market. The increase in the demand from multinational corporations, as a result of the massive increase of FDI inflows,[79] is one of them. Moreover, it appears that a new breed of business executive now aspires to establish Spanish businesses in European markets, and is on the look-out for methods of doing so.[80] At the same time, business executives might have realised the need and the advantages of using external experts.[81]

From the interviews conducted, it would seem that consultancy firms are now changing their approach. Among larger consultancies in particular, there is a strong drive to develop 'long-term relationship consulting', to promote long-term relations by focusing on a smaller number of clients, while trying to provide all the consulting services which a client may require.[82] On the one hand, consultancy firms have been merging with companies in other areas of specialisation; while on the other, they have been establishing alliances and contractual agreements with firms supplying complementary or substitute services (such as business media).

CURRENT MARKET STRUCTURE

The main beneficiaries of the demand growth for consulting appear to have been consultancies of American origin. In 1996, six out of the ten largest consulting firms in Spain were American (see Table 3). International consultancies have come to dominate the Spanish market in recent years. The interviews suggest that this is because of the first-mover advantage of foreign firms, as well as their reputation and knowledge, and 'the connectors'[83] they have used to gain access to potential clients. Many presidents and consultants of leading consultancies are former top managers of large companies, with good contacts within the Spanish business system.[84] Moreover, public institutions and multinationals appear to have preferred the services of multinational consultancy firms.[85] However, today, much of the 'sex-appeal'[86] of these big consulting firms has worn off.

Recent events have had a negative impact on international consulting firms. It is possible to refer, for instance, to the massive transfer of ninety-one employees from Coopers and Lybrand into Ernst & Young in 1995 and the lawsuit brought by Aserlocal against Delloite & Touche for presenting Aserlocal work as its own to potential clients. At the same time,

Table 3: The Ten Leading Consulting Firms in Spain (1996/97)

Consultancy Ranked by revenues	Year Est.	Origin	Revenue (ESP/mn) 1997	1996	Growth Rate (%)
1. Andersen Consulting	1989	US	40,322	32,576 Dec 96	13.2
2. Price Waterhouse	1956	US/UK	7,920	9,980 Jun 96	26.9
3. Grupo CP	1966	SP	11,300	8,500 Dec 96	19.7
4. Sema Group	1970	F	12,774	7,709 Dec 96	38.2
5. Idom Ing./cons.	1957	SP	6,047	4,576 Dec 96	8.0
6. Gemini Consulting	1971	F/US	4,169	3,790 Dec 96	16.5
7. Coopers and Lybrand	1963	US/UK	3,199	3,199 Aug 97	7.9
8. Ernst & Young	1989	US	2,489	2,489 Jun 97	77.7
9. McKinsey	1977	US	9,000*	2,260 Dec 96	13.0
10. Boston CG	n.a.	US	n.a.	1,642 Dec 96	n.a.

Source: Management Consultant International, various issues.
* Portugal and Spain in 1997 (AE: 1998 1–99).

domestic firms (such as IDOM established in 1957 or CP Group established in 1966) seem to have undergone significant restructuring, aligning them more closely to big international companies such as Andersen Consulting.[87] Apart from these large firms, there are also very active smaller and medium firms whose success rests either on regional orientation or on specialisation, and upon agreements made with other specialist firms where a range of expertise is necessary. For instance, Europa MC works with different partners, including McKinsey and Arthur Andersen.[88] Some of these firms were established recently by former consultants of larger firms,[89] or by former business managers[90] and politicians. Overall, the considerable number of domestic firms (large, small and medium) learn from the large groups, and are challenging their pre-eminence. However, as revealed by more than 50 per cent of the Spanish consultancies, the Spanish market is peculiar with respect to Andersen Consulting's (AC) leadership. As a result, for AC in 1996, Spain was already its third-largest market in turnover, after the United States and Britain.[91] The interviewees revealed that the reasons behind this leadership appear to be related to AC's more assertive strategy, with its first-mover advantage, as well as with the reputations of AC's Spanish partners.

Another distinguishing feature of the business in Spain is the regional asymmetry. Consultants are predominantly concentrated in Madrid, Cataluna and the Basque Country.[92] However, a regional presence seems to be important to succeed in certain places, since in some regional communities preference is given to firms established in the region. As a result, in order to reach clients in some regions, and in particular the regional public administration, consultancies need a large net of offices. As mentioned by the interviewees, this is a barrier to the development and growth of consultancies.

As far as business areas are concerned, development and implementation of systems and market research are the areas that have grown most. However, IT has been a fast-growing business as well, and systems development and implementation is by far the major contributor to the total turnover (42.5 per cent in 1997). This result reveals not only the increasing role of consultancies in the diffusion of IT technologies, but also a generalised interest in IT within the Spanish business system. More than half of the interviews revealed that IT 'became a fashion' among Spanish managers. The weight of IT-related consulting is, in fact, the highest within the group of FEACO members.[93] IT consultancy and IT systems development and integration account for 59 per cent of consultancy fees in Spain, followed by the UK, where the same services accounted for 39 per cent of FEACO members' fees in 1997.

Within the group of clients, financial services are the largest users of management consulting in Spain, and in 1997 they accounted for 35 per cent of the total consulting fees.[94] This figure confirms our predictions that the sectors experiencing major restructuring, and those facing increasing competition, have been pressured into searching for external support. However, the interviews revealed that, in Spain, the privatisation of public firms has fostered the demand for consulting to only a small extent and that public administration is not yet aware of the need to reorganise its internal structure. While private sector demand for consulting is booming, public sector demand declined as a proportion of the total, dropping from 24 per cent in 1993 to 12.8 per cent in 1997.[95]

Spanish demand for consulting services grew steadily but remains underdeveloped compared to other European countries. Consulting business accounts for only 0.25 per cent of GDP,[96] while in other European countries (such as Germany, France and in the UK) it is nearly 1 per cent of GDP.[97] More than 90 per cent of the interviewees affirmed that the low level of consultancy usage is related to the late and slow industrial development process as well as the behaviour of managers. Spanish managers seem reluctant to resort to professional advice and are sceptical of external intervention.[98]

With the proliferation of small and medium-sized firms – known as PYMES – there has also been a boom in terms of public and semi-public bodies aiming at the promotion of R&D, the strengthening of communications at European level and the simplification of often bureaucratic management structures.[99] From the interviews it can be adduced that these organisations may not be in direct competition with the large consulting firms[100] but that they are important competitors for those whose clients are mostly PYMES.[101] Consulting firms are also currently undergoing change. Departments have given way to multidisciplinary teams. Small and medium consulting firms are co-operating in order to face the competition. Indeed, consultancies are changing not only in structure but also in the services provided.[102] With the private sector demand for consulting services strong in all areas, the interviews revealed that leading Spanish consulting firms are predicting at least two years of robust growth.

As expressed above, the evolution and role of consultants has been essentially demand driven, which has itself been largely determined by changes in the economic situation and business system. Among other factors, government intervention, competition, firms' organisational structure and even national innovation policies have all contributed. However, other supply characteristics have also come into play. The evolution of the Spanish consultancy market after 1946 has been largely determined by the existence of semi-public institutions, such as INOT or NCIP, which has played an important role in the promotion of scientific management. In addition, the penetration of large international consultancies has been a determinant factor. All these events have been accompanied by the development of business schools and managers' educational background. All the above, together with the ideals of leading academics and managers, sometimes fuelled and at other times mitigated the diffusion and attraction of certain management models.

CONCLUSION

The above overview has revealed a number of insights concerning the development of consultants' activities and their role in Portugal and Spain after the Second World War. First of all, it has confirmed the later development of the consulting business in these two countries, involving a time lag of at least two decades. It is, therefore, a relatively new profession with a short tradition, without statutory regulation or the standards of a professional body. In Portugal and Spain, the upsurge did not occur before the 1950s and 1960s. The earlier consultants appear to have been engineering consultants and accountants who were also providing more general advice on business-related issues. Most of the subsequent developments in the consultancy business occurred under foreign influences. Many of the dominant consultancies have indeed been of foreign origin, not only from the US but also from Germany and France. Another group of consultancies was founded by consultants who had either worked with or for foreign consultancies. Additionally, as in many other countries in the European Union (EU), the large international consulting firms dominate the market. However, there are a large number of active domestic consulting firms playing an important role in the diffusion of new management methods and techniques (for example concerning human resources, quality certification and operations research).

Different features of the systemic context have played an important role, either mitigating or fuelling the role of consultants in both countries. Government policies and public institutions have been important actors in the process of diffusion of management practices, either through direct consultancy or through seminars and so forth, boosting the attraction for new management models. All the interviewees mentioned that a few public institutions became more active and nowadays they compete directly in the consultancy market with private ones. This market characteristic has been cited by a large number of the interviewees as a barrier for their firm's development. Aside from this, the lack of competitive behaviour during certain periods, and certain aspects of the business system itself (in particular the small size of firms), have been major constraints on the development of the consultancy business in both countries. However, the business appears to be more developed in Spain than in Portugal. This may be related to the structure of the Portuguese business system, dominated by smaller firms and constrained by a smaller market. Indeed, most of the interviewees in Portugal identified this fact as a barrier to their firm's development. Moreover, in the early 1970s the two countries were already quite distinct. In the 1970s, Spain joined the group of industrialised countries,[103] while Portugal was still a developing country going through the controversial post-revolution period. Furthermore, since the EC accession Spanish companies have shown more dynamism. On the surface, the differences in the consultancy markets in Portugal and Spain are ones of size. As mentioned by partners of large consulting firms from both countries, the larger size of Spanish companies and the larger market create better opportunities for consulting firms.

Despite the apparently increasing predominance of Anglo-American service providers in each of these countries, a careful analysis reveals deeper differences in the consultancy markets between Spain and Portugal. Even the large international consultancies tend to carry out different activities. Partners of large consulting firms suggested that their firm's activities largely depend on the systemic context in which they operate. The majority of their consultants are of national origin recruited from the same universities from which domestic firms recruit. Furthermore, there are differences concerning the principal services offered. One partner of a large consulting firm mentioned that while in Spain the labour negotiations and labour legal advisory has been very active, in Portugal this was not so much the case. In another example, the Portuguese branch does not operate in the health sector although the firm is known internationally for its activities in that area. Moreover, the Spanish firms seem to emphasise 'soft' technology issues much more, such as information, quality and marketing.

To conclude, this analysis confirms the impact of the systemic context on the evolution of consultants' activities in both countries. There are signs that the lack of an appropriate network of business and technical services has been one of the weaknesses of the Portuguese and Spanish business systems. However, there are also signs that these institutions have played an important role as 'outsiders' contributing to the dissemination of management know-how. Signs of change have become clear in the last decade but only a further convergence of national social, legal, institutional framework and business systems in general can lead to a further narrowing of the differences in the consultancy market between Portugal and Spain, and between them and the nations in which the consultancy business is more developed.

Despite these differences, in both countries managers increasingly look for external sources of know-how with a view to competing successfully in a global market. As a result, they may use consultancies more intensively if they recognise in them valuable expertise and knowledge. The penetration of international consulting firms, their aggressive strategies combined with a more national approach may help to enhance confidence in consultants' and consultancies reputations. Moreover, as firms become larger and managers more open to external advisors, the potential for management consulting may also increase.

APPENDICES

Appendix 1: Penetration of Some of the Larger International Consultancy Firms in Portugal

Consultancy	Origin	Open office
Price Waterhouse	US/UK	1951
Arthur Andersen	US	1969
Coopers & Lybrand	US/UK	1972
Hay Management Consultants, SA	US	1972*
Mc Kinsey	US	1987 (1967**)
Ernst & Young	US/UK	1988
Andersen Consulting	US	1989 (Split from AA)
Roland Berger, S.A.	G	1989
Mac Group	F/US	1990 (1986***)
American Management Systems	US	1993
Boston Consulting Group	US	1995

Source: Authors' own elaboration, based on business press and company reports.

    *   some company documents refer to 1972. However, during the interview with HCG, 1979 was cited.

   **   first assignment in Portugal with CUF, Mello Group.

 *** from 1986 to 1990 Mac Group operated in alliance with the domestic consulting firm Iberconsult.

Appendix 2: The Large Consortia in Engineering Consulting in Spain – 1976

Industry	Dominant Consortia	Foreign Participation	Partners	Main Client
Nuclear				
	Empresarios Agrupados	Direct	Banco Urquijo; Gibbs & Hill; Banesto; Hidroelectrica Espanola	Spanish Hydroelectric
	Auxiesa-Inypsa		INI – FECSA	FAECSA business
	Sener		Family Firm	Iberduero
Chemical Engineering				
	Intecsa-Eyser	Indirect	Banco Central; Grupo Huarte	
	Técnicas Reunidas	Direct	Banco Urquijo; B. de Bilbao	
	Herida y Moreno		Procou; Herida y Moreno	
	IPQ-Técnicas		INI; Banco Urquijo;	
		Reunidas	B. de Bilbao	
	Foster Y Wheler	Direct	American Private Company	
Civil Engineering				
	EDES		INI	
	Eptisa	Indirect	Banco Urquijo	

Source: Authors' own elaboration based on information provided by Egurbide (1976, 136).

Appendix 3: Penetration of Some of the Large International Consultancy
Firms in Spain

Consultancy	Origin	Open Office
TEA-CEGOS	F/S	1952 (TEA)
Price Waterhouse	US/UK	1956
Coopers & Lybrand	US/UK	1963
Arthur Andersen	US	1965
Bossard Consultants, SA	F/S	1968–1970
Sema Group	F/UK	1970
Gemini Consulting	F/US	1971 (Cap Gemini)
KPMG Peat Marwick	US	1971
Hay Management Consultants, SA	US	1972
American Appraisal, SA	US	1976
McKinsey	US	1977
Arthur D. Little	US	1978
Development Systems	US	1981
European Consulting Group	?	1985
Roland Berger, SA	G	1985
Deloitte & Touche	US	1987
BDO Binder	US	1988
Ernst & Young	US/UK	1989
Mercer Consulting Group	US	1989
Andersen Consulting	US	1989 (*Split from AA)
American Management Systems	US	1995

Source: Authors' own elaboration, based on business magazines and company brochures

Appendix 4: Management Consultancy in Spain (1989–97)

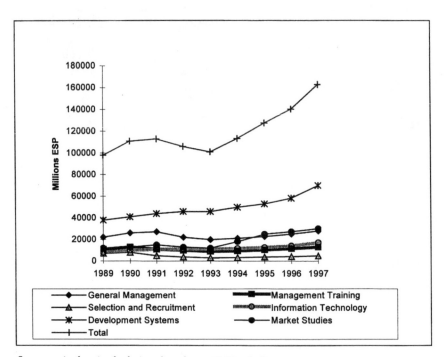

Source: Authors' calculations based on AEC *Yearly Reports*

NOTES

1. This research is a contribution to the project *Creation of European Management Practice*, funded by the EU TSER programme. I gratefully acknowledge financial support from the Subprograma Ciência e Tecnologia do 2°Quadro Comunitário de Apoio and from the CEMP project.

2. J. Cantwell, *Technological Innovation and Multinational Corporations* (Oxford, 1989); K. Pavitt, 'Strategic management in the innovation firm' in R. Mansfield (ed.), *Frontiers of Management – Research and Practice* (London, 1989); W. Cohen and D.A. Levinthal, 'Absorptive capacity, a new perspective on learning and innovation', *Administrative Science Quarterly* 35 (1990), pp. 128–52.

3. For example, G. Hofstede, *Culture's Consequences, International Differences in Work-related Values* (London, 1980); N. Adler, *International Dimensions of Organizational Behavior*, 2nd edition (Belmont, California, 1991); C. Lane, *Management and Labour in Europe: The Industrial Enterprise in Germany, Britain, and France* (Aldershot, 1989); M. Maurice, F. Sellier and J.J. Silvestre, 'For a study of the societal effect universality and

specificity in organisations research', in C.J. Lammers, D.J. Hickson and P. Keagan (eds), *Organisations Alike and Unlike* (London, 1979), pp. 42–60.

4. P.J. DiMaggio and W.W. Powell, 'The iron cage revisited: institutional isomorphism and collective rationality in organizational fields', *American Sociology Review* 48, 2 (1983), pp. 147–60; M.F. Guillén, *Models of Management. Work, Authority and Organization in a Comparative Perspective* (Chicago 1994); F. Mueller, 'Societal effect, organizational effect and globalization', *Organization Studies*, 15, 3 (1994), pp. 407–28.

5. E.g. R. Florida and M. Kenney, 'Transplanted organizations, the transfer of Japanese industrial organizations to the US', *American Sociological Review* 56 (June, 1991), pp. 381–98; R. Fincham, 'Business process reengineering and the commodification of managerial knowledge', *Journal of Marketing Management* 11 (1995), pp. 707–719.

6. J. Morris, 'The transfer of Japanese management to alien institutional environments', *Journal of Management Studies* 32, 6 (November 1995), pp. 719–30; and N. Brunsson, *The Standardization of Organizational Forms as a Cropping-up Process*, 3 (1996).

7. R.G. Havelock, *Planning for Innovation. A Comparative Study of the Literature on the Dissemination and Utilization of Scientific Knowledge* (Ann Arbor, 1969).

8. J. Bessant and H. Rush, 'Building bridges for innovation, the role of consultants in technology transfer', *Research Policy* 23 (1995) pp. 97–114; and J.R. Bryson and P.W. Daniels, 'Business link, strong ties, and the walls of silence, small and medium-sized enterprises and external business-service expertise', *Environment and Planning C: Government and Policy* 16 (1998).

9. Guillén, *Models of Management*; Fincham, *Business process reengineering*; E. Abrahamson, 'Management fashion', *Academy of Management Review* 21 (1996), pp. 254–85; T. Clark and G. Salaman, 'Telling Tales, management consulting as the art of story telling'; D. Grant and C. Oswick (eds), *Metaphor and Organizations* (London, 1996).

10. M.E. Arias and M. Guillén, 'The transfer of organizational techniques across borders, combining neo-institutional and comparative perspectives' in J.L. Alvarez (ed.), *The Production and Diffusion of Business Knowledge in Europe* (London, 1998); M. Kipping, 'The US influence on the evolution of management consultancies in Britain, France, and Germany since 1945', *Business and Economic History* 25, 1 (1996), pp. 112–23; and C. McKenna, 'The origins of modern management consulting', *Business and Economic History* 25, 1 (1995), pp. 51–8.

11. M. Kipping, 'The US influence on the evolution of management consultancies in Britain, France, and Germany since 1945'.

12. Boisot, 'The revolution from outside – Spanish management and the challenges of modernization', D.J. Hickson (ed.), *Management in Western Europe: Society, Culture and Organization in Twelve Nations* (Berlin, 1993); R. C. Cunha and C.A. Marques, *Portugal*, I. Brunstein (ed.), *Human Resources Management in Western Europe* (Berlin, 1995); A. Carreras and X. Tafunell, 'Spain, big manufacturing firms between state and market, 1917–

1990'; A.D. Chandler, F. Amatori and T. Hikino (eds), *Big Business and the Wealth of Nations* (Cambridge, 1997).

13. I. Kovács, *Sistemas Flexíveis de Produção e Reorganização do Trabalho* (Lisbon, 1992); A.P. Inácio and D. Weir, 'Portugal, a developing country', D.J. Hickson (ed.), op. cit.; Carreras and Tafunell, 'Spain, big manufacturing firms'.

14. E.g. AEC (issues 1990–97), *Yearly Reports*, Madrid, AEC; Sismet, *O Sector da Consultoria e Projectos em Portugal*, SISMET, APPC (Lisbon, 1993); K. Vogler-Ludwig, H. Hofmann and P. Vorloou, 'Business services', *European Economy* (1993), pp. 281–401; DN, 'Santos da casa fazem milagres', *Diario de Noticias* (1998), Especial, (June), pp. 22–3.

15. M. Buesa and J. Molero, *Innovación Industrial y Dependencia Tecnológica de España* (Madrid, 1989); A.B. Moniz, 'Mudancas tecnologicas e organizacionais em Portugal, analise das duas ultimas decadas', *Organizacoes e Trabalho* 1 (November, 1989), pp. 7–23; J.M.C. Ferreira, 'Novas tecnologias e tendencias de mudanca organizacional do trabalho em Portugal', *Organizacoes e Trabalho* 516 (1991); V.C. Simões, 'Innovation in Portuguese manufacturing industry', J. Molero (ed.), *Technological innovation, multinational corporations and new international competitiveness: the case of intermediate countries* (Australia and United States, 1995).

16. E.g. business media, empirical studies and available statistics.

17. E.g. Inácio and Weir, *Portugal*; Simões, *Innovation*.

18. V.C. Simões, 'Portugal' in J. Cantwell (ed.), *Multinational Investment in Modern Europe: strategic interaction in the integrated community* (Aldershot, 1992); Inácio and Weir, *Portugal*; Cunha and Marques, *Portugal*; W. Chislett, *Portugal: Investment and Growth* (Euromoney Publications, 1997).

19. APPC, *APPC Directory 1995/1996* (Lisbon, 1995/96).

20. E.g. EU, *Panorama of EC Industry: Management Consultancy*, EU (issues 1989–96); Sismet, *O Sector da Consultoria*.

21. Sismet, *O Sector da Consultoria*.

22. Sismet, *O Sector da Consultoria*.

23. A partner of one of the largest consultancies founded at that time and operating in the field also confirmed this fact. Sismet, *O Sector da Consultoria*.

24. E.g. Cooperativa Uniao Fabril (CUF), Espirito Santo Group and Champallimaud.

25. Ferreira, *Novas tecnologias*; Inácio and Weir, *Portugal*; G. Correia, J. Fiel and R. Nunes, 'Onde eles se fizeram gestores', *Exame* 6, 64 (1994), pp. 42–50; A.S. Silva, 'O sistema financeiro Português e o movimento de internacionalização de empresas', *Economia e Prospectiva* 1, 2 (1997), pp. 59–70.

26. Correia et al., 'Onde eles se fizeram gestores; Silva, O sistema financeiro Português'.

27. Correia et al., 'Onde eles se fizeram gestores; Silva, O sistema financeiro Português'.

28. Correia et al., 'Onde eles se fizeram gestores'.

29. Cunha and Marques, 'Portugal; Silva, O sistema financeiro Português'; Correia et al., 'Onde eles se fizeram gestores'.
30. Cunha and Marques, *Portugal*; Chislett, *Portugal: Investment and Growth*; Silva, 'O sistema financeiro Português'.
31. Ferreira, *Novas tecnologias*; Silva, 'O sistema financeiro Português'.
32. E.g. Moniz, *Mudancas tecnologicas*; Kovács, *Sistemas Flexiveis*.
33. P.P. Tordoir, *The Professional Knowledge Economy: the Management and Integration of Professional Services in Business Organisation* (Netherlands, 1995).
34. Sismet, *O Sector da Consultoria*.
35. Cunha and Marques, *Portugal*.
36. Sismet, *O Sector da Consultoria*.
37. Cunha and Marques, *Portugal*; Silva, *O sistema financeiro Português*.
38. Inácio and Weir, *Portugal*; Silva, *O sistema financeiro Português*.
39. Some companies had been paying above the union rate for qualified personnel; Cunha and Marques, *Portugal*.
40. Cunha and Marques, *Portugal*.
41. Silva, 'O sistema financeiro Português'.
42. *Exame 6*, 65, pp. 25–32.
43. DN, *Santos de Casa*.
44. DN, *Santos de Casa*.
45. DN, *Santos de Casa*.
46. G. Correia, 'Quem sao as rivais da McKinsey', *Exame 5*,51 (1993), pp. 130–34.
47. M. Kipping and C. Sauviat, 'Global Management Consultancies, Their Evolution and Structure', Discussion Paper in International Investment and Business Studies, Series B, IX, (University of Reading, 1996).
48. Correia, *Onde eles se fizeram gestores*.
49. Correia, *Quem sao as rivais da McKinsey*; DN, *Santos de Casa*.
50. Referred to by Iberconsult Partner.
51. E.g. Sismet, *O sector da Consuloria*; Business press.
52. This was the case for a large proportion of the firms interviewed.
53. They were cited by private consultants as important competitors in the market for SMEs.
54. Sismet, *O sector da Consuloria*; Simões, *Innovation*.
55. DN, *Santos de Casa*.
56. Cunha and Marques, *Portugal*.
57. António Bernardo, President of Roland Berger Portuguese Unit. Expansao, 'Competir num mercado global', *Expansao* 22 (1994), pp. 90–93.
58. Simões, *Innovation*.
59. DN, *Santos de Casa*; AEC, *Yearly Reports*.
60. P. Buiges, F. Ilzkovitz and J.F. Lebrun, *The Impact of the Internal Market by Industrial Sector: the challenge for member states* (Brussels, 1990).
61. Molero, *Innovación Industrial*.
62. ASEINCO, created in 1962/3, experimented with a major internal restructuring process which involved broadening out its expertise. As a result of this process, the association was renamed as TECNIBERIA. The develop-

ment of management consulting businesses promoted the increasing autonomy of the organisation and the studies department of TECNIBERIA. These developments led to the creation of AEC, an independent association of management consultants in 1996. AEC, *Yearly Reports*.

63. FEACO, *Survey of the European Management Consultancy Market* (31 December) (Brussels, 1997).

64. P. Egurbide, 'El consulting en España', *Información Comercial Española* 513 (May 1976), pp. 133–7; J. Molero, 'Las empresas de engenieria', *Información Comercial Española*, 552, (August 1979), pp. 59–71.

65. However, in 1950 the Spanish bureaucratisation ratio was approximately at the same level as that of Germany during the early 1920s; but on average Spanish companies were only somewhat smaller than in Japan, Italy, Britain or France; Boisot, *The revolution*; Guillén, *Models of Management*; Carreras and Tafunell, *Spain, Big Management Firms*.

66. Boisot, *The Revolution*; Guillén, *Models of Management*; Carrera, *Spain, Big Management Firms*.

67. Egurbide, *El consulting en España*; Molero, *Las empresas de engenieria*; Boisot, *The revolution*.

68. Bedaux, which was founded by the French emigrant Charles Bedaux in the US in 1916, achieved considerable success from the mid-1920s and continued to expand during the first half of the 1930s. But its success in Europe did not last for long (M. Kipping and C. Sauviat, 'Global Management Consultancies, Their Evolution and Structure').

69. Guillén, *Models of Management*.

70. Boisot, *The revolution*; Guillén, *Models of Management*; Carreras, *Spain, Big Management Firms*.

71. Boisot, *The Revolution*; Carreras, *Spain, Big Management Firms*.

72. Guillén, *Models of Management*; Carreras, *Spain, Big Management Firms*.

73. Boisot, *The revolution*; Guillén, *Models of Management*.

74. Buesa and Molero, *Innovación Industrial*.

75. ASEINCO, *Noticias ASEINCO* VI, 28, March (Madrid, 1983).

76. ASEINCO, *Noticias ASEINCO*.

77. The other country was Italy; Kipping and Sauviat, *Global Management Consultancies*.

78. FEACO, *Survey*.

79. G. Gidron, 'Consulting en España', Management Consultant International (1997).

80. K. Bruton, 'The business culture in Spain', C. Randlesome, W. Brierley, K. Bruton, C. Gordon and P. King (eds), *Business Cultures in Europe*, 2nd edition (Oxford, 1994).

81. Interview with E. Mendicutti.

82. Interview with E. Mendicutti.

83. M. Kipping, 'Bridging The Gap? Management Consultants and Their Role in France', Discussion Papers in Economics and Management, Series A, X , University of Reading, (1997).

84. For instance, Léon Benelbás, former general manager of Tabacalera, is

director of Price Waterhouse and Vicent Bort, former top executive in ATT, is the current president of Arthur D. Little.

85. Gidron, *Consulting en España*.
86. Mr. Huesa, Europa MC partner, (*MCI*, 1997).
87. Gidron, *Consulting en España*; Robredo, J. (1998); 'Control Presupuestario', *Nueva Empresa* 427, pp. 54–7.
88. S. Brown, 'Full stream ahead', *Management Consultant International* 99 (1997).
89. As Mr E. Mendicutti mentioned, this was the case mainly during 1990–93.
90. Aristóbulo de Juan, former General Inspector of Spanish Central Bank, and José Ignácio Lopez, former top manager in General Motors and Volkswagen are examples of such exchanges; S. Franco and L.J. Rosell, 'Directivos que se pasan a la consultoría', *Expansión* (1997), at www.recoletos.es/economica/info/052497directivosaconsultore.htm.
91. I. Lozano, 'Andersen Consulting se aplica su propria medicina', *Actualidad Economica* (June 1996), pp. 35–6.
92. Miner, *Catalogo de La Oferta de Servicios Tecnologicos Por las Empresas de Ingenieria y Consultoras*, Ministerio de Industria y Energía (1996).
93. FEACO, *Survey*.
94. AEC, *Yearly Reports* (1997).
95. AEC, *Yearly Reports*; S. Brown, 'Full stream ahead'.
96. AEC, *Yearly Reports*.
97. FEACO, *Survey*.
98. Boisot, *The Revolution*; Guillén, *Models of Management*.
99. Bruton, *The Business Culture in Spain*.
100. Interview with E. Mendicutti.
101. This fact was referred to us during the interview with the director of Portugal's leading firm in the glass industry. This firm asked for support from 'Sociedad para el Desarrollo Industrial de Extremadura' to set up their operations in Spain.
102. Gidrón, *Consulting en España*.
103. Bruton, *The Business Culture in Spain*; Guillén, *Models of Management*.

Relational Capital and Economic Success in Early Modern Institutions: The D'Este Courts in the Sixteenth Century

Guido Guerzoni and Alessandro Usai

University 'Luigi Bocconi', Milan*

INTRODUCTION

This article rests on two premises, the first historical, the second methodological. We are particularly interested in studying, from diverse points of view, the history of complex pre-industrial organisations. The Renaissance court represents one of the most interesting examples, capable as it is of drawing together both historians (particularly scholars of business history) and scholars of organisational theory in a debate that we anticipate being extremely fruitful. We believe that, to date, these organisations have not been fully investigated – aside from the courts we could cite the great royal factories, the ports, arsenals, building yards, monasteries, armies, by way of example – and we hope that our contribution will stimulate debate in this area.

The second premise lies in the profitable and reciprocal methodological information exchange which historians (including those who are furthest away from a chronological point of view) and scholars of organisational disciplines can achieve, one that permits them to transcend normal time scales and fill in important lacunae.[1] More specifically, we would like here to test our ability to bring about a positive convergence between the research areas of economic history and economics itself, a practice that has already served to emphasise the commonalities between historians and economists on issues where it is hard to discern clear disciplinary boundaries. However, because we are unable to apply the classic techniques of network analysis, we have sought to derive from such methods analytical tools, the application of which will be of interest to both disciplines.

METHODOLOGY

In our article we attempt to apply research methodologies that enable us to assess the role and the importance of 'relational capital' in determining

the economic success of certain individuals, all of whom had close relationships within the environment constituted by the various networks
making up the d'Este courts in the early sixteenth century. In doing so, we
have divided our work into three parts – historical background, compilation of data-sets, and the cross-referencing and interpretation of the data
collected.

(1) A description of the historical background. Not everyone has a clear
idea of the complex structure of an Italian Renaissance court or the extent
of the network of courts that made up the house of Este. Thus, in order to
define more clearly the framework of our historical subject, we have
decided to describe briefly the most relevant social and economic aspects
of our subject.

(2) Relational capital associated with attachment to the circuit of d'Este
courts may have conferred upon individuals great advantage from an
economic point of view. To verify this assertion, we have constructed three
data-sets,[2] making constant use of a prosopographic approach.[3]

In the first database, we reconstructed the identity and careers of all the
members of the courts of the dukes of Ferrara from 1471 to 1559, tran-
scribing and elaborating data from forty-four ducal court payrolls (*bollette
dei salariati*).[4] These documents were written annually using the traditional double-entry book-keeping system, and consisted of the simultane-
ous compilation of a *registro di bolletta*, an *indice*, and a *giornale di
bolletta*. The first of these was a ledger prepared *ex novo* every year, in
which was recorded the title, name, surname/patronymic, place-name,
position, monthly salary, and current account movements for each *salariato*
of the ducal court. The *salariati* were listed not only according to the office
to which they belonged – for example, *spezieria*, *tinello*, *stalla*, *cucine*,
guardaroba, *magistranze* – but also by reference to hierarchical principles.
So, the first pages contained the accounts of the princes and princesses of
the house of Este, followed by those of lords and gentlemen, and then
those of equerries, squires, barbers, doctors, and so on. Obviously, we
concentrated our efforts on the type of register that is most convenient and
useful from the point of view of computer transcription. Unfortunately,
only twelve such specimens were available, those for the years 1475, 1484,
1488, 1494, 1511, 1512, 1513, 1521, 1523, 1525, 1528, 1559, and 1560.
For further help, we were obliged to use the six *indici* (1471, 1478, 1485,
1499, 1500, 1502), as well as the alphabetical section of each master
ledger. These were small registers consisting of two pages for each letter of
the alphabet. Under the appropriate letter of the alphabet were listed the
names of the courtiers, in order of increasing number of pages, so making
the task of compiling the master ledger easier. Since they record only title,
name, surname/patronymic, place-name, and on occasion an individual's
position, these documents provide less information than the master ledger.

However, by looking at these indices we could trace the presence or absence of courtiers, as well as their function. That said, the master ledgers and the alphabetical sections could not satisfy in full our information needs. We required other sources to develop our research into the careers of the people under consideration. Thus we devised a method for using the data of the *libri giornali* as well. These registers were the natural companions to the master ledgers; they contained, in chronological order, payments made to the courtiers from 1 January to 31 December for every year, and always gave the page number of the corresponding master ledger in which the recipient's account was kept. We have been able, by means of an effective transcription technique, to elaborate the data of twenty-six such journals (1504, 1506, 1508, 1509, 1510, 1515, 1518, 1526, 1530, 1531, 1532, 1533, 1534, 1535, 1536, 1537, 1539, 1542, 1543, 1544, 1547, 1550, 1553, 1555, 1558, 1560). All the data from individual files (master ledger, journals and alphabetic sections) were included in one database, from which it was possible to calculate the duration of an individual's stay at court and to outline the career development of each of these courtiers. This is clearly a method to be perfected; but we are satisfied that we can display forty-four annual lists for the eighty-eight year period from 1471 to 1559. The gaps are usually less than three years, and in only one case are they greater than five (1478–84). The same procedure was then used for another thirty-five payrolls relating to members of other princely courts of the house of Este.[5]

In the second database, we reconstructed the names, surnames and yearly invoices of the cloth suppliers (velvet, damask, satin, and so on) who dealt with the ducal court's purchasing office, the *fontico dei panni*, for the period 1533–57. The purchase of these goods was one of the most conspicuous outgoings from the ducal balances and employed a truly enormous sum of money. This expenditure attracted the attention of numerous merchants from Ferrara and elsewhere who, wanting to assure themselves of supply profit, selected mark-ups generally greater than 15–20 per cent.[6] We used information from the following sources to construct this database: two ducal treasury *libri di uscita* (1533 and 1534), and nineteen *autentici del fontico* corresponding to the transactions realised in the years 1535, 1537, 1538, 1539, 1540, 1541, 1545, 1546, 1547, 1548, 1549, 1550, 1551, 1552, 1553, 1554, 1555, 1556, 1557.[7] These were classic master ledgers compiled annually and containing current account movements for each supplier. They recorded, in chronological order, balances, liabilities, sales and incomes. We calculated the value of goods for every supplier during each accounting year,[8] and included these in a general database. This allowed us to identify 206 suppliers active for the period 1533 to 1557. From these, we selected the eighty-one with the highest total invoices. Further, to examine the scale of their relations with other d'Este courts, we followed the same procedure with the data of a further three registers showing the cloth purchases of the officials of the courts of Don Alfonsino (1545–46), Don Alfonso (1550) and the Cardinal Ippolito II (1556–58).[9]

In the third database, we placed the names and invoices of the fifty-six tax contractors active in the Ferrara district from 1493 to 1527 and from 1539 to 1558.[10] The contract for the collection of every category of duty was a profitable activity, with a usual return on capital greater than 15–20 per cent per annum. It was based on multi-annual contracts (3, 5, 7, 9), between the d'Este ducal chamber and a contractor or group of contractors (2, 3, 4), and contained clauses designed to strengthen the reciprocal obligations of the parties concerned. By the due date, for example, the contractors were obliged to deposit a large part of their future income in the ducal chamber treasury. Obviously, rents were lower than the final sums, and huge fortunes could be founded on this differential; explaining why the position of tax contractor was so highly prized. In order to reconstruct the names of the contractors and the total value of their tax, we used the data from twenty-five registers called *significati* and six *libri delle entrate e uscite*.[11] These registers are a year-by-year record, giving – for each type of duty – the first name and surname of the contractor or group of contractors, the duration of the contract and the starting and finishing terms, and the monetary value. Once the values of individual years were established, we gathered these into a database, which was then sorted by decreasing values.

(3) On the basis of the above, we cross-referenced the data, checking how and to what extent the presence of relational capital, based on assessments of relationships within the court environment, could contribute to economic performance. This cross-referencing was done in the knowledge that the economic interests involved in duty collection were greater than those determined by cloth supply. Thus, we tried to measure relational capital statistically by identifying key parameters and focusing both on the group of tax contractors and the suppliers.

For each tax contractor, we listed:

a) Name and surname.
b) The total value of the invoices, equal to the sum of the annual rental fees of the tax collected during the contractor's career.
c) The period in which the contractor worked (to see if it preceded or followed the period of court employment).
d) The number of years employed as a contractor.
e) The type of position held in the ducal court.
f) A dummy variable (1 for court position, 0 otherwise) to see whether or not the individual had a ducal court position.

g)   The duration of the court position.
h)   The duration of the ducal court position, expressed in years.
i)   The number of relatives active in the ducal court between 1493 and 1559.[12]

For each cloth supplier:

a)   Name and surname.
b)   Total value of the invoices.
c)   The average annual invoice.
d)   The longevity of the career as supplier, calculated as the difference between the first and the last year as a supplier.
e)   The number of years as a supplier (note that only the most important merchants obtained large-scale supply contracts every year, the other had to manage with periodic or small value transactions).
f)   The number of other d'Este courts these people supplied, as a way as of assessing the extent of their network of knowledge and influence.
g) i) m)   The *total* value of sales to the courts of Don Alfonsino (1545–46), Don Alfonso (1550), and Ippolito II (1556–58).
h) l) n)   The *average* annual value of sales to the courts of Don Alfonsino (1545–46), Don Alfonso (1550), and Ippolito II (1556–58).
o)   A dummy variable to account for whether the individual had a position at the ducal court or otherwise (1 for court position, 0 for otherwise).
p)   The number of relatives at court from 1471 to 1532 (see note 12).
q)   The number of relatives at court from 1532 to 1558 (see note 12).
r)   The total number of relatives at court (see note 12).

Historical framework

One of the first tasks confronting scholars of the Italian Renaissance court is the delineation of the boundaries of the institution and the related criteria of inclusion and exclusion. However, these boundaries were actually far more distinct than we had expected; the court was not just a place in which men, classes and authorities mingled, but also served as the venue in which social differences were established and controlled. Its real essence was the creation and removal of differences. To help us understand this tendency towards the establishment and maintenance of order, it is necessary to ascertain both who was present in the d'Este courts, and who could legitimately style himself a courtier.

One category comprised those who served the duke permanently within the private and domestic space, as well as those serving the duchesses and several princes and princesses of the d'Este house. The continuity of the relationship between prince and courtier, and their physical and residential proximity were the first selection criteria, independent of service motives. These simple distinctions allowed for the creation of several categories of individual who had work relationships with the court. The continuity requirement excluded more than 1600 suppliers of goods and services, and the cohabitation and 'personal service' criterion excluded those who were not considered as 'salary-earning courtiers', even if they were regularly paid by the duke, because they worked away from his house and person. Also among those excluded were 600 state officers (stewards, governors, commissaries, administrators of the ducal territory, members of the outlying financial courts), 500 members of the permanent armies (nearly all knights), members of the ducal fleet, professors of the University of Ferrara, more than 2000 people working in agriculture, 200 employed in technical farming activities, 2500 people working in the ducal factories (wool and silk works, glass furnaces, soap factories, the mint, foundries, brick-kilns), as well as 800–900 people working in the Longastrino rock salt mine, in the Comacchio valleys, and in the mines and kilns on the lower slopes of the Apennine. While all these individuals depended on the duke, they were not regarded as members of his court.

THE COURT AND THE COURTS

It is important to note that there was not just one court at Ferrara, but that the d'Este house comprised a group of courts. This is of vital importance because all the members of the various d'Este courts were subject to the same economic and legal regimes, and enjoyed the same privileges, such as those of a fiscal nature. It is, then, helpful to identify at the very least the size of each court, starting with the ducal courts. Table 1 shows the annual number of salary-holders in the d'Este ducal courts between 1470 and 1560.

The numbers in Table 1 are undoubtedly underestimates since they include as salary holders only those receiving a salary in money. If we also include those individuals who received only food rations, the so-called *bocche* (mouths), namely 25 to 30 pages, 20 to 30 servants of the ducal chamber, 120 to 150 gentleman's servants, and the servants and relatives of workers and officials, the final figure comes to between 550 and 750. In contrast, the duchesses' courts were rather smaller. Those of Eleonora of Aragon and Lucrezia Borgia show evidence of having contained only about 110 to 120 members, *bocche* included, while that of Renata of France had only 150 to 160 members, *bocche* included.

Table 1: Number of *salariati di corte* of the dukes of Este, 1471–1560.

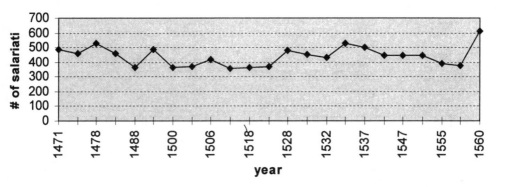

Source: Guerzoni, G. (1996), 'La corte estense 1471–1559', Aspetti economici e sociali, Ph.D. thesis, University 'Luigi Bocconi', Milan, Chapter 1, p. 31.

In addition to the two major courts were the minor, or non-ducal, courts. This category of court included those of the other princes and princesses of the blood. Even if these lacked the size, the undoubted political clout, and the social cachet of the ducal court, the courts of the various dynastic branches reproduced – on a reduced scale – the same organisational, economic and relational layout. Table 2 provides an impression of this general phenomenon, showing some of the principal d'Este courts and the number of people employed therein.

EFFECTS OF THE SPREAD OF NON-DUCAL COURTS

The existence of a veritable network of d'Este courts produced positive effects of considerable importance. For instance, it promoted the spread of consolidated organisational models and administrative procedures, which not only helped redistribute technical knowledge but also physically redis-

Table 2: Courts of Este and number of their members in 1495–1500 and 1555–60.

1495–1500

Sigismondo (duke's brother) 90 members	Rinaldo (duke's brother) 25 members	Alberto (duke's brother) 25 members
	Ercole I (duke) 550 members	Eleonora d'Aragona (duchess) 110 members
Alfonso I (crown prince) 90 members		Ippolito I (duke's 2nd son, cardinal) 120 members
Lucrezia Borgia (Alfonso I' wife) 70 members		Ferrante (duke's 3rd son) 35 members
		Sigismondo (duke's 4th son) 50 members

1555–1560

Ippolito II (duke's brother, cardinal) 250–300 members	Francesco (duke's brother) 90 members	Don Alfonso (duke's brother) 130 members
	Ercole II duke 520 members	Renée de Valois (duchess) 150 members
Alfonso II (crown prince) 300 members		Luigi (duke's 2nd son, cardinal) 120 members
Lucrezia Medici (Alfonso II's wife) 80 members		Laura Eustochia Dianti (2nd wife of Ercole II's father) 70 members
		Lucrezia and Eleonora (duke's daughters) 30 members

Sources: G. Guerzoni, 'The Courts of Este in the first half of XVIth century. Socio-economic aspects', in M. Aymard and M.A. Romani (eds), *The court as economic institution* (Paris, 1997).

tributed the very men who were paid to implement this technical knowledge. This led to the creation of a valuable uniformity of management practices, whilst boosting the labour markets and expanding the professional horizons of the personnel involved. This prevented staff from getting "stale", led to a salutary level of turnover, and brought into being what could be termed an 'internal market' within the court professions. That groups from a similar cultural background were skilled at carrying out virtually identical tasks meant that these individuals could offer their services at any d'Este court, and this encouraged the exchange and circulation of functionaries between the different establishments. Such opportunities widened the scope of client bonds. While the Duke's court offered 500–550 posts, the group made up of all the other courts represented a potential labour reservoir of another 1000–1200 people. This simple fact explains the establishment of client networks which sometimes maintained themselves independently of ducal networks. Each court maintained preferential relationships with specific economic workers, well-defined family groups, and fixed suppliers. Our analysis of the careers of functionaries at various courts has pointed up the existence of diversified strategies of appointment-seeking. For, though the middle to low ranks (book-keepers, craftsmen, small traders, generic servants) concentrated on establishing long-term relationships with just one *pater* or *mater familiae*, the powerful aristocratic and bourgeois groups (bankers and large-scale merchants) adopted a speculative policy. They were trying to acquire adherents in each court, so as to strengthen their group's control of the entire activity and boost its contractual power. One simple example is provided in Table 3.

THE COURTIERS: SOCIAL EXTRACTION, CAREERS AND CLIENTELE

When discussing the families, factions and careers of courtiers, it is also necessary to take into account a more strictly socio-demographic dimension. The first aspect of this is the immediately apparent sluggishness of the courtiers' progress up the ranks. This demonstrates the existence of a formidable system controlling access to courtly ranks, independent of the social origins of the individuals involved, as can be observed in Table 4.

The reasons for slow upward progress lie both in the idiosyncrasy of the skills developed and in the preference given to long-term dealings founded on fiduciary relationships. Loyalty and knowledge of administrative procedures and cultural practices went hand-in-hand. The duke could not allow himself to be surrounded by anyone other than servants of proven loyalty and undoubted ability. The princes and princesses of the d'Este house chose their own courtiers with enormous care, and once selected, they remained bound to their lord. In such circumstances, court service did

Table 3: Courtiers belonging to different families, active in the Este courts between 1554–58.

Family	Ercole II	Alfonso II	Ippolito II	Luigi	Don Alfonso	Renata
	Court					
Ariosto	Francesco Ludovico		Antonio Claudio	Attilio		
Beloncini	Gaspare Gianfrancesco				Ippolito	
Gatti	Gianbattista Rinaldo		Ercole	Vincenzo		
Giglioli	Alfonso	Ercole	Annibale			
Putti			Ippolito Ercole			Alfonso Guidobaldo
Silvestri				Ercole	Andrea	
Tassoni	Camillo Galeazzo Giulio Ludovico	Nicola Scipione	Lucrezio			
Vincenzi		Nicola	Alberto			
Zerbinati	Tommaso		Carlo	Antoniomaria		

This example is taken at random from a limited number of courts and a rich spread of families. *Source*: State Archive of Modena (A. S. Mo), A.E, C.D.E, B.S, registers no. 60 (Ercole II, 1558) and 58 (don Alfonso, 1554) and Amministrazione dei Principi (A.P), no.s 493 (Alfonso II, 1558–59), 901 (Ippolito II, 1556) and 1260 (Luigi, 1559); State Archive of Turin (A.S.To), Art. 806, paragrafo 2, Inventario 365, no. 90 (Renee de Valois, Duchess of Ferrara, 1558).

not come as just an option. It was, presumably, a duty which no one could refuse without seriously damaging his own family's prospects. Further, by examining the lists of members of the non-ducal courts – the officials working in the territory and the men-at-arms – we see how careers diversified. The great families succeeded not only in placing their members at all levels of the d'Este authority, but also in getting them appointed to the financial administration. For this reason, those who were in the duke's service remained the primary points of interest for family and faction

Table 4: Years of service at court for the period 1506–34 for socio-professional classes. The data refers to 1248 courtiers out of 1459 (85.53 per cent), already in service in 1506 and employed before 1534.

Office/Department	Individuals	Percentage	Average Years
Signori-Gentiluomini-Ambasciatori-Fattori Generali-Segretari-Consiglieri di Giustizia	124	9.94	16.42
Camerieri-Scalchi-Scudieri-Medici-Barbieri	95	7.61	14.69
Cancelleria	33	2.64	14.55
Camera ducale	167	13.38	15.27
Castaldi e Saltari	30	2.40	10.81
Musicisti ed Ecclesiastici	115	9.21	12.55
Magistranze:Armaioli-Tornitori-Fabbri-Falegnami, Ebanisti-Liutai-Sarti	62	4.97	13.11
Staffieri-Portonari-Chiavieri-ai Servizi	90	7.21	10.31
Falconieri-Uccellatori-Cacciatori-Montieri Canattieri-Pardieri	141	11.30	13.38
Giardinieri e Ortolani	36	2.88	8.86
Stalla: Maestri di Stalla-Ufficiali di Stalla-Cavalcatori-Maniscalchi-Sellari	48	3.85	14.75
Spezieria	9	0.72	18.56
Guardaroba	15	1.20	18.53
Spenderia-Grassa-Panetteria	24	1.92	15.25
Credenza-Bottigliaria	17	1.36	11.53
Tinello	38	3.04	9.97
Cuochi-Aiutocuochi-Sopracuochi	40	3.21	12.93
Granai e Depositi delle Farine	14	1.12	13.93
Cantine	16	1.28	16.25
Legnaie	8	0.64	10.13
Marinareza: Capitani-Ufficiali alle Barche-Nocchieri	26	2.08	8.46
Facchini-Massari-Massare-Servi-Carrettieri	100	8.01	7.71
Total	1248	100	13.08

Source: Guerzoni, G., (1996), 'La corte estense 1471–1559', Aspetti economici e sociali, Ph.D. thesis, University 'Luigi Bocconi', Milan, Chapter 4, p. 15

strategies. They could defend the positions the family had acquired and ensure the expansion of its sphere of influence. They could also sponsor those they protected and strive to increase the strength of the coalitions to which they belonged, while struggling against those of competing factions.

This phenomenon explains both the socio-relational centrality of courtiers who were the representatives of linked interests, and the tenacity with which those who were excluded tried to place their own people within the ducal circle. It was not easy to overcome the – understandable – resistance of the already established families, who were determined to maintain a firm control over recruitment processes. Yet, these processes could certainly not be entirely controlled by established families and remained more or less open to influence. In this respect, the duke would skilfully exploit existing mismatches, asserting his multi-faceted role of arbiter and player, judge and spectator of his courtiers' ascents and descents on the ladder of success.

Looking again at the data in Table 4, one can, however, see the extreme heterogeneity of the social rankings that could find opportunities at court: reigning princes, aristocrats, men-at-arms, churchmen, notaries public and men of law, doctors, intellectuals, artists, craftsmen, administrators from banking and merchant families, and ordinary people. In this sense, far from being an arena in which only the aristocracy struggled, to a more or less bloody degree, to win or defend positions, the court was a 'clearing-house' for all the dynamics of promotion and social down-grading, it was the 'chamber of compensation' where old and new assets were skilfully brought together, a genuine parliament in which all ranks found their natural place. Within the courts, there was a space for any expression of requests, wishes, interests and aspirations. In this regard, see Table 5.

The courts contained, therefore, lineages of squires, equerries, gentlemen, doctors, herbalists, treasurers, bookkeepers, craftsmen, stewards, counsellors, falconers, horsemen, collectors, treasurers, and so on. This phenomenon is fully explicable without recourse to interpretations from the traditional theory of the venal nature of work roles. It is possible that some people paid for their acceptance at court, but the family nature of the selection mechanisms encouraged the association of people who were already part of the d'Este power system. There were, in this sense, two converging desires at work. The courtiers were interested in sponsoring relatives or clients in order to strengthen the negotiating power and the influence of their own group, while the dukes supported the recruitment of known elements, whose fealty was guaranteed by those who introduced and recommended them. Moreover, the secrets, the dangers, and the interests were such as to impose the very loyalty which was the criterion for the selection and the promotion of employees. It therefore seems very logical that there should have been a willingness to keep to a minimum the

Table 5: Members of certain families in service at the ducal court between
1471 and 1559, excluding aristocrats.

First year	Last year	First Name	Surname	Office/Department
1500	1500	Battista	Beccari	camera ducale
1518	1560	Ludovico	Beccari	camera ducale
1521	1523	Antonio	Beccari	camera ducale
1528	1537	Lattanzio	Beccari	camera ducale
1533	1558	Vincenzo	Beccari	camera ducale
1534	1534	Giovannino	Beccari	
1535	1560	Giovanni	Beccari	camera ducale
1544	1553	Giovanni	Beccari	magistranze
1550	1560	Agostino	Beccari	camera ducale
1555	1560	Nicola	Beccari	camera ducale
1475	1475	Marano	Bellaia	camera ducale
1475	1493	Gianmaria	Bellaia	camera ducale
1471	1485	Gerolamo	Da Castello	
1475	1515	Ludovico	Da Castello	spenderia, panetteria e grassa
1488	1488	Francesco	Da Castello	medico
1493	1511	Francesco	Da Castello	medico
1499	1502	Bernardino	Da Castello	medico
1535	1537	Bartolomeo	Da Castello	
1513	1544	Giacomo	Da Signa	spezieria
1521	1544	Gerolamo	Da Signa	spezieria
1528	1535	Alberto	Da Signa	spezieria
1539	1539	Francesco	Da Signa	spezieria
1515	1528	Nicola	Di Raganello	musici e religiosi
1518	1546	Gerolamo	Di Raganello	musici e religiosi
1526	1533	Giacomo	Di Raganello	musici e religiosi
1538	1546	Riminaldo	Di Raganello	musici e religiosi
1478	1478	Zaccaria	Ferraio	
1513	1553	Bartolomeo	Ferraio	castaldi e saltari
1528	1537	Antonio	Ferraio	castaldi e saltari
1530	1533	Gianmaria	Ferraio	castaldi e saltari
1550	1559	Gianfrancesco	Ferraio	castaldi e saltari
1478	1494	Giovanni	Perinati	marinareza
1506	1522	Filippo	Perinati	marinareza
1511	1513	Antonfrancesco	Perinati	marinareza
1542	1544	Cesare	Perinati	camera ducale
1494	1534	Marco	Pigante	guardaroba
1528	1531	Bartolomeo	Pigante	castaldi e saltari
1528	1560	Marchetto	Pigante	guardaroba
1535	1558	Gerolamo	Pigante	spenderia, panetteria e grassa
1485	1494	Filippo	Prosperi	camera ducale
1494	1511	Francesco	Prosperi	Cancelleria
1508	1528	Bernardino	Prosperi	Cancelleria
1511	1513	Gianbattista	Prosperi	Cancelleria
1518	1518	Benedetto	Prosperi	Cancelleria
1530	1553	Bartolomeo	Prosperi	signori/gentiluomini/oratori
1506	1539	Francesco	Serafini	Stalla
1525	1560	Gianmaria	Serafini	Stalla
1528	1528	Bartolomeo	Serafini	Stalla
1555	1560	Cesare	Serafini	Stalla

Source: Guerzoni, G. (1996), 'La corte estense 1471–1559', Aspetti economici e sociali, Ph.D. thesis, University 'Luigi Bocconi', Milan, Chapter 4, pp. 35–41.

number of outsiders, and to recruit from among those already linked to people in service, in such a way as to be useful as further instruments of control.

THE ROLE AND WEIGHT OF RELATIONAL CAPITAL

The desire to minimise the number of outsiders was a logical extension of attempts to defend the vast economic interests of members of the house of Este, as can easily be seen from the data in Table 6, which illustrates the size of the ducal patrimony, production, type of management, and the number of people employed.

What is immediately striking is the wide spectrum of activity which was managed directly, or started, by ducal initiative, a fact which explains why a sizeable part of that which was consumed came from ducal farms and works. Food and wine, glass and ceramic crockery, firewood and clothes, bricks and roofing tiles, cannons and powder, soaps and perfumes, weapons and ships, carriages and horses, all bore the unmistakable sign of the *impresa del diamante*, the house of d'Este's mark. The result of these ambitious projects was the patient construction of a genuine 'd'Este economy', able to contain an impressive number of people, and to exploit every possibility of establishing profitable connections with outlying members. But this frenetic activity did not just benefit a small number of economically-privileged workers. Neither was it in opposition to the development plans of local economic frameworks: the courts were not parasitic on the cities which hosted them, in fact, the opposite was true. The manufacturing activities, together with more traditional types of consumption, involved an enormous number of people. These ranged from the suppliers of goods and services, merchants and intermediaries who supplied the d'Este court with finished products or merchandise, through to those who bought the products of the d'Este workshops, along with technicians, craftsmen and other hands involved in projects of different types (porters, carriers, water-carriers, workers employed in specialist maintenance and repair, boatmen, mule-drivers and carters). There was, however, a precise hierarchy which fixed the position of the various economic operators who were in contact with the d'Este entourage. Not all the merchants or suppliers enjoyed the same entrée. Not all the financiers succeeded in standing in the breach for many years. Thus, in order to understand the reasons for the success of those who did well, and to understand if social relations with the court networks may be invoked as a major explicative factor, we decided to test and measure the weight and role of these relationships by analysing the group of cloth suppliers and tax contractors.

Table 6: Ducal wealth, productive results, type of management, and number of employees

Sectors	Type of management	# employees
Agriculture – crops and animals		
110 farms with *pertinentie* (vine-yards, meadows, farmhouses, stables, granaries, cellars, backeries, warehouses, wells, etc.). They produced on annual average 1040 tons of wheat, 230 of barley, 290 of corn, 40 of millet, 480 of spelt, 80 of pulses.	70 farms were directly administered with harvest contracts, 40 farms were leased	2500
meadows, gardens, kitchen-gardens, orchards, orange-groves, lemon-groves, garden centres (mulberry-trees)	directly administered	30
Woods	those of Garfagnana, San Felice and Mesola were leased	
1050 head of horses, 2000 beef cattle, 7000 sheep	directly administered/ contracts agistment	50
about 10 lakes, valleys (*valli*) and fishfarms	leased	
The 35–40 valleys (*valli*) of Argenta and Comacchio, which produced an annual average of 50 tons of eels between 1513 and 1562	directly administered	350
Extractive activity		
The salt works of Comacchio and Longastrino, produced and annual average of 4000 tons between 1527 and 1566. At Ferrara alone in 1562 there were 12 warehouses for storage and sale of salt	directly administered	350
6 to 7 mines in the Apennine dedicated to the extraction of gold, silver, iron, copper and vitriol	leased	
Transport activity		
3 to 4 *bucintori*, 15 to 16 transport craft, 3 large ships for Mediterranean and Atlantic navigation. At Ferrara the duke also had a dockyard	the *Mediterranean* and *Atlantic* ships were jointly owned with shipowners and sailors	30

Table 6: continued

Sectors	Type of management	# employees
Manufacturing and commercial activity		
various urban establishments for accomodation	provided free and on lease	
warehouse and pickling business (eel pickling)	directly administered	5
warehouses, cellars, granaries, shops	almost all in Ferrara, mostly leased	30
30 hotels	leased	
more than 20 mills (the 3 mills of Ferrara of san Paolo, san Benedetto, san Giovanni Battista operated in conditions of monopoly)	directly administered	12
4 'slauter-houses (Argenta, Ferrara, Modena e Reggio)	directly administered only at Ferrara	45
4 iron furnaces at Garfagnana and other metalurgical works (in the '40s they produced an annual tonnage of 400–450 of cast iron per year	leased	
1 ceramic kiln and laboratory	directly administered	5
furnaces for lime and bricks (in Ferrara were 12)	directly administered	110
1 glass furnace	leased	
soap works from 1540 (producing 15 to 16 tons per year)	leased	15
2 artillery foundries	directly administered	15
ducal factory for the production of woolen clothes (Arte della lana), which operated 1540–60	directly administered	1200
ducal factory for the production of silk clothes (Arte della seta), which worked during first half of the 1500s	directly administered	300
Ferrara mint	leased	

Source: G. Guerzoni and M. A. Romani, 'Looking for a Model: The Court as an Economic Institution. The Cases of Gonzaga, d'Este and Farnese from the XVth to the XVIIth Century', paper presented at the conference *Beyond Elias? Court Society: The Center as Symbol and Locus of Power*, UCLA (2–3 May 1997).

DATA ANALYSIS

Many authors have analysed the impact of what one might call 'the embeddedness argument' on modern economies.[13] In this study we have tried to use the relational approach in the context of an historical analysis. As Granovetter observed, most sociologists, anthropologists, and historians have taken the strong embeddedness position with regards economic action in primitive or non-market societies; claiming that such action was heavily embedded there, but has become much more autonomous with modernisation.[14] Our preliminary findings seem to confirm this classic assumption: embeddedness was a more significant factor in ancient economies. Our data also shows how the d'Este court was not only the source of political power but also of economic power. In addition, the cross-study of the careers data set and of the court economic transactions data set (tax contractors and cloth suppliers) shows how these two aspects of the court's centrality were often linked. The career and the transaction sides were not separate.

In this sense the court seems to have been – for its economic counterparts – the source of a form of capital different in kind from those considered by the neo-classical economists. This is relational capital[15] a concept vital for understanding economies such as that of the d'Este courts. Relational capital is comprised of the set of relations an individual maintains in his dealings with a system, another individual, or the rest of the world. We can include within relational capital not only social relations but also formal relations springing from association, work, affiliation and collaborative agreements such as contracts.

In our opinion, the concept of relational capital is more helpful in interpreting this particular economic environment than are other types of capital such as financial, human,[16] or social.[17] One is not dealing here with an analysis of the capacity or the personal competence that permitted suppliers or contractors to prosper, or with a study of the relations between the financial strength – employment or material capital – of a cloth merchant or contractor and his ability to improve his activity. Nor can we limit our attention exclusively to relations of a social type, such as friendship or kinship, in order to see how these influenced the economic progress of different suppliers and contractors.

In other words, if we study the economies of the tax contractors and the cloth suppliers we should not limit our study to the attributes of the individual contractors and suppliers themselves. If we did so, we would lose sight of a very important element: the degree to which they controlled relational capital in dealings with the d'Este courts. We stated that the d'Este courts were the largest potential sources of earnings for economic operators who lived in the dukedom territories. There was thus a clear asymmetry in the potential relation with the courts, or more precisely, a situation of resource dependence.[18] It is therefore logical to assume that every form of relation – direct or mediated – between economic operators on the one side, and the courts on the other, represented an exceptional form of capital for the economic operator.

This form of capital could not be quantified in monetary terms, nor was it easily transferred from one subject to another as applies to physical or monetary forms of capital. It represented, nonetheless, an indispensable asset which, like other forms of capital, guaranteed income and other useful returns over long periods of time. Relations were direct and multiple and, governed by the norm of reciprocity,[19] favours or services delivered in one aspect of a particular relation were paid for, or reimbursed, within another. It might have been the case that an individual who performed a distinguished long-term role at court, was repaid either with exclusive supply contracts or with the concession to collect duties. Nothing prevents us from hypothesising that the converse could also occur – that a long-term and satisfactory supplying relationship could be rewarded with a court position. Relational capital is, therefore, measured in terms of the number, the type and the intensity of the relations between external agents and the court: the network considered was a very highly centralised one whose heart was the ducal court.

It seems reasonable to hold, then, that the activity of economic agents[20] linked to the courts was correlated with the amount and nature of the relational capital they controlled. Yet, a fuller picture of the correlation between economic and relational capital is harder to construct. It remains to be shown whether the relational wealth of an agent itself determined their business success; or whether the inverse true, and court ties were a simply a reward for those who had excelled in their own fields. In addition we need to ask which relations were important, and which were less important to individual economic success?

From a methodological point of view, there are a number of ways in which the phenomenon of relations can be studied. Attention can be focused on the network of relations, or on the nature of the relations between a generic pair of agents, from whom one may extrapolate to all agents involved in analogous relationships. The typical methodological approaches of network analysis[21] did not seem applicable for our case; in fact, network analysis concentrates mainly on the structural characteristics of networks,[22] and, with regard to the individual actors, provides only measures (such as centrality and structural equivalence) which in this case were of little interest. In the present case, the form of the network is very clear from the beginning: the ducal courts are the primary sources of relational capital served as the central hub of the network. Moreover, in order to have made a structural approach more interesting, we would have had to analyse each of an individuals' relations and not only the sum of dyadic relations pertaining to the courts. We concentrated, instead, on making a comparative analysis of the economic biography of agents and their relational history with the courts. Objection could be made to our distinction between the spheres of exchange and relation, on the grounds that economic exchange is also a kind of relation between actors. While not denying the validity of this objection, we wish to stress that our purpose is to distinguish between the economic sphere in the strict sense – pure exchange – and other possible relational spheres. We therefore refer to as 'relational' the set of links that are different from one-off or repeated economic transactions.

Moving on to the data analysis, we should point out that the data at our disposal cannot be interpreted in a strictly deterministic manner but, nevertheless, supplies us with some interesting indications. The most interesting results are the following. For the first group, that of the tax contractors, we found a significant correlation (0.473 ** Pearson 2-tailed sign) between the presence – as an employee – at the court and the number of invoices that this person had earned in the period. We found an even stronger correlation between presence at court and the length of the tax contract. In other words, employees enjoyed greater economic stability and longevity of service.

If we assume a structural point of view in studying these relationships, we cannot limit our attention to the analysis of just the direct relational capital (the coincidence of relations of commission and relations of court dependence). Structural analysis assumes, in the majority of social relations, that a transitivity property exists within social relations. For this reason, we also considered the indirect methods by which relational capital could be controlled. In order to do that, we considered the number of ducal dependants related to each contractor. This result provides a preliminary, if crude, impression of the potential impact belonging to a family with rich court relations could have on economic performance, or even simply an individual's ability to establish a contractual relationship with the d'Este court.

In this case the data considered concerned not only the presence or absence of relatives at court, but also the number of relatives in attendance at court.[23] The information gathered suggests the following frequencies. Among the first fifty-six tax contractors, 39.3 per cent were at the same time contractor and employee at the court and 67.9 per cent had at least one relative employed at the court. Only 26.8 per cent were neither direct employees nor related to an employee at the court. In other words, only one contractor out of four did not control any form of relational capital with the court. Almost 33.9 per cent enjoyed both direct employment and relatives at court. The top ten contractors in terms of invoices – among the first fifty-six – made up 62.2 per cent of the total number of invoices, and

Table 7: Summary of data analysis for the contractors cluster

Cluster of contractors	% of the 56	Average Invoices
Employee/without relatives at the court	5.4	119.543
Employee (with ad without relatives)	39.3	98.121
Employee/with relatives at the court	33.9	94.739
With relatives (employee and not employed at the court)	67.9	54.626
Average Contractor	100.00	53.717
Not employed/without relatives at the court	26.8	38.248
With relatives at the court/not employed	33.9	14.514

nine where also employed at the court. In Table 7 we have summarised some of the more interesting results. We have also introduced data of the average invoices for each cluster of contractors.

From looking at this data, it would appear that the two types of relational capital had different roles. The presence of relatives at the court seems to have been a virtual *sine qua non*. Even if we cannot prove directly the necessity of this indirect capital we could say that, in any case, it does not seem very likely that an individual could have become a tax contractor were he totally outside the court network. Yet, this indirect type of capital does not show any influence on the economic performance of the contractors. In descriptive terms, we found direct access to the network – as an employee of the duke – to be a much better indicator of the economic success of the contractors. Those contractors with relatives at court but without a direct position, however, were found to have the smaller contracts. Indeed, it almost seems as if these contracts represent, as it were, the crumbs of the consensus system. Curiously, this cluster is, from an economic point of view, of smaller average size than that of the isolated individuals, though the latter does show lower average invoices than the first fifty-six. It is necessary to look more closely into the reasons for this discrepancy between the economic status of those outside of the court and those indirectly connected with it.

In terms of economic success, having a position at court was of decided importance. The sum of the invoices of those with a court position – 39.3 per cent of the contractors – account for 72 per cent of the invoices of the first fifty-six contractors. Court position seems, then, to have had a strong influence on the economic performance (economic size) of the contractor. In other words, if the existence of a family relationship could, in some way, favour access to the generic position of contractor, where there was a direct relationship the duke was significantly more likely to award contracts of large size – those for which the risks deriving from opportunism were greater and from which the contractors' profit could be far higher. From another point of view, it could be argued that economic success called for a court position, and not the other way around. In this second case, a position would become a genuine instrument by means of which the duke could develop the economic relation into another type of long-term relation: that of dependence.

This evidence would therefore seem to support the hypothesis that social capital guaranteed trust on the part of the duke towards his tax contractors. However, the role of those whom we have termed 'isolated', whose earnings were below average, demands clarification, and we need to explain why those in possession of indirect capital (relatives at court) had contracts for diminutive amounts even in comparison to the isolated. It seems likely that their contracts were given – we are speaking here of the crumbs – between network relatives, with the sole purpose of guaranteeing a constant but limited profit.

As far as cloth suppliers are concerned, we have produced the following data: only 9.8 per cent of them had a court position, while about 28.39 per cent had at least one relative at court. Those with a court position had at least 23.35 per cent of the total income of the first eighty-one suppliers, which is to say that a court position guaranteed – to the few who possessed one – a high supply level. We are therefore a long way from the 72 per cent of the total enjoyed by court-connected tax contractors. In general, the importance of relational capital seems less important in this sector than with respect to the tax collectors, and this seems to be consistent with the argument that trust was an important ingredient of the relation between tax collectors and the duke. It is therefore clear that the majority of suppliers had neither court position nor relatives at court. Despite this, the data for cloth suppliers show two interesting correlations between the following variables: the length of supply to the ducal court and the number of deliveries to other courts (0.401** 2-tailed significant), and the number of deliveries to the ducal court and number of deliveries to other courts (0.416 ** 2-tailed significant). From the point of view of organisational theory, we can confirm that the diverse nature of the economic activity taken into consideration may have led to the adoption of different selection criteria by the duke's counterparts.

In the case of tax contractors, the first necessity for the duke was not to achieve the best service at the least cost, but was to be able to guarantee non-opportunistic behaviour on the part of his employees. The collection of tax duties was one of the principal sources of income from the dukedom and could not therefore be entrusted to unreliable individuals. 'Reliable' referred to not just reputation, but also the extent to which an individual's loyalty had been secured by advantageous and reciprocal economic relations. Social and direct controls were, in this case, the best methods available to the duke of managing this delicate activity. From the point of view of the contractor, relational capital seems to have been the privileged condition for gaining access to the contract (relatives) and for obtaining it in high values (employee). In contrast, in the case of cloth suppliers, the court needed good quality cloth but accepted the small risk of opportunism. It was not the case then, that for cloth suppliers the context of reference was more similar to that of a market, even if it was embedded in relations other than exclusively economic ones. The correlation between court deliveries and the number of deliveries to other courts is probably evidence of the fact that the success of a cloth supplier was relatively interlinked with his exclusive link with the court of reference.

One can also formulate some hypotheses about the function of relational capital with regard to this second group of actors connected to the court. It is arguable – but here we are really just within the field of hypotheses – that the relational capital in this case was established on the basis of existing social network between the elites of the various courts. The network became capital to the extent that it could supply what we would today call 'promotion' for the cloth of a specific supplier. In other words, the relational networks served to enhance the reputation of suppliers and therefore secure for the lengthy supply contracts (duration of supply to the ducal court and number of other courts supplied – 0.401 ** 2–tailed significant).

If for contractors, then, useful relational capital resided exclusively in the network established by the ducal court, and seems to have been the necessary condition for obtaining the contract, for clothing suppliers, on the other hand, we have not found any correlation between the possession of relational capital at court and economic success. Here, in fact, useful relational capital seems to have resided principally in the network established by the elite governing the different courts. The nature of the social capital seems to differ between the two networks. In the first case, social capital was able to guarantee trust. In the second, relational capital was able to guarantee reputation.

Apart from the hypotheses proposed in this preliminary paper, which require further empirical examination, the usefulness of this analysis lies, in our opinion, in demonstrating the importance of a structural or relational approach to economic phenomena, particularly those of the past. In those periods when the embeddedness of economic relations was total, it seems important to take into account less obvious, but perhaps more significant, forms of capital, principally social or relational capital.

Appendix A: 56 tax contractors active in the Ferrara district 1493–1527 and 1539–58

A	B	C	D	E	F	G	H	I
Benedetto Brugia	350200	1498–1508	11	fattore generale	1	1510–13	4	5
Tito Strozzi	315000	1501–08	8	fattore generale	1	1511	1	12
Lazzaro Marzi	221837	1540–44	5	superiore valli Comacchio	1	1558–66	9	0
Gaspare Macchiavelli	168000	1491–1500	10	fattore generale	1	1493	1	5
Ludovico Orsini	167595	1493–1503	11	m.o generale dei conti	1	1478–1512	33	1
Gianpaolo Macchiavelli	161962	1538–49	12	fattore generale	1	1547–60	14	5
Giovanni Dalla Pena	148170	1553–56	4		0			0
Bernardino Cestarelli	125400	1493–1503	11	consultore	1	1493	1	3
Pietro Capellini	108000	1504–09	6	ragioniere	1	1499ᵃ–1512	14	1
Ludovico Brugia	106900	1493–96	4	massaro di camera	1	1485–93	1	5
Nicola da Angera	97853	1539–59	21	esattore generale	1	1528–60	33	2
Zaccaria Spanopoli	93326	1539–44	6		0			0
Pietro Soncini	87660	1545–49	5		0			1
Cristoforo Correggiari	75600	1498–1502	5		0			0
Giovanni Dal Miaro	72000	1501–03	3		1	1493	1	0
Paris di Rigo Antonio	64793	1503–17	15	capitano della piazza	1	1511–28	18	0
Giovanni Rodi	62422	1506–24	19	esattore	1	1521	1	2
Sebastiano Zaninelli	61636	1536–49	14	tesoriere	1	1535–57	23	1
Galasso Coccapani	58600	1504–1508	5		0			0
Ludovico Coccapani	58600	1504–08	5		0			0
Rinaldo Morelli	56624	1543–59	17		0			6
Gerolamo da Treviso	50850	1491–1500	10		0			0
Francesco Correggiari	31250	1491–95	5		0			0
Nicola Lavezzoli	31200	1539–44	6		0			6
Nicola da Savana	22765	1549–56	8	notaio in spenderia	1	1550–59	10	3
dall'Angelo Giovanni	18280	1501–10	10		0			2
Paolo di Rigo Antonio	15513	1503–08	6		0			1
Andrea Rodi	15280	1502–37	36	esattore	1	1523–28	6	2
Ludovico dai Sacchi	13600	1501–09	9		0			1
Gianmaria da Copiano	12800	1495–1500	6		0			0
Francesco dale Anguille	12447	1494–99	6		0			5

Appendix A: continued

A	B	C	D	E	F	G	H	I
Benedetto Ugolini	9600	1493–1500	8		0			4
Belino Bruson	9350	1501–06	6		0			0
Giovanni Cuogo	8804	1543–44	2	notaio ai memoriali	0			0
Pellegrino Munaro	8350	1501–11	11		0			0
Alessandro Biondi	8200	1501–02	2	ufficiale alle fornaci	1	1493–1511	1	4
Teodosio Brugia	8200	1500	1	fattore generale	1	1502–10	9	5
Biagio Rossetti	8200	1501–02	2	ingegnere ducale	1	1484–1502	19	4
Angelo Cuzuola	6700	1504	1		0			0
Gianmaria dale Anguille	6134	1494–96	3		0			5
Battista Franzosi	6000	1492–1500	9		0			0
Bartolomeo Morelli	5250	1505–09	5		0			6
Matteo Cappelli	4875	1522–45	24		0			0
Bartolomeo Sogaro	4800	1491–95	5		0			2
Lionello Sogaro	4800	1491–1495	5		0			2
Michele di Netto	4700	1515–33	19	ufficiale sopra le munizioni	1	1558–60	3	3
Nicola Sadoleti	4000	1501	1	fattore generale	1	1478–1502	25	2
Baldissera dal Sale	3720	1501	1	gentiluomo	1	1511	1	6
Giambattista Palmieri	3600	1499–1503	5		0			2
Gianmaria Bellaia	2500	1493–96	4		0			9
Antonio Caleffini	1775	1502–10	9		0			5
Antonio Rodi	989	1494	1		0			3
Taddeo Ugolini	664	1502	1		0			4
Francesco dal Basso	450	1494–96	3		0			0
Leonardo Novelli	270	1494	1		0			1
Alessandro Cultri	66	1494	1		0			2

Legend: A) Name and surname of the contractor; B) The total value of the invoices, equal to the sum of the annual renting fees of the tax collected during the contractor's careers; C) The period in which the contractor worked; D) The number of years employed as a contractor; E) The type of position held in the ducal court; F) A dummy variable (1 for court position, 0 otherwise) to see if the individual had, or did not have, a ducal court position; G) The period of the court position; H) The duration of the ducal court position, expressed in number of years; I) The number of relatives active in the ducal court between 1493 and 1559.

Appendix B: Top 81 cloth suppliers 1533–1557

A	B	C	D	E	F	G	H	I	L	M	N	O	P	Q	R
Francesco Contugi	46868	24	19	2467	3	1387	194	14	14	300	150	0	0	2	2
Antonio da Vento	14464	24	14	1033	1					2240	747	1	0	1	1
Alberto e Gianbattista Masi	12736	25	15	849	0							0	1	0	1
Bongiovanni Marigella	8749	16	10	875	0							0	0	0	0
Andrea Rodi	8315	6	5	1663	0							1	1	1	2
Giulio, Sebastiano e Zaninello Zaninelli	7748	24	16	484	1			5	5			1	0	0	0
Francesco, Gerolamo e Vincenzo Vincenzi	5278	24	20	264	1					40	40	1	1	1	2
Battista Venturini	5249	14	11	477	2					25	25	0	0	0	0
Isacco e Leone di Lazzaro ebrei	4911	18	12	409	0	1686	843	2123	2123			0	0	0	0
Ippolito Tesini	4760	24	10	476	0			5	5			0	0	0	0
Giacomo Tombesi	4721	24	18	262	1					298	149	1	3	3	4
Odoardo Balbo	4249	26	18	236	0							0	0	0	3
Giangerolamo Cappelli (eredi)	3697	10	8	462	0							0	0	3	0
Camillo Galiera alias da Parma	3333	17	8	417	1	314	157	47	47			0	0	0	0
Giovanni Bonetti detto il Rosso	3240	24	17	191	2					889	296	0	0	0	0
Domenico Maria dalle Balle	3139	5	5	628	0							0	0	0	0
Antonio e fratelli Rasini	2697	24	17	159	3	181	90,5	113	113	143	72	0	0	0	1
Bernardino da Monte	2552	8	5	510	0							0	0	1	0
Andrea Correggiari	2429	18	10	243	0							0	0	0	0
Albertino e Francesco Picchiati	2423	25	12	202	1			18	18			0	0	0	0
Giulio dal Moro (eredi)	2147	25	18	119	0							0	0	2	2
Tiberio Rizzi	1678	24	18	93	2	80	40	12	12			0	0	0	0
Lorenzo Guicciardini	1573	7	3	524	0							0	0	0	0
Bassano Burri	1354	3	3	451	0							0	0	0	0
Michele Valiero	1274	11	6	212	1					11	11	0	0	1	1
Nicola Scuri	758	4	4	190	0							0	0	0	0
Matteo Prandi	1220	14	4	305	0							0	0	0	0
Maggio Bordella Levita ebreo	730	10	6	122	0							0	0	0	0
Alfonso Raimondi da Reggio	718	2	2	359	0							0	0	0	0
Pietro Antonio dalla Seta	711	13	4	178	1					57	57	0	0	0	0

Appendix B: continued

A	B	C	D	E	F	G	H	I	L	M	N	O	P	Q	R
Ludovico Zipponari	710	23	11	65	0							0	3	2	5
Francesco Gambertino	708	3	2	354	0							0	0	0	0
Ippolito Linarolo	696	2	2	348	0							0	0	0	0
Gabriele Ariosti	685	1	1	685	0							0	14	3	17
Giovanni Scotti	580	2	2	290	0					1256	628	0	0	4	4
Alfonso Silvestri	564	10	3	188	1							0	5	0	5
Paolo Biondi	527	1	1	527	0							0	0	0	0
Francesco Mona	518	23	8	65	1					124	124	1	0	7	7
Gerolamo Cavalieri	508	1	1	508	0							0	0	7	7
Isacco rabbino ebreo	505	7	5	101	1					2950	983	0	0	0	0
Domenico Gallo da Venezia	474	2	2	474	0							1	1	4	0
Francesco dall'olio	474	3	2	237	0							1	1	0	5
Angelino ebreo	433	8	4	108	0							0	0	0	0
Abramo de Luna ebreo	403	14	9	45	0							0	4	8	12
Tommaso Nigrisoli	403	11	4	101	1					106	106	0	2	3	5
Francesco Bianchi	389	1	1	389	0			10	10			0	2	3	4
Giacomo Novelli	344	12	7	49	1							0	0	4	4
Giovanni Magni	339	1	1	339	0			59	59	89	89	0	0	0	0
Pietro Francese	327	3	2	164	2	214	107					0	0	0	0
Pietro Maria Mantovano	323	5	2	162	2			306				0	1	0	1
Giovanni Maria Maganza	308	17	5	62	2				306			0	1	0	1
Nicola Dolcetti	308	2	2	154	0							0	1	1	3
Ugo Boiardi	306	1	1	306	0							0	2	0	0
Alfonso Prosperi	301	16	4	75	0							0	1	5	6
Francesco Calzetta	298	14	5	60	0							0	0	0	0
Pietro Maria Gardo dalla Seta	242	7	2	121	0							0	2	1	3
Alessandro Rodi	240	1	1	240	0							0	0	0	0
Ippolito Argoati	218	6	3	73	0							0	0	0	0
Mengino Patella	212	5	4	53	0							0	0	0	0
Alberto Corregiari	208	2	2	104	0							0	0	0	0

Appendix B: continued

A	B	C	D	E	F	G	H	I	L	M	N	O	P	Q	R
Mosè Sacerdoti ebreo	205	4	4	51	1					50	50	0	0	0	0
Bacchio Tolomei fiorentino	204	12	6	34	2	423	212			493	164	1	0	0	0
Giacobbe Capritti ebreo	188	6	5	38	1			87	87			0	0	0	0
Venturino dal Finale	186	1	1	186	0							0	0	0	0
Vincenzo da Cremona	179	1	1	179	0							0	0	0	0
Giovanni Magnon	178	11	4	45	0							0	1	0	1
Patrizio Muzzi	173	5	3	58	0							0	0	0	0
giovanni di per	169	1	1	169	0							0	0	0	0
Francesca di Simone da Trento	166	1	1	166	0							0	0	0	0
Gerolamo dalle Carte	165	1	1	165	0							0	1	0	1
Giacomo Boiardi	165	21	6	28	2			259	259	266	266	1	1	2	3
Antonio Marigella	164	2	2	82	1			3	3			0	1	2	3
lionello dal sale	159	21	6	27	0							0	2	6	8
Albertino Da Vento	159	2	2	80	0							1	1	1	2
Giovanni Mastellaro	156	10	2	78	0							0	0	0	0
isacco levita ebreo	156	3	2	78	0							0	0	0	0
Giovanni Maria Mazzolini	151	3	2	76	0							0	0	3	3
Giacobbe Todesco Hebreo	150	17	5	30	1			87	87			0	0	0	0
Terzo Terzi	141	11	2	71	1			19	19			1	0	0	0
Gerolamo Casanova	135	3	3	45	0							0	1	1	2
Giacomo Filippo Cultri	132	3	2	66	0							1	0	1	1

Legend: A) name and surname of the supplier; B) The total value of the invoices (expressed in lire); C) the yearly average invoice (in lire); D) the longevity of the career as supplier (in number of years); E) The number of years of supply; F) The number of the other d'Este courts with whom they had a relationship as suppliers; G), I), M) The total value of sales to the courts of don Alfonsino (1545–46), don Alfonso (1550), Ippolito II (1556–58) in lire; H), L), N) The average annual value of sales to the courts of don Alfonsino (1545–46), don Alfonso (1550), Ippolito II (1556–58) in lire; O) A dummy variable (1 for court position, 0 otherwise) to see if the individual had, or did not have, a ducal court position; P) The number of relatives at court from 1471 to 1532; Q) The number of relatives at court from 1532 to 1558; R) The total number of relatives at court

NOTES

*   Alessandro Usai wrote the section 'Data Analysis', Guido Guerzoni is the
      author of the rest of the article.

1.   See for instance P.S. Bearman, *Relations into rhetorics: local élite structure in
      Norfolk, England, 1540–1640*, (New Brunswick, 1993); R.V. Gould, 'Multi-
      ple networks and mobilization in the Paris Commune, 1871', *American
      Sociological Review* 56 (1991), pp. 716–29; J.F. Padgett and C.K. Ansell,
      'Robust action and the Rise of the Medici, 1400–1434', *American Journal of
      Sociology* 98 (1993), pp. 1259–319; D. Postles, 'Personal pledging: "medi-
      eval reciprocity" or "symbolic capital"?', *The Journal of Interdisciplinary
      History* 26 (1996), pp. 419–36; N. Rosenthal, M. Fingrutd, M. Ethier, R.
      Karant and D. McDonald, 'Social movements and network analysis: a case
      study of nineteenth-century's Women's Reform in New York State', *Ameri-
      can Journal of Sociology* 90 (1985), pp. 1022–54; B. Wellman and C.
      Wetherell, 'Social networks analysis of historical communities: some ques-
      tions from the present to the past', *History of the Family: an International
      Quarterly* 1 (1996), pp. 97–121 and C. Wetherell, A. Plakans and B. Wellman,
      'Social networks, kinship and community in Eastern Europe', *The Journal of
      Interdisciplinary History* 24 (1994), pp. 639–63.

2.   See on these matters J.A. Barman, R.J. Barman and W.T. Kershaw,
      'Prosopography by computer; the development of a data base', *Historical
      Methods* 10 (1977), pp. 102–8; J. Bradley, 'Relational database design and
      the reconstruction of the British medical profession: constraints and strate-
      gies', *History and Computing* 6 (1994), pp. 71–84; L. Breure, 'Interactive
      data entry: problems, models, solutions', *History and Computing* 7 (1995),
      pp. 30–49; G. Croenen, 'Prosopography and source oriented data processing
      with KLEIO', in K. Goudriaan, K. Mandemakers, J. Reitsma and P. Stabel
      (eds), *Prosopography and Computer* (Leuven, 1997), pp. 195–210; P. Denley,
      'Source oriented prosopography: KLEIO and the creation of a data bank of
      Italian Renaissance university teachers and students', in F. Bocchi and P.
      Denley (eds), *Storia e multimedia* (Bologna, 1994), pp. 150–60; J.P. Genet,
      'Entre statistique et documentation: un système de programmes pour le
      traitement des données prosopographiques', in N. Bulst and J.P. Genet (eds),
      Medieval Lives and the Historians: Studies in Medieval Prosopography
      (Kalamazoo, 1986), pp. 359–75; J.P. Genet and M. Hainsworth, 'Prosop: un
      système de traitement automatique des données prosopographiques', in H.
      Millet (ed.), *Informatique and Prosopographie* (Paris, 1985), pp. 279–97;
      D.I. Greenstein, 'A source oriented approach to history and computing: the
      relational database', *Historical Social Research* 14 (1989), pp. 9–16; D.I.
      Greenstein, 'Multi-sourced and integrated databases for the prosopographer',
      in E. Mawdsley, N. Morgan, L. Richmond and R. Trainor (eds), *History and
      computing III: historians, computers and data applications in research and
      teaching* (Manchester, 1990), pp. 60–66; C. Harvey and J. Press, 'The Busi-
      ness élite of Bristol: a case study in database design', *History and Computing*
      3 (1991), pp. 1–11; C. Harvey and J. Press, 'Relational data analysis: value,
      concepts and methods', *History and Computing* 4 (1992), pp. 98–109; C.

Harvey and J. Press, *Databases in historical research. Theory, methods and applications* (London, 1996); O. Itzcovich, 'Masters and apprentices in Genoese society, 1450–1535', in P. Denley, S. Fogelvik and C. Harvey (eds), *History and Computing II* (Manchester, 1989), pp. 209–219; G. Price and A. Gray, 'Object oriented databases and their application to historical data', *History and Computing* 6 (1994), pp. 44–51; J. Winchester, 'What every historian needs to know about record linkage for the microcomputer era', *Historical Methods* 25 (1992), pp. 149–65.

3. On this aspect see: F. Autrand (ed.), *Prosopographie et genése de l'état modern* (Paris, 1986); G. Beech, 'Prosopography', in J.M. Powell (ed.), *Medieval studie* (Syracuse, 1976), pp. 151–84; N. Bulst, 'Prosopography and the computer: problems and possibilities', in P. Denley, S. Fogelvik and C. Harvey (eds), *History and Computing II*, (Manchester, 1989), pp. 12–19; T.F. Carney, 'Prosopography: payoffs and pitfalls', *Phoenix* 27 (1973), pp. 156–79; A. Demurger, 'L'apport de la prosopographie à l'étude des mécanismes des pouvoirs XIIIeme–XVeme siècles', in F. Autrand (ed.), *Prosopographie et genése de l'état modern* (Paris, 1986), pp. 289–301; J.P. Genet and G. Lottes (eds), *L'Etat moderne et les élites XIIIe–XVIIIe siècles. Apport et limites de la methode prosopographique* (Paris, 1996); K. Goudriaan, K. Mandemakers, J. Reitsma and P. Stabel (eds), *Prosopography and Computer* (Leuven, 1997); J. Hamesse (ed.), *Methodologies informatiques et nouveaux horizons dans les recherches médiévales* (Turnhout, 1992); K.S.B. Keats (ed.), *Family trees and the roots of politics: the prosopography of Britain and France from the tenth to the twelfth century* (Woodbridge, 1997); H. Millet (ed.), *Informatique and Prosopographie* (Paris, 1985); H. Millet, 'From sources to data: the construction of a prosopographical data-bank', in P. Denley and D. Hopkin (eds), *History and computing I* (Manchester, 1987), pp. 63–6; C. Nicolet, 'Prosopographie et histoire sociale: Rome e l'Italie à l'époque républicaine', *Annales* 25 (1970), pp. 1209–28; A. Paravicini-Bagliani, 'Pour une approche prosopographique de la cour pontificale du XIIIeme siècle. Problémes de méthode', in N. Bulst and J.P. Genet (eds), *Medieval Lives and the Historians: Studies in Medieval Prosopography* (Kalamazoo, 1986), pp. 113–120; T. Schijvenaars, 'Computerized prosopographical research', in K. Goudriaan, K. Mandemakers, J. Reitsma and P. Stabel (eds), *Prosopography and Computer* (Leuven, 1997), pp. 1–24; L. Stone, 'Prosopography', *Daedalus* 100 (1971), pp. 46–79 and R.F. Wevers, *Isaeus: chronology, prosopography, and social history* (Paris, 1968) and K.F. Werner, 'L'apport de la prosopographie á l'histoire sociale des élites', in K.S.B. Keats (ed.), *Family trees and the roots of politics: the prosopography of Britain and France from the tenth to the twelfth century* (Woodbrige, 1997), pp.1–22.

4. These registers are preserved in the State Archive of Modena (A. S. Mo), A.E, C.D.E, B.S, registers no.s 6–19, 21, 23, 25–, 29–34, 37–9, 41–9, 51–3, 55, 58–60. The *salariati* were courtiers who also received a salary in money.

5. These registers are preserved in the A. S. Mo: A.E, C.D.E, B.S, registers no.s 28, 50, 56, 58, 60, 61 and A. P, no.s 492, 493, 899, 901, 902, 903, 904, 1130, 1131 and 1260; other pay-rolls have been found in the State Archive of Turin (A. S. To), Articolo 806, paragrafo 2, Inventario 365, 'Conti e

Ricapiti delle Case de' Signori Duca di Genevois, Nemours, Amule, Chartes, e Gisors dal 1397 al 1686, no.s 44–55 and 59–64.

6. These registers are preserved in A.S.Mo, A.E, C.D.E, L.C.D., registers no.s 327 and 328.

7. These registers are preserved in A. S. Mo, A.E, C.D.E, A.C, Fontico, registers no.s 3, 5, 6, 7, 10, 13, 18, 19, 21, 23, 24, 26, 28, 30, 32, 34, 35, 37, 40.

8. These amounts are equal to the value of all the goods sold throughout the year. The decision to consider the value of goods sold was based on the fact that the officials of the ducal *fontico dei panni* tended to pay the larger suppliers in different tranches, often deferred for extended periods of time.

9. This data was obtained from registers contained in A. S. Mo, A.E, C.D.E, A.P, no.s 387 and 170 and A. C, Guardaroba, no. 152.

10. The d'Este dukedom, of which Ferrara was the capital, was subdivided into different administrative sectors. Different contractors worked within these subdivisions: as well Ferrara, there were the districts of Argenta, Brescello and Castelnuovo, Carpi, Cento e Pieve, Comacchio, Finale, Frignano e Grafagnana, Modena, Reggio Emilia, Romagna, San Felice. The 56 tax contractors therefore constituted a portion of the whole population, of more than 400 people. However, for political reason the d'Este preferred to concede the contracts for district tax collection to indigenous contractors. This fact explains our decision to focus exclusively on Ferrara operators. The chronological interruption of the period examined (1528–39) is due to a lack of documentation. Further references in F. Bayard, 'La carriére des financiers français dans la premiére moitié du XVIIe siècle', in F. Autrand (ed.), *Prosopographie et genése de l'état modern* (Paris, 1986), pp. 195–208; A. Greeve and J. Storjohann, 'Innkeepers, brokers and moneychangers in Bruges during the 14th Century', in K. Goudriaan, K. Mandemakers, J. Reitsma and P. Stabel (eds), *Prosopography and Computer* (Leuven, 1997), pp. 167–84; P. Hamon, 'Le personnel financier subalterne sous François Ier: cour ou marge de l'administration monarchique? Les apports de la prosopographie', in J.P. Genet and G. Lottes (eds), *L'Etat moderne et les élites XIIIe–XVIIIe siècles. Apport et limites de la methode prosopographique* (Paris, 1996), pp. 181–8; J. Kerherve, 'Prosopographie des officiers de finances: L'exemple des tresoriers de l'Epargne bretons du Xveme siecle', in N. Bulst and J.P. Genet (eds), *Medieval Lives and the Historians: Studies in Medieval Prosopography* (Kalamazoo, 1986), pp. 376–89; J.L. Le Cam, 'Prosopographie d'éleves boursiers en Allemagne protestante au XVIe siècle', in H. Millet (ed.), *Informatique and Prosopographie* (Paris, 1985), pp. 19–38 and M. Van Den Noortgate, 'A database as an instrument for a prosopographical study on elite groups of financial experts in fifteenth-century Ghent', in K. Goudriaan, K. Mandemakers, J. Reitsma and P. Stabel (eds), *Prosopography and Computer* (Leuven, 1997), pp. 87–96.

11. These registers are preserved at the A. S. Mo, A.E, C.D. E, A.C, Significati, nos 1–24 and 27 and L.C.D, no.s 343, 358, 364, 370, 381, 396.

12. The analysis of the d'Este courtiers did not always allow us to identify exactly the relationship and degree of kinship between individuals with the same surname. We therefore decided to adopt a strong hypothesis that a shared surname presupposed a kinship link. For a serious analysis of these

aspects see F. Bayard, 'La carriére des financiers français dans la premiére moitié du XVIIe siècle', quoted; A. Demurger, 'Carrières normandes: les vicomtes (1350–1450)', in J.P. Genet and G. Lottes (eds), *L'Etat moderne et les élites XIIIe–XVIIIe siècles. Apport et limites de la methode prosopographique* (Paris, 1996), pp. 97–110; H. De Ridder-Symoens, 'Possibilités de carriére et de mobilité sociale des intellectuels-universitaires au moyen-âge', in *Medieval Lives and the Historians: Studies in Medieval Prosopography* (Kalamazoo, 1986), pp. 343–57; O. Matteoni, 'L'apport de la prosopographie á la connaissance des carrières des officiers de la Chambre des Comptes de Moulins (environ 1450 et environ 1530), in J.P. Genet and G. Lottes (eds), *L'Etat moderne et les élites XIIIe–XVIIIe siècles. Apport et limites de la methode prosopographique* (Paris, 1996), pp. 123–38; J.C. Passeron, 'Biographies, flux, itinéraires, trajectories', *Revue Francaise de Sociologie* 31 (1989), pp. 3–22 and S. Zulstra, 'Studies and professional careers of Frisian students, 1375–1650', in K. Goudriaan, K. Mandemakers, J. Reitsma and P. Stabel (eds), *Prosopography and Computer* (Leuven, 1997), pp. 61–72.

13. See M.S. Granovetter, 'The strength of weak ties', *American Journal of Sociology* 78 (1973), pp. 1360–80; 'Economic action and social structure: the problem of embeddedness', *American Journal of Sociology* 91 (1985), pp. 481–510; 'Problems of explanation in economic sociology', in N. Norhia and R.G. Eccles (eds), *Networks and Organizations: structure, form and action,* (Cambridge, 1992), pp. 25–56. Furthermore in H. White, 'Where do Markets Come From?', *American Journal of Sociology* 87 (1981), pp. 517–47; M.N. Zald, 'Political economy: a framework for comparative analysis', in M.N. Zald (ed.), *Power in Organizations* (Nashville, 1992), pp. 221–61 and in S. Zukin and P. Di Maggio, *Structures of Capital: The Social Organization of the Economy* (Cambridge, 1990).

14. In M.S. Granovetter, 'Problems of explanation in economic sociology', quoted, p. 27.

15. On this aspect see G. Soda and A. Usai, 'The dark side of dense networks: from embeddedness to indebtedness' in A. Grandori (ed.), *The Game of Network* (London, 1997).

16. We refer to G. Becker, *Human Capital* (New York, 1993).

17. See J.S. Coleman, 'Social Capital in the Creation of Human Capital', *American Journal of Sociology* 94 (1988), pp. 95–120.

18. See J. Pfeffer and G.R. Salancik, *The external control of organisations: a resource dependence perspective* (New York, 1978).

19. In A.W. Gouldner, 'The Norm of Reciprocity: a preliminary statement', *American Sociological Review* 25 (1960), pp. 161–78.

20. We use this generic name for the set of agents who were involved in economic exchanges with the courts.

21. See for instance S. Wasserman and K. Faust, *Social Network Analysis: methods and applications* (Cambridge, Mass., 1994).

22. See R. Burt, *Toward a Structural Theory of Action* (New York, 1982).

23. It is obvious that an important element to be borne in mind is the power and prestige of each individual, but this data is not readily available, and, further, would be difficult to measure. So, for now, it will not be considered.

The Convergence of History, Organisation and Networks:
An Introductory Research Note

Giuseppe Soda

University 'Luigi Bocconi', Milan

In this article I will attempt to clarify some points relative to the relationship between business history, organisational theory and network analysis. The first point regards the *rapprochement* of economic history, business history and organisational theories. In recent years, the research areas of economic history and economics itself have increasingly converged. This phenomenon has considerably increased the points in common and the points of difference between historians and economists on issues where it is hard to distinguish clear disciplinary boundaries. There are numerous reasons for this, pointing both to the specific, epochal, change in the gnosiological nature of individual disciplines, as well as the increasing meeting of the respective areas of enquiry.

Let us begin with economic history. Here there seem to be two important indicators: the first is the decisive liberation of economic history from a long-lasting subordination to economics, which reduced its role to that of a valuable – but substantially submissive – researcher of evidence for the economic paradigm. Economic history provided the first hard, but justified, critical reactions to the limits of the most orthodox economic approaches. The second indicator is the growth of studies dedicated to contemporary economic history, of which business history is the most visible form. This has forced many economic historians to carry out a careful and comprehensive revision of methods, language, methodology, and training, moving ever closer to arguments which had, for a long period, remained almost completely the prerogative of economic research.

Organisational science, on the other hand, was born as a paradigm for integration between distant and different disciplines. In analytic models developed in the course of research in the organisational field, the multidisciplinary roots of the organisation emerged very clearly – at once sociology, psychology and economics. While discovering the 'foundations' of this body of knowledge, it is impossible to ignore the profound links with historical method and content. Max Weber, for example, was more a historian than a sociologist. He was convinced that it was necessary to study institutional history in order to understand the functioning of institutions.

The development of organisational theory was a sort of revolution parallel to that of the revision of neo-classical economic theory. Organisational theory absorbed contributions from other social sciences, moving ever closer to a 'sensitivity' typical of historians – it had also courageously challenged the limits of the economic approaches which had, up to then, predominated, in the attempt to explore new paths of research. Thus, those in organisational studies were perhaps the first among economists to have abrogated the dogma which considers economics to be a 'science without history', beginning by considering the 'Time O' of economic models as a boundary to the understanding of complex phenomena, rather than the absolute prerequisite of every 'scientific' proof. The 'parallel course' has only begun. If economics owes to the 'organisational' Simon the concept of bounded rationality, economic history has, for a long time, advised economists against assuming as constants the sorts of behaviours and mind-sets of which no significant traces have been recorded historically.

Starting from this background, organisational scholars have extended the concept and the predictive value of historical explanation with respect to one key question: Why does the organisation of economic activity take various forms?

One of the most effective proposals to come from organisation scholars revolves around the concept of path-dependency. This explanation of organisational variety considers the dynamic effects of an organisational system's development and history on its organisational configuration at a particular point in time. This approach has focused the attention of scholars on interactive processes both within the organisation and the organisation. It is but a small step outside from this to the convergence with the relational perspective. The organisation thus learns to recognise the role and weight of all those 'non-economic' components of 'economic action', components which economic history has already fully described – albeit at the level of the economic system or, in the case of business history, without full methodological support. The theory is fundamentally that of the relational network as a conceptual tool[1] for describing and exploring the vast range of social relations in the community, in groups and in institutions. It was only later that the network became a methodology and a very powerful analytical instrument for describing relational structures between organisational agents (Social Network Analysis).

The use of social network analysis within organisational studies has allowed research to be focused on what has generically been defined as the 'informal' and 'social' elements within and between organisations. Much research has demonstrated the importance of non-formalised relations and uncodified schemes of action. As an example, from a more analytical understanding of uncodified internal organisation relations, one can gain a deeper understanding of factors such as the following: group or organisation performance; strategy formulation processes; conflict and mobility; and inter-functional integration. Links between the formal and the informal, as well as those between the structuralisation and formalisation of ways of collective action with behavioural tacit norms and social and communicative relations, are recurring themes in organisational studies.[2] Some of the studies contributing to the foundations of organisational theory, such as Mayo's work at the Hawthorne plant,[3] have taken as their particular domain the links between formal and informal organisations – social relations.[4] Early efforts at developing methods of network analysis, such as sociometrics, formed part of this pioneering research programme. Throughout the course of its development, the link between 'formal' and 'informal' organisations has been at the centre of scholarly attention. Even the most normative component of research in the organisational field has retained this distinction: for example Mintzberg[5] recognises that all organisations are comprised of social relation networks, and that even the most prescriptive types, such as bureaucracies, depend on informal relational structures. To conclude, network analysis has made a definite contribution to understanding the structure, nature, content and environmental conditions of the relations which an organisational agent has with others.

Similarly, having emphasised the role of another well-noted presence to historians, that of complexity, the organisationalists rediscovered the role of institutions and institutional assets, which for historians had, since time immemorial, been the daily bread of their own research. Coming to the present, what of the discovery of 'trust' or 'reputation' and of 'relational capital'? How could one get by without trust, the very elegant mechanism of currency exchange from the fifteenth century onwards? And what of a nineteenth-century banker who had lost 'honour and reputation'?

In this sense economics, and above all organisational theories, are now discovering the role and significance of all those 'non-economic' components of 'economic action', which for decades economic history has stressed and defended against the criticisms of most economists.

It is regarding this confluence of studies that a unique and beneficial *rapprochement* between history and economics is taking place; and business history is perhaps the most researched and fruitful field of interaction among subjects which, for a long time, limited occasions for exchange and debate. One thinks of the attention paid by many scholars from organisational disciplines to texts that are now canonical in economic history (this is the case of Chandler), or of the close dialectic link created in industrial districts and network structures.

It is really with the theme of networks that the second part of my remarks is concerned. In this brief note I shall attempt to achieve two objectives. The first consists of a methodological contribution, an attempt to clarify both the many meanings which historians and scholars of organisation studies attribute to the terms 'network' and 'networking', and possible applications in the historical field of methods and techniques usually employed in organisational studies. I will present an introductory discourse, a brief series of judgements identifying the potential points of intersection between the arguments presented by historians and the survey methods of the relational approach.

The second objective is, however, more ambitious: to illustrate the need to integrate organisational studies and history in an effort to overcome what is, at the moment, the most serious weakness of network analysis – the absence of the diacronichal, the historical dimension, in the full sense of the term 'historical'. The most severe criticism of network analysis is that, to date, it has only been able to 'take a snap-shot' of relational structure, but does not manage, without help from other methodologies, to take account of development and transformation. This is a limit of importance, which does not lie in obvious difficulties of a technical nature, but in the absence of the sensitivity and know-how possessed by historians. In this sense, business history can be of use not only to our understanding of past dynamics, but also in furnishing methodological suggestions and operating tools.

The study of networks offers an alternative explanation of organisational behaviour, such as that of individuals and groups. These are interpreted not so much in terms of individual attributes but in terms of relations which individuals, groups or organisations have with other individuals, groups or organisations (from now on we will use the concept of organisational actor to indicate individuals, groups and organisations).

Network theory is based on the following hypotheses: the reasons for the behaviours, decisions and actions of all types of organisational actors are not only the result of internal characteristics or processes, but are to be found in the relations which the actor has with other actors. This concept is anchored to two fundamental propositions of the network perspective:

1. The relations an actor has with the external environment can condition or determine, in a way which can to some degree be known, obligations which modify decisions and behaviours.[6]
2. Relations are a resource which the actor can use and manipulate to obtain benefits.[7]

Early network studies were executed within disciplines usually considered distant from the organisation of economic activity. The available material is vast, and network analysis presents a multiplicity of forms, interpretations, schemes of reference and perspectives. It began as the study of social networks in extra-organisational environments. Social networks were considered to be: 'Specific sets of interpersonal links characterised by the fact that the nature of relations within the whole could be used to predict and interpret the social behaviour of individuals'.[8] This idea came about in opposition to the hyper-rational vision of individual decision-making which saw the individual as 'autonomous, independent and solitary'.[9] Despite this, it was only after the Second World War that the study of social networks assumed importance both in the quantity and quality of studies, albeit there had been some interesting attempts to research the theme at the beginning of the century. Particular attention was focused on communication and personal interaction networks among individuals. Communication processes, and the transfer of knowledge, values, culture and languages by means of social exchange were regarded as fundamental elements for understanding social dynamics, above all in pre-industrial societies. One can already guess that the theoretical basis and empirical interest for the study of networks was grounded on the observations of 'social concentrations',[10] from which societies and organisations are formed. These are aggregations of individuals which can take different forms, and have diverse contents and objectives. Networks can seem to have different degrees of formalisation. Relevant here are the first studies conducted into businesses, and the social and interpersonal networks connecting the world of industry and finance. Examples include the research conducted at the beginning of the century in Germany into the networks between large industries and the banking system, or the investigation into the anti-competitive effects of business collusion in the USA in the first half of the century.[11]

The network approach later found different stimuli for greater strengthening. A significant impulse came from the adoption of functionalism in sociology. The functionalists paid considerable attention to the study of the determinants of individual and group behaviour, usually by observing social and informal networks. One of the key ideas of functionalism was that of the existence of informal lines of communication both within an organisation and with other organisations. The organisation is seen as an 'adaptable, social structure'. From the functionalist viewpoint, every behavioural adaptation of the organisation takes place in relation to a presumably stable system of needs.

The functionalist approach presented certain difficulties, however, with regard to the study of relational networks and the concrete forms assumed by social systems. First, it was a static vision of the boundaries of social systems which were assumed to have well-defined and unchangeable limits if not subjected to radical transformation. In the second place, it was an excessively deterministic interpretation of individual adaptation to prescriptions and norms. This approach seemed particularly inadequate in situations of great environmental dynamism, and in contexts such as factories or mines which often have strong informal connotations and uncodified schemes of action.

On the theoretical and empirical levels, the need to deepen the study of social networks, and the early integration between disciplines (anthropology, sociology and social psychology, certain organisational 'schools' such as Taylorism, the bureaucratic school and the human relations school), led over time to two important developments: first the birth of the Manchester school; and second the birth and development of structural analysis.

In line with the aims of the present work, I will concentrate on the first of these developments. The second is certainly more important, not least in the light of my own experience, but it is the first which provides the more interesting considerations as far as the study of convergence between history and organisations is concerned.

The 1930s and 1940s saw the development of the school of English anthropologists. These concentrated not on cultural aspects of social groups and communities, but on the structural systems of social relations between individuals, groups and organisations.[12] Many of the insights gained in this school were not integrated into a system or analysis of the global characteristics of networks. Further, most of the research was focused just on informal interpersonal relations of a community type. Anthropological research played a fundamental role in the later development of methods of analysis of relations systems. It is to anthropology, in fact, that many of the basic concepts and mathematical and measurement methods have been attributed: one example being that of network density. The early applications of network analysis derived from the scholars in the Manchester school. After a largely metaphorical usage of the idea of social networks, this became an analytical concept to which the mathematical formulae of graphs theory could be applied. Anthropological research also demonstrated the need to differentiate relational analysis into different fields: institutional structures, social category aggregations and interpersonal relations.

Institutional relations are those deriving from, belonging to, or simply working within, a specific institutional structure. Barnes[13] cites as an example the neighbourhood, the local authority, the factory, the missionary society, or the crew of a ship. Mitchell[14] adds to these: the family, the mine, the voluntary association, the trade union, and the political party. Social aggregations refer to an individual's membership of a given social category – class, profession, race, and so on. Interpersonal relations refer to the set of interpersonal links such as friendship, emotion, and relatives.

Finally, anthropological research demonstrated how individuals operating within a system, or set, of relations are not conditioned only by those relations. They can, in fact, modify and manipulate that set of relations for individual objectives. The position occupied within a relational network can be modified or used to obtain individual benefits. Like the individual, the organisation as well can work on the system, or set, of relations to modify or manipulate the nature, intensity and form of the connections through which it is linked to other organisations. This is an important issue because this idea suggests a vision of the organisational actor, whether as individual or as organisation, untrammelled by excessive socialisation and therefore equidistant both from the individualist or under-socialised idea of human action, and from that of the over-socialised perspective.

The legacy which these studies leave in the economic field has led to diverse normative and interpretative perspectives. The methodological value of these theoretical perspectives is visible in the following: analysis of the position of an actor within a relational network – whether that actor is an individual or organisation; the examination of the opportunities for actor movement within a network; the study of pseudo-groups, of roles within networks and of central-peripheral relations.

Other conclusions which have left a significant resource for network development research include the following:

1. The behaviours of organisational actors are conditioned by the group relations within which these actors operate.
2. The actions of organisational actors, in so far as they are consistent with their objectives, can manipulate and modify the relational system to which they belong.
3. These processes of relations manipulation can change the functioning of the groups, the organisations, and the institutions themselves.
4. The groups and organisations are complex systems of interdependence: operating on interdependence means operating on the whole organisation.

From the historian's point of view, the study of networks ascribable to anthropological research have strong links to history, because they do not study 'network forms' but the processes of activation of exchange and interaction networks. It is clear that the processual study presents strong analogies to history, because it is researched over a temporal dimension.

This interpretation enables the whole potential of the relational approach to be used. The approach goes beyond the study of networking, to the process of relational interaction. The approach, in fact, thanks to its methodological resource, permits relational systems to be studied on the basis of certain specific characteristics – this is to say that networks are one way of organising activity, whether they be a multinational, a group of friends, or a sixteenth-century court. There are, then, two parallel levels of significance of the network concept: the level of the relations and that of the links or network as a whole. On the one hand, the need to understand the structure, the nature, the content and environmental context of the relations held by an organisational actor with other actors in order to interpret actions and behaviours. On the other hand, the demonstration of the role played by the way relations are organised and the need to understand the functioning, the conditions for formation, the contingencies determining effectiveness or efficiency with respect to other ways of organising economic and non-economic activity. Both meanings assume, however, significant value on the level of historical analysis. Now there is a need to work together.

NOTES

1. W.W. Powell and L. Smith-Doerr, 'Networks and Economics Life' in N.J. Smelser and R. Swedberg (eds), *The Handbook of Economic Sociology*, (Princeton, 1994), p. 369.
2. C.I. Barnard, *The Functions of the Executive* (Cambridge, Mass., 1938).
3. E. Mayo, *The Human Problems of an Industrial Civilisation*, (Cambridge, Mass., 1933).
4. P.M. Blau, *Exchange and Power in Social Life* (New York, 1974).
5. H. Mintzberg, *The Structuring of Organisations* (New Jersey, 1979), p. 53.
6. E. Botte, *Family and Social Networks* (London, 1957).
7. R.S. Burt, *Toward a Structural Theory of Action* (New York, 1982).
8. J.C. Mitchell, *The Concept and Use of Social Networks* (Manchester, 1969), p. 2.
9. J. Glaskiewicz and S. Wasserman, 'Social Network Analysis: Concepts, Methodology and Directions for the 1990s', *Sociological Methods and Research* 22, no. 1 (August 1993), pp. 3–22.
10. A. Rugiandi, *Organizzazione d'Impresa* (Milan, 1979).
11. O. Jeidels, *Das Verhaltnis der Deutshen Grobbanken zur Industrie mit besonderer Berücksichtigung der Eisenindustrie* (Leipzig, 1905).
12. J.A. Barnes, 'Class and Committees in a Norwegian Island Parish', *Human Relations* 7 (1954), pp. 39–58; Barnes, *Three Styles in the Study of Kinship* (London, 1971).
13. J.A. Barnes, 'Networks and Political Process', in J.C. Mitchell (eds), *Social Networks in Urban Situations* (Manchester, 1969), pp. 51, 76.
14. J.C. Mitchell, 'Networks, Norms and Institutions' in J. Boissevain and J.C. Mitchell (eds), (The Hague, 1973).